'THIS HOLY MAN'

'THIS HOLY MAN'

Impressions of Metropolitan Anthony

Gillian Crow

DARTON · LONGMAN + TODD

First published in 2005 by
Darton, Longman and Todd Ltd
1 Spencer Court
140–142 Wandsworth High Street
London
SW18 4JJ

ISBN 0 232 52568 4

A catalogue record for this book is available from the British Library.

Designed by Sandie Boccacci
Phototypeset in 10.75/13.5pt Minion
by Intype Libra Ltd

Printed and bound in Great Britain by
The Cromwell Press, Trowbridge, Wiltshire

CONTENTS

List of Illustrations   vii

Acknowledgements   ix

Introduction   xi

Part One: Early Life

1. Background   3
2. Early Childhood (1916–1923)   11
3. Schooldays in Paris (1923–1929)   23

Part Two: New Life

4. Conversion (1929–1932)   39
5. Student Years (1932–1939)   55
6. Doctor, Soldier and Monk (1939–1949)   69

Part Three: London – The Early Years

7. Priesthood (1949–1957)   95
8. Bishop of Sergievo (1957–1966)   117

Part Four: At the Height of his Powers

9. Metropolitan of Sourozh (1966–1976)   137
10. A Man of Vision   154
11. Looking Outwards (1977–1992)   171
12. Starets   191

Part Five: 'Weeds Never Die' – Final Years

13. Looking to the Future (1992–1999)   215
14. Looking to Eternity (2000–2003)   227

Epilogue   241

Glossary   245

Recommended Reading   247

Index   249

LIST OF ILLUSTRATIONS

Between pages 144 and 145

This photograph, taken in 1966, was reproduced in *School for Prayer*. (Copyright © Sir Richard Bowlby.)

As a medical student in 1935 (middle row, third from left). (Estate of Metropolitan Anthony.)

In scout uniform, 1927 (far right). (Estate of Metropolitan Anthony.)

Walking down Bond Street, 1949. (Estate of Metropolitan Anthony.)

With Xenia, 1954. (Estate of Metropolitan Anthony.)

Consecration as Bishop of Sergievo, 1957. (Estate of Metropolitan Anthony.)

Exarch of Western Europe, 1964. With Patriarch Alexis I. (Estate of Metropolitan Anthony.)

Metropolitan Anthony of Sourozh, 1966. (Estate of Metropolitan Anthony.)

With Father Michael Fortounatto, at Summer Camp, 1979. (Copyright © Deacon Peter Scorer.)

Playing volleyball at Camp, 1985. (Copyright © Deacon Peter Scorer.)

At the first service held in the Kremlin Dormition Cathedral, Moscow, since the Revolution, 13 October 1989. (Estate of Metropolitan Anthony.)

On the 40th anniversary of his consecration as bishop, flanked by Archbishop Anatoly (left) and Bishop Basil (right), November 1997. (Copyright © Nick Hale.)

The last photo. Metropolitan Anthony with Bishop Mark of Berlin. (Estate of Metropolitan Anthony.)

ACKNOWLEDGEMENTS

I should like to thank all those people who have provided me with material for this book, both written and oral, including:

Bishop Basil of Sergievo, Father Michael and Mariamna Fortounatto, Father Sergei Hackel, Father John Lee, Deacon Nicholas and Véronique Lossky, Deacon Peter Scorer, Archbishop Rowan Williams of Canterbury, Bishop Richard Chartres of London, Canon Donald Allchin, Rev. Michael Bourdeaux, Tatisha Behr, Xenia Bowlby, Kelsey Cheshire, Jim Forest, Gwynneth Gosling, Mariane Greenan, Anastasia Heath, Bridget Hickey-Williams, Boris Khazanov, Irina Kirillova, Elena Maidanovich, Tanya Maidanovich, Ivo Morshead, Eddie Roberson, Irina von Schlippe, Sophie Tanner, Mary Tate, Sarah Walker, the Monastery of St John the Baptist, the Taizé Community and the Estate of Metropolitan Anthony.

I should like to thank the following people who have lent photos:

Deacon Peter Scorer, Nick Hale, Elena Orlova and Nicholas Tuckett.

And special thanks to Virginia Hearn, my editor at Darton, Longman and Todd.

Metropolitan Anthony's description of himself was very different from the title of this book. 'I am not a good man,' he would say to people, aware of his shortcomings. This modesty sprang not from a downward-looking false piety but from his perception of the glory of God, in whose light he saw himself revealed as sadly wanting.

Yet for those around him he often appeared to reflect that light, so that many could describe him in the words of Archbishop Methodios, the former Greek Archbishop in London, on the occasion of his visit to the Russian Cathedral on 2 March 1986, as 'this holy man'. It was reminiscent of the way he was once described in a radio interview as 'a living icon', an impression referring not only to his physical appearance, with his full beard and intense gaze, but also to the challenge he presented as someone in whom the image of God could be patently discerned.

His holiness was, however, relative. He could be radiantly transparent to the Christian message; but on other occasions, when he was tired, ill or depressed – or simply worldly – he could be as opaque as anybody else and the divine image was clouded by the darker side of his nature. This book is not a hagiography, for he was not a saint but, like everyone, a human being with his sins and weaknesses, which could be irritating and at times distressing to those with whom he had dealings. There was a paradoxical contrast between the greatness of the man and the smallness of his character.

The focus of this book is the greatness of the man – in Christian terms the fruits he bore: his vision and preaching of the Gospel; his work as the foremost bringer of Orthodoxy to modern Britain, not only in the building up of his own diocese but in the wider influence of his writing and broadcasting and his ecumenical work; and his immense contribution within the Orthodox Church worldwide, not least in Russia.

During the Soviet era he broadcast regularly from Britain. The authorities tried to jam the programmes but were partially defeated by an irony which appealed to Metropolitan Anthony's sense of humour: a relative in Moscow told him how the jamming worked in solid pre-revolutionary buildings but had no effect on the more flimsy structures put up by the Soviets themselves. In this way many thousands of people were able to listen to his voice – at times the only voice – preaching hope in the dark days of the Soviet system. His writings, both his published books and the transcripts of his numerous talks and lectures, had a wide samizdat (underground) distribution, and it has been said that they were more influential in Soviet Russia than those of Solzhenitsyn. To all this he brought his distinctive style of Orthodoxy: not hidebound or reactionary, as it is often thought to be, but vibrant, open and burning with the truth of the Gospel.

His other major contribution was the vision he had for Orthodoxy beyond the bounds of traditionally Orthodox countries. He saw, rightly, the Orthodox faith as being nothing more or less than simple Christianity, the fullness of the Gospel, its message universal. Understanding the twentieth-century Orthodox diaspora as God's scattering of precious seeds over all the earth, meant to take root and flourish wherever they were cast, he sought to rid his diocese of the ethnophiletism that has been a heretical plague among Orthodox jurisdictions, and to open it to all people of whatever race, nationality or culture. This was his vision for Orthodoxy everywhere, beginning where he was, in Western Europe, and it was with joy that he welcomed the Moscow Patriarchate's proposal made in April 2003 that a Metropolia for Western Europe be formed, with him as its head, to make concrete this vision and to be the foundation for a future Orthodox Church of Western Europe. Unfortunately it came too late for him to realise – just four months before his death, when his cancer was already far advanced – but he saw in the Patriarch's letter an endorsement of all that he had stood for. It was a fitting if belated conclusion to his ministry.

Incipiently holy he may have been. He most certainly was not a pious man. Unlike some, he was not hung up on attending every possible service. By choice he did not say grace before meals. He did not affect a pious voice or vocabulary, or give anything other than totally practical spiritual advice. Despite his monastic profession, his was not the holiness of the cloister but of a man who lived among men and women and had as a result become more of a person, not less.

As for his sins and shortcomings – the smallness he never conquered, in common with most people – they were his own concern, and should largely remain so.

Metropolitan Anthony wished no one to write a formal biography of himself because he felt his life, both as a priest and as a doctor, was too bound up with other people to whom he owed professional confidentiality. He claimed not to keep a diary apart from an appointments book, and to destroy all letters he received, even official ones (though that was not entirely true). He did, however, suggest that I should write what he termed a 'lyrical biography': a collection of impressions and anecdotes in keeping with the informal style of his own books.

This is not a dispassionate account. Metropolitan Anthony was a person one could not meet without being moved, in one direction or the other. He was my spiritual father, to whom I owe my conversion, my Orthodox faith and my practice of it. I write so that others may share what he gave to his spiritual children: his wisdom, his teaching, his enthusiasm, his deep insight into prayer, his response of total commitment to the Gospel; and the sense – sometimes – of being in the presence of a man who radiated the divine fire with which he was aglow.

Metropolitan Anthony was known to apply the words of St Paul to himself: be followers of me, as I am a follower of Christ. The stories he told about his life were always to make a point relevant to his listeners. 'This Holy Man' is therefore concerned less with charting the official business of his career than with conveying something of his life, his faith and his spirituality and the impact they made on other people. I use the word 'something' deliberately. He was a very private man, with an inherent shyness he never conquered. He had a detachment and reserve proper to his monastic vocation, but he was also on his own admittance a lone wolf by nature, so that even apart from the excuse of confidentiality he had an inborn reluctance to bare his soul. True, from time to time he would give a piercing sermon which was little short of a confession, when he would speak of his falling short both in his work and in his personal life. Yet despite this he remained in many ways an enigma, both in thoughts and actions, and one felt this was deliberate.

With few exceptions he allowed no one into the simple rooms at the back of the Russian Cathedral in London where he lived during his middle and later years. When he closed the door behind him he retreated into a physical seclusion analogous to the privacy of his inner life. He often described his soul as a 'walled garden' that he wished to keep shut against all-comers. There were times when his work as a priest dictated that he allowed brief glimpses inside, but they were given out of obedience to God's will, and with the sense that it was a very costly exercise.

Without intruding beyond the bounds he set, this book sets out what he revealed about himself, either in words or actions, to people around him. He made great use of anecdotes, as a way of shedding light on how the experiences of his life had shaped him and how he had learned to cope with the problems his listeners faced. At first acquaintance this could appear trivial – it was the initial reaction, for instance, of the composer John Tavener, according to the latter's biography – and could disappoint those who were unwilling to persevere. In fact, Metropolitan Anthony's fondness for anecdotes was, far from being trivial, a genuine part of Christian tradition, akin to the stories of the Desert Fathers, for whom he had a special reverence. A child summed up what the sophisticated missed: 'He speaks to us in parables.' He used these anecdotal parables to put people at their ease, to instruct, to chide painlessly and often to bring a ray of humour into a serious conversation or talk. Taking his lead from the gospel parables and the Desert Fathers, he was aware that it was the anecdote which often remained in the memory long after learned discourses had been forgotten.

In all these ways his use of anecdotes was deliberate, a fact of which I was made strikingly aware when, at the end of an especially intense private appointment, he suddenly said in a tone of regret, 'We have talked so earnestly today that I haven't had time to tell you any anecdotes!' He also used them, whether subconsciously or otherwise, as reserved people do: as a way of giving an impression of intimacy while in reality keeping his inner self at a secure distance.

Although the stories became stylised during a lifetime of retelling, to every listener they would sound fresh and spontaneous because he always put his whole heart into his words. While the core of each episode would remain the same he could be less than consistent in peripheral details. I once challenged him on this tendency to inaccuracy, and the next time he told one of his stories during a talk he fixed his eyes on me with a look that in its sheepishness also reproved and said, 'Well, I may have told this differently elsewhere, but the essence of it is true.' On other occasions he might, through tiredness, muddle up a location or wrongly attribute something, as he sometimes did with his quotations from the Bible or the Fathers during a sermon. It was this kind of mistake which could be overlooked as trivial rather than his anecdotal style, because it was the truth behind the details that mattered.

I have not therefore striven impossibly to find the 'authoritative' version of each anecdote but have reproduced what best illustrates its essential qualities, in Metropolitan Anthony's own tradition and as far as possible in his own words spoken on a particular occasion. He was fond of recounting stories in the form of dialogue, sometimes mimicking participants' voices and accents, and on occasion employing a dry, sarcastic tone or dramatic facial expressions and gestures. He was, typically for a Russian, a born actor.

He was also a gifted speaker and preacher. He had an inspired understanding of Christianity, which he expressed clearly and with enthusiasm in whatever language he happened to be using. His own opinion was that he was good at public speaking but less successful in a one-to-one situation. The latter was certainly not felt to be true by the hundreds of people who clamoured for private appointments to see him for spiritual counsel, but his confidence in preaching and lecturing, virtually always without notes, was entirely justified.

In a sermon given in November 1987 Metropolitan Anthony repeated words familiar to his flock as the essence of his interpretation of the Christian life: that it was only by becoming the living message of the Gospel that anyone could truly say they had received that message. The disciples of Christ should be such, he said, that people looking at them would be puzzled, perturbed, challenged by the awareness that they had encountered men and women who were like no one else, not on account of their wisdom or reasoning but because they were different: they had become new creatures.

To his listeners those words were not a matter of rhetoric. Metropolitan Anthony himself embodied them to a measurable degree. Through his faith he had become a man who was indeed unlike ordinary men. Many, on meeting him for the first time, went through their own experience of being puzzled and perturbed by the overwhelming awareness that here was a man whose living faith had transformed him into something bigger than people around him. They saw in him a person who was strikingly different, who partook – incipiently – of that otherness which one calls holy.

Metropolitan Anthony did not think he lived out his message in a recognisable way. On the contrary, he often commented that every time he opened his mouth to speak of the Gospel he felt he was knocking a nail into his own coffin because his life belied his words. Certainly that was true in some respects. He lived intensely, putting his whole self into each present moment, which meant that his mistakes and failings were as intense as his virtues. He had the burning passion of a meteor, which was breathtaking so long as one was not the victim of his fire, as people and circumstances were from time to time.

Yet despite his failings many people were drawn to him, not only because his Orthodox teaching rang true but also because he seemed to demonstrate its truth. There was something obstinately different about him. He described it as a madness. 'But the strange thing is that other people want to catch it,' he would say. That was truly a puzzle and a challenge, and in seeking an answer many people found salvation. 'This holy man,' Archbishop Methodios summed it up; and others agreed.

He saw the life in Christ as a challenge simultaneously exciting, joyful but also demanding total self-dedication in life and, if necessary, in death. It was never a matter of knowing but of becoming.

This book records his visible struggle to embody the Gospel message and bring it to others. The invisible was his business. But although he wanted neither the light nor the dark sides of his life dissected, he did want the world to know that both existed. He would undoubtedly have approved of my quoting a mischievous comment he made to me, f ollowing an article I wrote for the *Church Times* in celebration of his seventy-fifth birthday. The piece was billed by the paper as 'A Tribute to Metropolitan Anthony'. Never much of one for tributes, he pointed out to me afterwards that there were a great many other, less complimentary things I could have said about him, which he summed up with the words: 'You could have called me a pig, which is also true.'

That is the aim of this book: to record not his outward career but his achievement in the Christian life, so that other people may be inspired by his example.

PART ONE

EARLY LIFE

CHAPTER ONE

BACKGROUND

M etropolitan Anthony of Sourozh, né André Borisovich Bloom, had what he called a 'background'. The son of a diplomat and nephew of the composer Scriabin he was born just before the First World War into the upper-class world of the Russian Empire, a world soon to die except in the hearts of the émigré milieu of which he was to become a part. The Russian Orthodox Church, tied to the old regime but largely marginalised by the country's agnostic elite, seemed destined to share the fate of the tottering imperial system. Yet Orthodoxy knows no death without resurrection, and the Church was indeed to rise and bear fruit, not only through the horror and persecutions of Soviet Russia and beyond into rebirth after the collapse of communism, but also, in the emigration, through the vision and example of people such as Metropolitan Anthony.

His birth, on 19 June 1914, took place in Lausanne, Switzerland, where his father and mother were staying with his maternal grandparents, Nikolai and Olga Scriabin.

Though untitled, the Scriabins counted themselves a noble family which could proudly trace its origins back to medieval Central Russia. For generations the men had followed military careers. Nikolai's father, Alexander Ivanovich (1811–1879), was a colonel in the Tsar's artillery and had been decorated with the Order of St George. In 1846 Alexander married Elizabeth Ivanovna Podcherkova, twelve years his junior, and they rented a house on the outskirts of Moscow. There they raised eight children, of whom Nikolai, born in 1849, was the second.

Alexander Ivanovich was said to be an unbending man who ran his household with military precision and who was rewarded by seeing all his sons, with one exception, follow him into the army. Life did, however, have its lighter side. A certain amount of amateur music-making provided welcome relaxation for the young officers; everyone in the family played an instrument, and this musical background was to have unforeseen consequences in Nikolai's life.

For he was the exception to the military rule. His sensitive ear helped give him a linguistic ability and, despite his father's displeasure, he insisted on breaking the family tradition to seek a non-military career which would harness this talent. After reading law at Moscow University he studied oriental languages in St Petersburg, where he quickly mastered Arabic and Turkish. A future in diplomacy beckoned. On graduating, Nikolai entered the imperial diplomatic service and was sent to Constantinople, capital of the Ottoman Empire, as dragoman (interpreter) at the Russian Embassy.

There was another break with family tradition. He married young, and his choice of bride – not the customary arranged marriage – betrayed an innate musicality: a young concert pianist, Lyubov Petrovna Shchetinina. In 1871 she bore him a son, Alexander Nikolaevich Scriabin, the future composer.

Tragedy struck quickly. Lyubov was suffering from tuberculosis. In 1872 in a last vain effort to find a cure Nikolai took her to Italy, where she died and was buried. Nikolai's brief spell of domesticity was at an end and, leaving his infant son in Moscow in the care of his sister (also named Lyubov), he continued his diplomatic career in Turkey and the Balkans.

Musicologists have often said that while the composer Scriabin inherited his soldierly bearing and shortness of stature from his father's family, his musical talent came exclusively from his mother. Several factors point to that not being the case. Nikolai's attraction to a pianist and the nurturing of his son's talent in the paternal grandfather's household substantiate a musical awareness among the Scriabins. The family certainly recognised the importance of the young Alexander's talent, taking the seven-year-old boy to Anton Rubinstein at the Conservatoire for evaluation. Nikolai was to choose a second wife who also played the piano – though as an amateur and 'ingratiatingly' according to one of Scriabin's biographers – and one of her sons, a half brother to the composer through his father, was later to consider a career as a professional musician. But the most convincing and perhaps surprising musical link, Scriabin's renowned synaesthesia, the gift of 'seeing' musical tones as colours, which played such a large part in the development of his composition, was without doubt inherited from Nikolai, not his mother. A generation later Metropolitan Anthony, Nikolai's grandson by his second wife, was to inherit the same strange ability.

In 1880 Nikolai remarried. He was by then the Russian Consul in Trieste, which was at the time part of the Austro-Hungarian Empire. His new wife was a local Italian named Olga Ilyinichna Fernandez (she took her Christian name and patronymic when she married), a short, dark-eyed girl of only seventeen. Like Nikolai's first union it did not follow the prevalent Russian custom of arranged marriages. Indeed, it caused some ill feeling in Olga's family because she was the middle of three sisters and traditionally the eldest should have married first.

That sister eventually married a Viennese and was to provide a brief home for the Blooms in the early 1920s. Many years later Metropolitan Anthony came to remember her for her sense of courage and selflessness, because when in old age she became a diabetic and developed gangrene in her leg she refused surgery, preferring to die and leave the cost of the operation to her needy relatives. The younger sister later made an unhappy marriage to a Croatian.

Olga's own future married happiness might have seemed just as doubtful. She was thirteen years younger than Nikolai. With a precocious step-son being brought up far away by a doting aunt, her own widowed mother to care for and her position as the teenaged wife of a Russian diplomat her new life could not have been straightforward. She was, however, a sincere and trustful person, as she was to remain throughout a very long life, with a natural inclination to take things at face value.

For instance, on one occasion before her marriage she paid a visit to a travelling circus which was boosting its attendance by advertising free admission. Olga did not suspect that this was anything other than a generous gesture on the part of the circus management until, having enjoyed the show, she was confronted by a sign at the exit demanding payment to get out. As a boy, Metropolitan Anthony would sometimes exploit this weakness for the sake of harmless amusement, as he found himself unable to resist telling her exaggerated tales to which she would invariably respond, wide-eyed, 'Is that really true?'

Other people were to find Olga no less endearing. Her stepson Alexander grew to call her 'mamochka' (Russian for 'Mummy'). Many years later he would ask for her to be present when his wife gave birth, even letting her override his wife's choice to name one of his daughters.

Although the Italian ancestry Metropolitan Anthony inherited from

Olga did not impress him – he disliked the temperament, he said – he did, however, inherit her dark looks, in particular her striking brown eyes, and he was familiar with the Italian language. He also retained into old age the ability to eat spaghetti with a proficiency that suggested her influence.

Having arranged Olga's conversion to Orthodoxy on their marriage – the Scriabins were not religious but there were certain conventions to be followed – Nikolai decided his new wife should also learn Russian, to complement the French they spoke to each other. He presented her with a grammar, a dictionary and the complete works of Turgenev and told her to get on with it. 'She never spoke Russian very well,' Metropolitan Anthony would say, 'but what she did speak was till her dying day in the language and idiom of Turgenev.'

The couple returned to Russia briefly in 1882. On that occasion the eleven-year-old Alexander is said to have mimicked by ear Olga's rendering of a Bach Gavotte and a Mendelssohn Gondolier's Song. By that time she was already the mother of one son and was to bear Nikolai three more, although all were eventually to die young in military action. In 1889 she gave birth to her only daughter, Xenia, who was to become Metropolitan Anthony's mother. Nikolai meanwhile continued his diplomatic career in various corners of the Ottoman Empire, finally rising to the rank of Consul-General in Erzerum, eastern Turkey. It was his signature which validated the imperial passport of Igor Stravinsky on the latter's first trip abroad in 1907. Settled into his second marriage and with a growing family Nikolai became less and less inclined to spend his leave in Russia, and in later life he and Olga often preferred to meet Alexander for holidays in Western Europe, although the composer tended to find his father increasingly boring and reactionary as time went on.

They sent the children home to St Petersburg to be educated. Their daughter Xenia was enrolled at the Smolny Institute, the foremost girls' school in Russia, which was later to achieve unforeseen notoriety when the Bolsheviks commandeered it to become their headquarters during the 1917 Revolution. Naturally Xenia was expected to learn several languages; besides Russian and French she became proficient in German and English. She developed into a resourceful and energetic girl, intelligent and cultured, who was taught the expected social graces of the day; she enjoyed tennis, she was a good horsewoman and, inheriting some of the family talent, a competent pianist. In short, Smolny equipped her admirably for the life of a young lady of the Russian upper classes, at home in diplomatic and society circles. That this was to leave her totally unprepared for the subsequent rigours of emigration was another matter.

During the summer holidays she would make the long journey by train and horse-drawn carriage to visit her parents in Erzerum. As she blossomed into womanhood she attracted the attention of a young dragoman at the Russian Embassy, Boris Bloom, who was to become Nikolai's secretary and her future husband.

Boris Edwardovich Bloom was born in 1884, the son of a Moscow doctor, Edward Bloom. Some of his ancestors had variously come to Russia from Holland and the north of Scotland during the reign of Peter the Great, who had encouraged such immigration in his drive to westernise his empire. The name 'Bloom' was said to have originated from the Dutch. Some people have wondered whether the name might have had distant Jewish connections. 'Metropolitan Anthony never said no and he never said yes,' one of his clergy, Father Sergei Hackel, maintained. In any case, with few exceptions Jews had to live 'beyond the pale' at a distance from Moscow, and were certainly not permitted to enter the diplomatic service. If there had been any Jewish antecedents they would have been some generations back. By Boris's time the Blooms were respectable, if nominal, members of the Russian Orthodox Church.

Although the Bloom family had soon intermarried with the local Russians, they maintained links with their Scottish relatives down the generations, and Dr Edward Bloom still corresponded with a distant cousin living alone in a remote cottage in the Western Highlands.

In one particular letter this fearless old lady recounted to her Russian cousin how she had one night discovered a prospective burglar outside her house. Looking out of the upstairs window she watched him climb up the drainpipe and along the wall. So she picked up an axe, waited until he took hold of the windowsill, chopped off his fingers, shut the window and went to bed. When telling this story many years later Metropolitan Anthony would remark mischievously that what impressed him most was the fact that the old woman could shut the window and go to bed, leaving the thief to deal with the consequences.

When Metropolitan Anthony was already established in England and made his first trip to Scotland to speak there, a member of the audience sent him a note claiming to be one of his Scottish relatives. He kept the letter, intending to reply eventually; but by the time he did so the man had moved and no contact was ever made. ('Well, you know me,' he would say to people, 'I never was one for writing letters!')

The household of the Moscow Blooms was run in a more sophisticated manner than that of their Scottish cousin. The doctor had his children, three boys and a girl, educated by tutors at home according to a strict discipline, which included his insistence on fluency not only in Russian but also in Latin, Greek and French. This laid the foundation for the young Boris's linguistic proficiency.

Boris Bloom went on to read mathematics at Moscow University before entering the diplomatic school of the Foreign Ministry, where he studied oriental languages. Both his brothers were to die young. His sister married one of the early Bolsheviks and lost touch with her surviving family.

After graduating from the diplomatic school Boris was posted to the Middle East, where he was to become secretary to Nikolai Scriabin in Erzerum and suitor to his daughter. Xenia, five years younger than Boris, did not share his retiring nature. She was more outgoing: uncomplicated and direct, as Metropolitan Anthony described her. Nevertheless, they married. At first the couple continued to live in Erzerum, enjoying diplomatic society and in their free time riding and hunting together in the mountains. When Nikolai Scriabin retired in 1913 he settled with Olga in Switzerland. The following year Boris was officially appointed Russian consul in Colombo. The post was, however, only nominal, and instead of heading east he took his wife to visit her parents. Xenia was by then pregnant, and their only child, a son André Borisovich, the future Metropolitan Anthony, was born in Lausanne on 19 June 1914.

The new baby was to inherit his grandfather Scriabin's short, upright bearing and his grandmother's beautiful brown eyes. As he grew older his hair would also take on her colouring, although as a young child he had cherubic golden curls. From his father would come his reserved nature and preference for solitude.

From both parents he took his nominal religion, being baptised in Lausanne by the local Russian Orthodox priest, Father Konstantin. At the time the ceremony appeared to have no more significance than that encountered in non-churchgoing families everywhere. The godmother, Boris Bloom's mother, was back home in Russia and was merely recorded as sponsor in her absence. That this particular perfunctory society christening was to be something of a time bomb never crossed the mind of Father Konstantin as he immersed the naked infant three times in the font according to the Orthodox rite.

Forty-seven years later, when a newly appointed Bishop Anthony from London paid a visit to the Lausanne parish, the old priest was taken aback to be greeted by the words, 'Father Konstantin, I am so glad to meet you again!'

'I'm sorry, there must be some mistake,' the bewildered priest replied. 'I don't recall our ever having met.'

'Oh yes, we certainly have met,' Bishop Anthony insisted. 'You baptised me!'

The old man dug out the parish register to show the relevant entry to his congregation, and in honour of the occasion he made a special effort at the Liturgy to read the Gospel in Russian, the rest of the service being in Greek. Unfortunately his Russian accent was so poor – his everyday language was French – that, had not an obliging parishioner pointed out the fact to the bemused young bishop, he would never have guessed it was Russian at all.

Metropolitan Anthony was to tell a similar story in relation to himself when he tried to celebrate in French-accented Greek to an uncomprehending congregation in Ireland.

Father Konstantin's neglect of his native tongue was not unusual among the westernised Russian upper classes of the day. No one could foresee the nationalist fervour that enforced emigration would soon bring. But what could be foreseen in the summer of 1914 was the threat of approaching conflict; and as the outbreak of war drew near, the Blooms and their two-month-old son were summoned from the peace of Lausanne to return to Moscow.

There they lived with the other members of the Scriabin family in a house rented by the composer, now the Scriabin Museum (11 Vakhtangova Street, near the Arbat). Decades later, when Metropolitan Anthony visited the house, he claimed he instinctively felt at home there.

Grandfather Nikolai died, aged sixty-five, that year. A photograph taken towards the end of his life showed he had never lost his proud bearing and seemed to confirm his son Alexander's assessment of him as stiff, insensitive and despotic. However, Metropolitan Anthony, when himself in his eighties, took a different view. Looking at the same photo he was impressed by the upright appearance of the grandfather he had never known.

'When I look in the mirror at myself I don't see the same thing,' he would say wistfully. 'He seems so dignified: not the sort of man who would ever run for a bus!'

Metropolitan Anthony's parishioners could only be grateful that their bishop, despite his undoubted dignity in church, had been exactly the unpretentious sort of man who was ready to run for a bus in his younger days.

Nikolai's death was the first of a series of bereavements for Olga. Her eldest son was killed in action early in the war; then her stepson Alexander died in the spring of 1915 on the very day, it was said, that the lease ran out on the Vakhtangova apartment. The composer was only forty-three. There was a distant Scriabin relative who was to enjoy much greater longevity. Vyacheslav Mikhailovich Scriabin became an ardent Bolshevik and rose to high and notorious office in the Soviet regime. He was better known by his assumed revolutionary name of 'The Hammer': Molotov. However disconcerting the family found it at times, in later years Metropolitan Anthony felt a certain amusement at being related to someone so vehemently opposed to his own religious and political convictions.

Boris Bloom was now posted to Persia, where he was to remain as consul until the Revolution, working in a number of locations. He took with him his wife, infant son and widowed mother-in-law, who although only in her early fifties took on a very passive role within the household.

Persia was to furnish the young André with his earliest memories and his only childhood experience of normal home life. As for Russia, it became a distant object of nostalgia, a lost cultural and spiritual home to which the Blooms would never as a family return.

CHAPTER TWO

EARLY CHILDHOOD

(1916–1923)

'One of my earliest memories was of Persia, looking out over a great plain stretching to the horizon; and in the middle of it, very small, a shepherd leading his flock of sheep as shepherds do in the Middle East.'

That childhood picture was one which Metropolitan Anthony would later recall as an image of the biblical shepherd, and in particular of Christ the Good Shepherd walking ahead of his sheep. It was all the more relevant since not only was his own life to be devoted to being a spiritual shepherd, but the cathedral in London where he spent almost his entire ministry bore the mosaic inscription 'I am the Good Shepherd' over the west door. So the shepherd image was to encompass the whole of his conscious life.

Persia provided other images, remembered as vivid interludes in a comfortable and comparatively happy childhood. Boris Bloom's diplomatic career entailed frequent travelling and many changes of residence; the family lived in about ten different places during their six-year stay, although exactly where they all were Metropolitan Anthony, who professed to have no interest in geography, could not say. Among a kaleidoscope of memories he would recall big city gates, possibly he thought at Teheran or Tabriz, and something of the bustle of the Middle Eastern way of life with its dusty roads and the melee of horses, donkeys and human traffic. Home was invariably spacious premises abutting the embassy or consulate, such as a house that he could remember going to inspect before yet another move. One of its prime features, as far as the five-year-old was concerned, was a large overgrown garden, and he relished the crackling sound as he dragged his feet through its long, dry grass.

Two years before that the tragedy of the Revolution had struck Russia. Yet although the adult world was at this time plunged into chaos, André's nursery life was cocooned from the threats which were of such concern to his parents. While his father struggled with the diplomatic situation the rest of the family continued to live a leisurely life surrounded by servants. Metropolitan Anthony looked back on it as a blissful existence.

It was, however, not altogether without its darker moments. Outside the diplomatic *pairidaeza* – the Persian word for a walled garden from which is derived the English word 'paradise' – the world was a dangerous place, and not only on the political level. There were the wild animals which his parents hunted and wild dogs, which on one occasion mauled his pet dog to death. His other pet, a sheep, eventually suffered the same fate. This raw cruelty he would later refer to as 'tragic' without elaborating on the impact it had made on his sensitive nature.

What he was happy to enlarge on was the sheep's eccentric habits, which remained imprinted on his memory into old age. Every morning the animal would come into the dining room, take all the flowers out of the vases with its teeth and lay them carefully down on the table, before climbing on to the sofa where it would settle comfortably until it was chased out – indignantly on the first few occasions, but with a certain laisser faire as it became part of the daily routine.

One animal that stayed firmly outside was a donkey. This perverse beast was meant to furnish André with his introduction to horsemanship, and the boy spent many hours in the company of the Persian servants attempting to ride it. After a lengthy ritual of finding it in the large grounds and saddling it, getting it to obey him was not an easy task. It had what Metropolitan Anthony referred to as its 'principles', a stubborn intent on going in the opposite direction to its young rider's wishes. So in order to get it to move forward André would have to give its tail a vigorous jerk backwards.

Horsemanship was an essential skill since four-legged transport was the norm in the Middle East of the early 1920s. In Persia, where pedestrians counted for little, André also had to learn to keep out of the way of passing riders. He would be seven before he saw a car.

There was, however, a train, running a short distance to the town of Kermanshah, and riding on it was an exciting event not only for a little boy but for all its passengers. Travelling away from the town was downhill and uneventful; the return was another matter. The engine would puff its way up the gradient as far as a humpback bridge, where it came to an undignified halt. All the men would get off and the nobles and the Europeans would walk beside the train while the peasants got behind and pushed it over the bridge. Then everyone climbed back on board and the train chugged triumphantly into the town.

For the first four years of his life André had a Russian nanny. One incident which occurred during her appointment was an early manifestation of his natural tenacity, in this instance showing itself as a childhood tantrum. Refusing to do something on which his mother was insistent, he threw himself on to the floor and spent a couple of hours howling in rage and frustration. The hapless nanny tried to intervene but Xenia had other ideas. She sent the woman out of the room, sat back in an armchair with a book and waited for her son to cry himself to exhaustion. When he eventually stopped she simply said, 'Have you finished? Now do as you were told.'

Unlike some children he did not store this incident in his mind to hold against his mother. On the contrary, he claimed this was one anecdote he did not remember himself; it was she who told him of it years later. Despite the occasional rebellion he felt his parents were reasonable in their discipline and sensitive to his fears. Like many children he was afraid of the dark; and they accepted it without making any attempt to cure him by ridicule. He in turn was sensitive to their quiet and genuine affection. He claimed he was never tempted to retreat into an inner world of dissimulation as many children do when they are subjected to unfair or excessive discipline.

Honesty was a virtue instilled into him from the cradle, both by instruction and by example, although much later in life he was to discover that lying might be necessary in extreme situations – and he would quote a chilling example of an unthinking, literal honesty that could kill. During the Second World War a member of the French Resistance was being hunted by the occupying Germans across some fields. Running up to a farmer he asked for help, and the man let him hide in the farmhouse. When the German soldiers arrived they asked the farmer whether he had seen the fugitive run past the house.

'No,' said the farmer truthfully. The Germans, however, were convinced the man had passed that way, and asked him a further question. 'Well, did anyone go into the house?'

'Yes,' admitted the farmer, again truthfully. The Germans set about searching the house and soon found their quarry. As the man was being dragged away he called out to the farmer, 'Why oh why did you tell them I was here?'

'I am a Christian,' replied the farmer. 'I do not lie.'

Metropolitan Anthony was to tell this story at one of his parish talks in answer to a question about the necessity for white lies. 'I offer it without comment,' he said, although he went on to add that even when expedient, lying was not the ideal of a disciple of Christ who was the Way, the Truth and the Life; and he would often, as a priest, remind people that Satan was The Liar and the father of lies.

In 1918, following the Revolution, the nanny departed and André was left in the day-to-day care of his mother and grandmother, who continued to shield him from the turmoil of the outside world that was impinging more and more on their own consciousness. His life went on peacefully as before – on his own admission somewhat lethargically. In later years he would quote his grandmother's comment, 'You were born tired.' It was a trait he saw as natural to the Russian character; he would describe Russians as people who were never oppressively active if they could avoid it.

In his case there was also a physical reason for his lack of energy. During his time in Persia he suffered from bouts of dysentery. He became very frail and was lucky to survive, although at the time he did not see survival as luck. 'I used to crawl into bed at night thankful that the misery of the day was over, and just wishing I could die,' was how he described his feelings about his illness. It was the first of many situations in which he expressed the desire to go to sleep and not wake up again.

Sickness apart, his early childhood might have seemed the perfect upper-class expatriate existence. However, it suffered from one deficiency: there were no playmates of his own age. He remained an only child, brought up among adults. It was characteristic that he never commented unfavourably on that; it suited his introverted, shy disposition.

Inevitably there were moments when loneliness got the better of him, but from an early age he was taught to overcome it. When on one occasion he ventured, 'Gran, I'm bored,' her prompt reply was, 'Well, go to your room and learn not to be bored.'

Olga's usual response was, however, more constructive. She was happy to play the part of the doting granny and would spend hours reading to him, and this quickly became his favourite pastime. She read all the children's classics while he sat listening beside her or lying, ears pricked, on the floor drawing illustrations to the stories. He had a natural affinity with a pencil which he was never to lose.

Olga read and spoke to him in French. With his father he spoke Russian, and with his mother both languages. From the servants he picked up Persian, and although he apparently forgot it within a short while of leaving the country he retained it for some time on the subconscious level. When, as a nine-year-old, he had nightmares at boarding school in Paris he was said to cry out in Persian in his sleep, although he could no longer recall a word of it during the day.

While there was no other attempt by his family to 'develop' him, as he put it, in the formal educational sense, he was unwittingly learning the skills of concentration and understanding. He readily absorbed everything he heard his grandmother read to him; not only the subject-matter of the books but the expressive way she read, which even as an old man he would recall with admiration, and the way in which she would discuss with him what they had read, so that he could draw real moral value from it.

Another virtue his family instilled in him was tidiness. Putting away his toys was a prerequisite to any other activity. This discipline, strengthened in time by his love of all things military, was to follow him into adulthood. As a youth leader in the camps in France, for instance, he would insist on a high standard of orderliness, and as a priest and bishop he carried on this discipline in the way he cared for the church.

Despite their comfortable lifestyle his parents taught him from an early age to value small things and they were never tempted to spoil him with too many toys. That was to prove doubly useful during the ensuing years of emigration when their material possessions were at a minimum.

André was also beginning to learn about the virtues valued by the diplomatic social stratum into which he had been born: honour, and courage, and duty to one's fellow men. Boris Bloom would spend time with his young son telling him heroic tales in order to develop in his son an admiration for the manly qualities of his day. From the very beginning he was at pains to inculcate André with, as he saw them, beautiful and lofty ideals, in particular the importance of living not for oneself but for a cause. It was partly because of that training that Metropolitan Anthony always professed to be uninterested in and forgetful of the details of his own life, unless they could be used as a parable to illustrate a moral or spiritual lesson. History for its own sake was of little concern to him. It was life, and a life lived honourably, that counted.

As an example of the moral ideals he absorbed he recalled being taken by his parents one evening to visit a local nobleman's rose garden. Their host received them with all the hospitality of the Middle East, taking them round his *pairidaeza* to admire the flowers, serving them abundant refreshments and sending them away feeling he had been the most attentive and charming host imaginable. It was only the following day that they learnt how the unfortunate man's son had been murdered a few hours before their arrival, and had been lying dead in an upstairs room while the father had been entertaining the Russian consul and his family so magnificently in the garden below.

This incident made a deep impression on André, who saw in it even at his young age the absolute obligations of the living towards one another, even when surrounded by the grief of bereavement. It was to influence his own attitude and actions as an adult.

This was a time when bereavement was all around, in the carnage of the First World War, followed by the turmoil of the Revolution and consequent Civil War in Russia. Another incident with a similar moral which Metropolitan Anthony would quote from this period was a conversation between a young bride and her sister-in-law. The bride's new husband had been killed in battle, and the young woman came to his sister with the words, 'Rejoice, your brother has died heroically, fighting for his country.' Metropolitan Anthony described how this had impressed upon him the greatness of the human spirit and the vastness of human courage, as well as the sharpness of death.

On all sides, heroism and self-sacrifice were at the forefront of qualities being urged on young males. The Blooms found it natural to imbue their son with the ideals common to their day and their class. These were based on the moral rectitude of the secular world; religion played no noticeable part in André's early upbringing. For instance, Bible stories did not feature among the books he recalled his grandmother reading to him.

By 1920 Boris Bloom's position as consul had become untenable. He represented an imperial government no longer in existence; and Persia, itself in the middle of political upheaval, bordered the fledgling Soviet State and was a strategic posting. Like thousands of other upper-class Russians the Blooms found themselves faced with the prospect of dispossession and exile.

Boris arranged for his wife, young son and mother-in-law to leave the country on a diplomatic passport while he stayed behind to supervise the handing over of the embassy. The plan was to send the family to England, but in the prevailing conditions this would be no straightforward journey.

There were two possibilities for women travelling unaccompanied. They could either be put in the care of the military who, they were warned, would more likely than not rob them and even, if the convoy were attacked by bandits, desert them; or they could be entrusted direct to the bandits, who were hardly worse than the soldiers and who might just prove a little more reliable. In a desperate situation Boris Bloom chose the latter option, and the family began packing up its belongings. Whatever they took would become their only worldly possessions, since anything left in Russia had been seized by the Soviet authorities. Space was at a premium; they could only pack the most important objects. Because they would have to face the extreme cold of the Persian winter on their journey, sensible underclothes naturally took precedence over trinkets or treasured toys. At the last minute, however, sentiment overcame practicality and they threw into the final wooden chest a number of their most cherished personal belongings.

Xenia, Olga and André set out with their risky escort to traverse the north of Persia and Kurdistan in the depths of the harsh upland winter, travelling by carriage or on horseback depending on circumstances and the terrain. The weather was bitter, there was little food and progress was slow. Hungry and bored the seven-year-old André began to whine for something to eat and, in an age when there was no medical or social disapproval, his mother tried to distract his attention by the only means available: a cigarette.

This was to be the beginning and the end of his foray into smoking. He found cigarettes 'a pure deception'; they neither satisfied hunger nor provided any pleasurable diversion. Nothing was ever to change his mind about that. One obvious reason was the fact that he was asthmatic, but his forceful personality also played its part. As a teenager he was told he would no doubt take up smoking like everybody else, to which his resolute response was that he had no wish to be like everybody else. Later, his fellow students at medical school said he would be bound to smoke when he got into the dissecting room because nobody could endure it otherwise. His instinctive reaction, born of contrariness rather than virtue, was to decide, 'Not me. I'll die rather than smoke!'

Having traversed the mountains of Kurdistan they began the next stage of the journey away from Persia by barge down the Tigris and the Euphrates through present-day Iraq. At the confluence of the two rivers a beautiful sight awaited them. Where tradition sited the Garden of Eden the wide blue waters of the Euphrates were sliced through by the red current of the fast-flowing Tigris. For several hundred metres André watched this vivid phenomenon, storing it in his memory as a wonder never to be forgotten, as was the sight of a tiny desiccated tree fenced with a railing and festooned with pieces of cloth according to the Middle Eastern custom: the Tree of the Knowledge of Good and Evil, it was said.

At last the barge reached the port of Basra, and André's boredom was replaced by excitement as the journey took a series of unpredictable turns. They had intended to take a ship direct to England but to their dismay they found that was out of the question. The sea was still heavily mined as a result of the war. They were forced instead to continue travelling eastwards to India from where they would, they were assured, be able to find ongoing transport to Britain.

A month's stay in the languid heat of Bombay waiting for a ship provided more vivid memories: the deep red of the buildings, the oppressively hot weather and the grisly Towers of Silence where the Parsees laid out their dead to be a prey for the vultures wheeling overhead.

Passage was finally secured on an ageing vessel bound for Southampton. Even before the voyage began there were doubts as to the ship's seaworthiness. The adults boarded with misgiving, having been told by the captain to hope for fine weather, as it was too much of an old tub to survive any storm. To a boy of seven to whom his grandmother had read *Robinson Crusoe* that conjured up the thrilling prospect of shipwreck on some desert island. Why was his mother so prosaically hoping for fair weather? The captain, always the pessimist, had the novel idea of allocating André, Xenia and Olga to different lifeboats so that if the worst happened at least one member of the family would survive.

His precautions proved unnecessary. Slowly the ship ploughed its way through the Suez Canal to Alexandria and then onwards through the Mediterranean until after twenty-three days they limped into Gibraltar. Since the captain would not risk taking them through the Bay of Biscay the passengers were put ashore with most of their luggage. The only piece which went missing – it went on to Southampton and was retrieved fourteen years later after the Blooms had paid the £1 customs charge – was the very chest into which they had packed all their treasures.

Stranded in Gibraltar they began trekking overland in search of some kind of haven. They headed north across Spain, and the mosque at Cordoba was the next thing to imprint itself on to André's memory. This time it was not a visual image that he retained but a feeling for the atmosphere: breathtaking beauty and silence, he was to describe it as an adult. These were two qualities he would go on to find so perfectly expressed in Orthodoxy. Yet as a Christian bishop he was never slow to recognise the genuine spirituality of other religions and their very real awareness of God, and he was fond of recounting the story of the Muslim whose guests could talk as loudly as they liked all around him while he was at prayer because his concentration and inner silence were so intense. Indeed, it was that very inner silence which he insisted on bringing to his own cathedral in London, which became known across Europe for its unique sense of stillness.

From Spain they continued north through France to Paris, where the shock of European culture really made its impact. For the first time in his life André encountered electricity, and it was a fascinating discovery. They entered a room and he waited for the usual fuss of preparing and lighting the oil lamps. That was not necessary here, said his mother, there was electricity. And there was a click, and instant light.

To André it was an incomprehensible piece of wizardry heralding a new world. Another marvel was motor traffic. It was not only the cars that were a novelty. That there could be rules of the road was a new concept to him. Travelling from the station by taxi down the Champs Elysées he was astonished to see a man standing in the middle of the road waving his arms about. In Persia that would have meant certain death; he would have been mown down in an instant by a passing carriage. So the young boy shouted gallantly to his mother, 'Quick, let's haul him into the car and save him before he is killed!' She replied calmly that there was no need. The man was a policeman on traffic duty, and it was not allowed to kill a policeman. It was a staggering revelation. 'Marvellous!' André thought to himself. 'All I have to do is become a policeman and I'll be protected from accidents and live for ever!' It was not the sort of eternal life he would eventually come to desire.

Their financial situation was now such that Xenia had to look for work. When Paris proved unfruitful the trio made their way to Austria to Olga's elder sister, by this time married to a Viennese. From there they continued on to northern Yugoslavia to the vicinity of Zagreb and Maribor where they lived and worked for some time on a farm. Even the seven-year-old André was able to earn a little money doing odd jobs people found for him.

When the jobs ran out they returned to Vienna for eighteen months, and in this relative stability André was enrolled at a school. He could not understand the necessity. Why should he learn his letters when he could sit and listen to grandmother reading so beautifully? In fact, she had embarked on reading to him the whole of Dickens, a writer to whom at the time he warmed; it was only as an adult re-reading him in English that he came to view him critically as, he thought, sentimental.

His uncle tried to explain the value of education. He himself had done well at school and now he had a successful career and a good salary with which to support his family.

'In that case', the young boy retorted, 'why can't you support our family as well, and I can stay at home?'

The inevitable happened. Like all children starting school for the first time André found himself a small creature in a strange world, but for him this was also a foreign one where it was easy to misunderstand and be misunderstood. For instance, Xenia had registered his religion simply as 'Orthodox', and in pre-war Vienna that was assumed to mean Orthodox Jewish, especially for someone with the surname Bloom. So for his first religious education lesson he was sent to the rabbi.

The rabbi looked him up and down and asked why he was not wearing a little black hat. André replied innocently, 'I don't have a little black hat, but at home I do have an icon and a cross.'

'A cross?' the rabbi exclaimed in surprise. 'You're a Christian?' The man promptly threw him out of the class. André hung about in the corridor not knowing where to go. Eventually the headmaster came along and asked him what he was doing.

'The rabbi threw me out because I am a Christian', he replied.

'Oh, you're a Christian. In that case I'll take you to the priest.'

The priest asked him if he were a Roman Catholic.

'No, I'm a Russian Orthodox', André said.

'An Orthodox? Then you're a heretic!' Whereupon the priest also threw him out.

'And that', Metropolitan Anthony would say with a triumphant smile, 'was the end of my religious education!'

It was something he professed not to regret. Despite his icon and his cross he was not a believing child, and he was later grateful that he had not grown up with a borrowed faith foisted upon him by well-intentioned adults or indifferent schoolteachers.

There were other problems being a Russian in a Viennese school. Before he could learn to read and write he had to learn German. That he was able to do so in a native environment meant that he grew up speaking it without a foreign accent, to the extent that he could be mistaken for a German. He was particularly proud of the occasion when as a bishop he met a blind German cardinal who was intrigued to know how a fellow countryman had become Orthodox. Knowing that the blind are known for being particularly sensitive to sound Metropolitan Anthony took that as a special compliment.

The day came at school when he had become sufficiently competent in

German to be able to write his first essay. The subject was the familiar: 'What I want to be when I grow up.' All the other children produced the usual sort of answers: doctors, lawyers and other worthy if dull professions.

André's contribution was, on the other hand, totally original. By chance his family had taken him the previous day to the Tiergarten, Vienna's zoo, where the antics of the monkeys had particularly entranced him. So he wrote that when he grew up he would like to be a monkey. He described in detail how he would swing through the trees and hang by his tail, and he accompanied his words with what he considered were beautiful line drawings. He was sure the teacher could not fail to be impressed. When the following day she gave back the essays she did indeed call him to his feet, saying that his work had been quite unlike any of the others. He recalled feeling so proud as he stood up in front of the class, certain she was about to praise him not just for the excellence of his German but also for his outstanding imagination. Instead she let fly a tirade of abuse. The good little Austrian children had wanted to better themselves and improve the human race, but all this dirty foreigner, this Russian barbarian, could think of was to revert to his ancestors in the jungle.

This unexpected attack wounded him to a degree he never forgot. In later years he referred to it as the most humiliating experience of his life, saying that for ever after he never minded whatever insults people threw at him because they were 'like water off a duck's back' by comparison. Up to this point he had experienced the uncertainties of exile as exciting. Now he also discovered the other side of émigré life: the trauma of always being an outsider, a foreigner, a ready butt of cruel prejudice.

There was one more unexpected thing he learnt at the school in Vienna. To his utter disgust he was taught embroidery. 'And I unlearnt it as soon as possible!' was his response.

When he returned to Vienna fifty years later to record some radio programmes he discovered that the interviewer had by chance been at school with him, although neither recognised the other or made any further contact.

In 1923 André, his mother and grandmother left Austria for Paris, where they were to live for nearly thirty years. Boris had by this time joined the rest of the family after having been held up for some time in Istanbul. They were not alone. A flood of Russian refugees fleeing the Bolshevik victory in the Russian Civil War had settled in the French capital, where they were destined largely to eke out a sad and poverty-stricken existence. Penniless aristocrats had to take whatever work came their way. Being stateless they were not entitled to the French dole; those who did not work starved. The old Russia of whose society they had been the cream was gone, and with it their wealth, their status and their culture. In this desperate émigré community the Blooms endeavoured to find themselves a niche.

CHAPTER THREE

SCHOOLDAYS IN PARIS

(1923–1929)

T he Russian émigré community in 1920s Paris was a world apart. A hundred thousand or so impoverished members of the upper and middle classes were crammed into miserable conditions in which they created their own detached world, with no thought of integration into the surrounding French culture. In certain areas of the city, such as the 15th arrondissment, Russian was the lingua franca in shops and bars; churches appeared on almost every corner – and sometimes in the most unlikely buildings. An outpost of Mother Russia was created as a temporary resting place until they could defeat Bolshevism and return to their beleaguered homeland.

In the meantime, people lived on the breadline. In this difficult situation the first imperative for both Bloom parents was to find work; in Paris they had no comfortable relatives to fall back on. Xenia, educated for the life of a lady of leisure, knew that immediate employment prospects were not good. Once the mistress of the house with servants, she now found domestic work to be the only option. However, what she lacked in skill she made up for in resourcefulness and intelligence. In between scrubbing floors she set about teaching herself typing and shorthand which, once mastered, she used with her foreign languages to keep herself more or less constantly in work, even during the height of the Depression. But she barely earned a living wage. This was not an era of equal pay for women and inflated salaries for top-flight secretaries.

Boris Bloom had meanwhile turned his back on the diplomatic circle. In exile he began to brood over the causes of the Russian Revolution and the responsibility his social class carried for the ills that had led to the collapse of the imperial system. He found his way out of this moral crisis by seeing a role for himself in atoning for its sins, choosing to become a manual worker. For several years he worked on the railways and in factories, eking out a meagre material existence, and it was only as a result of poor health that he eventually turned to clerical work. However, he was never tempted to climb a new career ladder in order to provide a comfortable standard of living for his family. Whatever financial hardship his wife and son had to endure, he did not think it just cause for abandoning the austere and impoverished life he had chosen for his own peace of mind.

Neither parent could even provide a home. Each family member had to find some sort of lodging as best they could: Boris here, Grandmother there, Xenia somewhere else. For André there was nowhere at all, nor anyone with the time or resources to look after him. In later years he described this experience in stark terms: 'It was very unpleasant from a moral standpoint to feel not only that you were superfluous but also simply unwanted, with nowhere in the world to call your own.'

The practical answer was for his parents to put him into a boarding school. The Roman Catholic Church was offering scholarships to Russian children at their privilege schools, supposedly with no strings attached, and Xenia took her son along for an interview. It seemed to go well; indeed, André was offered a place, they were given a conducted tour and all the necessary arrangements were apparently finalised. Just as they were preparing to leave the interviewer paused and said, 'Of course, this is on condition the boy becomes a Catholic.' Horrified by what he saw as deliberate deception and an attempt at enforced conversion, André turned to his mother and said, 'Come on, let's get out of here. I'm not for sale!'

This incident had a profound effect on his attitude towards religion. Thereafter he viewed the Church – any church – as untrustworthy. Over the next few years his experience of the harsh émigré life in Paris was to harden this resistance to religion. While his subsequent personal conversion changed his views in general, he was always to retain a specific distrust of the Roman Catholic Church, which later ecumenical contact at times fuelled rather than assuaged. More importantly, as a result of this incident he remained throughout his life absolutely adamant that Christian charitable aid should be entirely without preconditions and was never to be accompanied by any form of religious coercion or material incentive. He had learnt at first hand the disastrous negative impression that could make.

Another school had to be found. The only option now open to them was a boarding school situated in an unsavoury quarter of Paris – the cheapest they could find. The first sight of the dormitory was like walking into a workhouse. Stretching the length of the room was a regimented line of identical bed, chair, bed, chair – more than seventy of them. One was to be André's, a cruel parody of what he had once understood as home.

The school's grim first appearance was but a foretaste of the horror that awaited him. As the new boy – this was the norm, he discovered later, and it would only cease when the next victim came along – he was bullied without mercy. Being a well-mannered upper-class child he was totally unprepared for the violence of a slum school where brutality was the only law. He did not know how to retaliate when he was beaten up by the other boys; and until he learnt to fight back he was beaten up with sickening regularity. On one occasion he tried to run to a teacher for protection, only to have the man push him back into the crowd of boys with his foot with the command, 'Fight!'

There were other agonies. It was forbidden to go to the lavatory at night; the dormitory supervisor did not want his sleep interrupted. Faced with absolute necessity André would have to pull back the bedclothes and slither as noiselessly as he could to the floor, tiptoe past all the other beds and try to open the door without a telltale creak betraying his movements. Failure meant another beating, this time by the staff.

Sometimes boys were so badly battered one way or another that they ended up needing hospital treatment. It was an accepted part of the school routine in an age when physical brutality towards children was not thought of in terms of abuse. The only possible way for André to survive in such conditions was to learn to play by the same rules: to exchange a loving, open disposition for distrust and animosity; to create a tough exterior and meet force with force. He could not learn that overnight, and until he did the intervening period was one of physical and emotional torture.

Looking back on this period towards the end of his life Metropolitan Anthony referred to it in language that still betrayed something of the horror: 'Never in the whole of my life have I endured so much fear and pain, both physical and emotional. And the things I learnt then, apart from endurance, were things I had to spend a long time unlearning later on: first, that every human being of either sex, any age and size is a danger to you; second, that you can survive only if you become stony, absolutely devoid of emotion; and third, that you can survive only by learning the laws of the jungle.' The shy boy content with his own company became of necessity a lone wolf, convinced that he was battling

against a hostile world. In adulthood he referred to the people who had surrounded him at this time, both children and adults, as 'hateful creatures'
and to himself, in the third person, as 'a young man hard as nails'.

He admitted that it had subsequently taken him years unlearning that
hardness of heart, although whether he ever truly conquered this destructive side of his nature was sometimes questioned by his spiritual children,
some of whom had occasion to encounter its residue. It was not merely
the physical battering that had scarred him.

One indication of the depth of this scarring was the occasion, decades
later, when during a visit to Paris he was travelling on the Metro.
Engrossed for some time in a book, he happened to glance up and find
himself at the nearest station to his old school, and fainted with terror.

Another negative, if less violent way in which his early schooling
influenced him in later life was the effect it had on his musical development. There might have been high hopes for the nephew of a composer.
Whether any pressure was ever put on the little boy to show signs of musicality he never said. What he was always quick to point out was how, from
the very beginning of his schooldays, he was recognised as being totally
lacking in any musical ability. When the class was taught to sing the notes
of the stave his efforts were, he said, so bad that after a while the teacher
pointed to him and said, 'You, just say the names of the notes and don't
sing any more.' He quoted this story as definitive evidence of his musical
ineptitude, which he insisted was later confirmed at medical school when
the professor of psychiatry referred to his absence of musicality as a
'specialised idiocy'. In fact, he seemed to consider himself physically
incapable of appreciating music.

This was not true. He suffered not from lack of musical ability but from
a lifelong mental block on the subject. This was a great pity because had a
good ear, a fine adult singing voice which he projected well with a pleasant vibrato and a nice sense of phrasing. But he was never able to accept
any judgement except that of his childhood teacher.

The hellish school life was punctuated by visits to his family. Weekly
boarders were let out of school at midday on Saturday, but his mother had
to get him back before nightfall on Sunday afternoon because it was not
safe to walk through the neighbourhood after dark. Yet even this one free
day, a brief respite from violence, was not without its own problems.
There was no home to which André could go. His mother occupied a tiny
room in the hotel where she worked as a receptionist. She was allowed to
take her son there during the day but the proprietor refused to let him stay
the night. In desperation Xenia invented a weekly ritual deception. Each

Saturday evening she would make a show of leaving the hotel with the boy, making sure the manager saw them go. Then she would come back alone and engage the man in conversation at the reception desk in order to distract his attention while André crawled in on all fours behind his mother, along the corridor and back into her room. Next day he would creep out in the same fashion before Xenia set off to fetch him from a mythical 'other place' where he had supposedly spent the night.

This sorry subterfuge made its own impact on him. He began to feel his very existence was nothing but a liability. For this mentally and physically tortured nine-year-old life had become unbearable. He began to spend his free days wandering the streets, crossing roads blindly in the hope that a car would knock him down and put him out of his misery. One nearly did: a taxi slammed on its brakes, the driver pulled him out from under his wheels and gave him a good hiding.

The long French summer holidays were a breath of heaven compared to school. They would spend them in the country where André was able to get a job on a farm to earn what was a pittance – 50 centimes – but which seemed to him a fortune. When he looked back on the experience it was not the hard work that he recalled but receiving his very first week's wages: the feel of the coins between his fingers, the way he walked back to the village swinging his arms with pride as boys do – and the next moment the precious money had flown out of his hand and into the grass by the roadside. He searched long and bitterly, without success. The whole week's effort was gone for good. It was one more painful incident to store in his memory, drawing him to the conclusion that the world was a hostile place.

There were, however, occasional brighter moments. Grandmother would sometimes come and read to him on Saturdays, there would be food such as grapes which he never had at school, and very rarely the money to buy a new book. He acquired a French translation of *Ivanhoe* and warmed to the excitement of the story, although in adulthood he was more critical of Scott's writing. His love of reading was never to diminish and throughout his life books remained one of the rare things he spent money on. Toys were few and all the more appreciated. One Christmas his parents gave him a small Russian flag. They explained the tricolor's significance: the white stood for Russian snow, the blue for Russian seas and the red for Russian blood. It became one of his most treasured possessions. He would run it through his fingers lovingly; even as an old man he could still conjure up the feel of the silky fabric in his hands.

He had some tin soldiers, and these became the focus of an intense interest in all things military. At the same time he joined the Russian scouts, where this interest found a ready outlet. The Russian youth groups and the summer camps they spawned became an important part of the émigré community's efforts to keep its culture and national identity alive. They were also a training ground for what it hoped would be the eventual liberation of Russia from the communist yoke – by conquest if necessary.

In 1925 a particularly painful event occurred. The Soviet government issued a decree depriving all exiles of their Russian nationality. It was, in Metropolitan Anthony's words, 'a shock and a catastrophe for us'. First physically cast out, they now no longer had the right either technically, or in Soviet eyes morally, to be called Russian. The very people who saw themselves supremely as Russian patriots were made stateless, not merely perpetual foreigners but non-people. They were subsequently granted a Nansen passport, which gave them an identity but no right to travel. It was a demeaning situation and only added to the exiles' nationalistic fervour.

Despite sharing the ideals of his fellow scouts, André made no close friends. While relating to them on an external level he claimed not to be interested in them as individuals. Heroic ideals could be cherished and fought for. People on the other hand remained enemies.

The Blooms found the resources to send their son along to his first camp, where for a month or more he could live in a totally Russian society and enjoy some welcome country air. The camps were run on pseudo-military lines with a strict discipline. Each morning the children would stand to attention as the imperial flag was run up. The daily routine included the learning of military skills, sports and lessons, and the endurance of spartan conditions, the latter in any case a necessity given the endemic poverty of the émigré community. Luxuries such as camp beds were unknown; the children slept on newspapers on the ground. On the first night they spread them out in innocence and settled down. The rough terrain did not make for a good night's sleep. The second evening the children smoothed the ground and removed any underlying stones first; but that was little better; next morning their bodies were still stiff and sore from the hard earth. At last, on the third night they found the answer: by scooping out hollows for their shoulders and thighs they were able to achieve a passable level of comfort. It was not surprising that as an adult Metropolitan Anthony claimed he could drop off to sleep anywhere, even on a stone floor or in the dentist's chair.

Food at camp was meagre and washing facilities nothing more than a dip in the nearby sea or river. That did not dampen the excitement which being in the country or at the seaside afforded to these inner-city children. One year when André arrived at a camp in the South of France, not having seen the sea for a long time, he did not even wait to take off his rucksack but hurried straight down to the water's edge and stood on a rock gazing out in wonder towards the horizon.

'And a big boy came up behind me and pushed me in!' As an old man he could relate the story to young campers from his own diocese as a joke, but at the time the spoiling of his new clothes and gear that his mother had provided with such sacrifice was anything but funny.

Another year, when the camp was held on an island off the coast near La Rochelle, Xenia was forced to let the ten-year-old André make the journey from Paris alone because she could not afford the train fare to accompany him. With a mother's natural concern she waited for a letter telling of his safe arrival, but it never crossed his mind to write. Anxious, Xenia despatched a telegram to the camp. The ambiguous reply came back from the leader: 'Arrived safely La Rochelle'. But La Rochelle was on the coast! Had her son ever reached the island? Meanwhile, André continued to enjoy his holiday oblivious of the panic his lack of communication had caused.

'I just didn't think,' he would explain lamely when recounting this anecdote as an adult. He continued not to think about letter-writing all through his life, and that was to become a major source of exasperation to would-be correspondents of every kind, whether official or personal.

School life continued much the same for three years. First, its outward hostile situation, then his inner state of self-destruction, he was later to call 'hell'. That was no casual use of the word, but a statement of what was for him a theological reality: the absence of God which spells total hopelessness and inner annihilation. He was to exist imprisoned in this hell for the rest of his childhood, facing a continuous struggle to survive in terms of procuring the barest essentials that had to be fought for almost on a daily basis, but with nothing beyond.

The time came when he was due to transfer to a lycée. The proviso was that poor scholars were forced to repeat a year. Desperate not to remain in the hated school a moment longer than necessary André made sure his schoolwork was up to the required standard. Beyond that he claimed not to show undue interest in lessons. Possibly, as sometimes happens with bright children, he was unwilling to stand out academically for fear of further victimisation. Possibly he was unaware of his own progress and aptitude. What he was certainly aware of was being a Russian boy in a French milieu, always the outsider. To that he responded with disdain.

There was nothing in the alien culture to hold his attention. On his own admission he was too lazy to be a troublemaker.

To his relief he entered the Lycée Condorcet on schedule. The new school seemed like paradise compared to the other. It also entailed more expense. Under the French educational system pupils had to buy their own books, and his parents could not provide the money. André solved the problem by giving private tuition to younger children. He started by teaching maths and, in his own words, 'whatever else I already knew and they didn't'.

As a polyglot his linguistic skills were obviously far above those of the average pupil and this enabled him to pick up Latin with ease. He developed a passion for it and this was to become one of the major subjects he taught. He was fascinated by its structure; the grammar and syntax which were the bane of many a schoolboy's career enthralled him. In them he saw a oneness with architecture, another subject which interested him and about which he read widely, to such an extent that for a time he found himself considering it as a future career. Always a natural draughtsman, he could appreciate the way a building was put together just as a Latin sentence was constructed.

Another favourite subject was German. At a certain moment he was given the choice of learning German or English. Xenia suggested English, an idea he immediately rejected. 'No, I will not learn English. It is such an ugly language – and besides, since I shall never go to England in my whole life, what use would it be?' He admitted in later years that his refusal was less to do with a genuine antagonism to English and more to do with the fact that, already being fluent in German, he knew he would be able to get good marks without having to do any work for the first couple of years. His love of German was also genuine. He came to develop an interest in medieval German poetry which was to last a lifetime; as an adult he claimed to read it for relaxation as other people listened to music.

At school his affinity with languages became so marked that his passion for architecture began to take second place and he decided early on at the lycée that he would like to pursue a career as a language teacher. Never one to waste any effort on the unnecessary, he began to show less than appropriate enthusiasm for other subjects.

That attitude culminated in his handing in some physics homework which was so substandard that the teacher told him bluntly, 'I never want to see another piece of work like this again.'

'Very well,' André replied, 'I'll make a bargain with you. If you promise never to ask me to do any more homework nor to ask me any questions in class, I promise to sit quietly, do nothing and not disrupt your lessons.'

Such a display of independence, not to say insubordination, might have earned a less determined pupil a severe dose of discipline. The teacher, however, was foolish enough to acquiesce, and from that day he and André ignored each other. The stubborn boy claimed to have sat through his entire school career of physics lessons getting on with other subjects without doing any physics at all.

This irregular situation was eventually to catch up with him, as he was required to take the physics exam for his baccalaureat. He also discovered that as a stateless person he would not, under the French system, be allowed to become a teacher, and so he had to set about finding an alternative career. When he eventually decided on medicine he found to his dismay that physics was essential. He had three months in which to swot up the whole syllabus from scratch.

'And I found it was actually quite interesting,' he admitted many years later. 'It was the teacher who was so terrible, not the subject!' Nevertheless, a less determined personality might have thought the task in hand impossible, especially with his continuing tutoring commitments, but to André it was one way of many in which he resolved to push himself to the limit. He passed the exam.

But all that lay in a totally unexpected future for the twelve-year-old boy settling into his new school. Although he found it much more congenial than the first, it still belonged to a world of which he did not feel a part. No amount of French education could dilute his passionate Russianness. His military fervour was undiminished and he began to teach himself the sort of physical endurance he imagined necessary for someone training to recapture his homeland.

In this Boris Bloom was a ready instructor. He insisted, for example, that if his son were to pick up a saucepan that was too hot to handle, he should keep hold of it. A couple of burnt fingers were incidental to the disgrace of dropping it. The same principle applied to being in any form of physical discomfort. André warmed to such manifestations of courage and dedicated himself to living up to his father's ideals. As he entered his teens he began sleeping without any blankets by an open window. When it grew too cold to sleep he would get up and do a few exercises, then lie down again still uncovered. Only in much later life did he admit that these attempts at heroism appeared trite to late twentieth-century perceptions.

In 1927 his scout group collapsed and he joined another organisation run by the Russian Student Christian Movement, which was an influential focus of émigré youth. There were political squabbles among the émigrés, which were reflected in the various organisations, but this one was to hold André's loyalty for the rest of his life. It demanded a higher standard of Russian culture than the scouts, a fact to which he had to adjust, sometimes painfully. The first time he was given an assignment in one of the discussion groups, when he was about fourteen, he disgraced himself. He was asked to prepare a talk on 'Fathers and Sons', which in his ignorance of Turgenev's book he took merely to be a topic of family values. For a whole week he tried desperately to come up with something to say on the subject, without success. When the day came for him to give his talk to the group he installed himself in a corner hoping in vain that he would be overlooked. Finally called upon to speak, he began, 'I have spent the week thinking about this subject – ' and looking around at the group waiting in expectant silence he was obliged to add, ' – but I have come up with nothing.' So began and ended his very first lecture.

His attempts at acting were more successful. It was an activity he came to enjoy and for which he had an aptitude. On one occasion he appeared in a play about a young man who was, in his words, 'cuckoo'. A tutor was engaged for the character, and when the mother heard her son was being taught geography she commented, 'What use is geography so long as one can take a cab?' In adult life Metropolitan Anthony would echo these words to explain his own lack of interest in geography. He would also reveal his part in the play: the boy who was cuckoo. His talent for acting was also apparent in the way he sometimes, even as a bishop, mimicked voices; for instance, he might put on a thick French accent when recounting words of Father Lev Gillet, or break into a falsetto to repeat a woman's comments. This he always did with humour, never malice. He also appeared in plays put on by his own diocese's camps, invariably playing the part of a surgeon – but still wearing his cassock. 'I always wear black when I operate,' he would comment in mock villainy.

His acting ability came naturally to a boy who had long since lost his openness and decided he would hide his inner self from the world. But not only was there a sense in which his outward life became a performance; he also warmed to the attention of an audience. In adult life these factors contributed to making him such a good public speaker and preacher.

Apart from the superior intellectual quality of the new scout organisation its other important difference was that being a specifically Christian group it included religion among its activities. One of the leaders was a priest and there was a chapel at the summer camp for services. At this stage in his life André's hostility to all things religious was well developed. Whereas many of his contemporaries had simply outgrown their childhood faith, as children often do, his own hostility was something more vehement. He had never believed in God. His unhappy experience at the Roman Catholic school interview had in the ensuing years been reinforced by the sort of religion he saw in the lives of both Catholics and Protestants around him. Not only was he convinced that God did not exist, he saw the Church in purely negative terms, as an object of hatred, and he had no qualms about showing his defiant feelings. So when the camp bell rang for the Liturgy on Sunday mornings he and others of like mind would roll back the tent flaps – and stay put, to make it plain to the camp leaders that they were indeed awake but had not the slightest intention of getting up for the service.

That was a common enough attitude among boys of his age, and André saw no reason for it ever to change, despite one occasion when he was challenged by something he admitted to finding puzzling. At one of his first SCM camps there was a priest who made a lasting impression on him. With his long hair and straggling beard in the traditional Orthodox fashion, the man seemed to the children to be ancient – on adult reflection Metropolitan Anthony judged him to be in his thirties. He was, however, certainly mature in the practice of his faith. In particular, what André found so remarkable about him was his capacity to love. It was something that was not dependent on the children's good behaviour but a constant, deep and unconditional love for all of them, even at the cost of pain to himself. That was a startling experience for a young boy who was used to seeing his fellow humans in hostile terms. It temporarily disturbed his embittered outlook on life. He was not able to draw any immediate conclusions from it, religious or otherwise, but he stored the memory of the priest in his mind as a question mark, something that did not make sense according to his own world view. This, he came to understand as a bishop, was a vital way to reach out to people: not to try giving them ready-made answers, but to provoke questions, and questioning within themselves.

None of the members of his family were regular churchgoers. Once a year, André's parents would take him to the Good Friday service at the Russian Cathedral in the rue Daru. For many Orthodox children this service is a beautiful experience. In the centre of the nave a 'tomb' is placed, surrounded by flowers, and a life-sized icon of the dead Christ is brought in procession from the sanctuary and placed there for the faithful to venerate. Even in the poorest church the flowers and the candles, the incense and the singing create an atmosphere to which children can readily respond. Many do. André remained stubbornly indifferent.

He soon discovered a foolproof way of escaping from this annual religious duty. Incense in sufficient quantities exacerbated his asthma and made him feel faint. Thereafter he never took more than a few steps inside the church before taking some deep breaths to inhale the incense, fainting and being taken straight home.

If the Russian Church did not act as a national focus for the exiled Blooms, Russian culture did. They referred to the French as 'the natives' – without, Metropolitan Anthony would hasten to stress, any racist overtones but simply as a fact of life, much as they referred to other things around them that they considered irrelevant. 'France would be a nice place without the French' was one of Xenia's sayings, which betrayed something of the attitude of ex-patriots everywhere.

There was a certain amount of animosity on both sides. In the difficult economic circumstances of 1920s France the local people had not been entirely happy with having their capital flooded with refugees. As commonly happens, large numbers of immigrants were not tolerated with the grace that might have been shown to a smaller group more willing to integrate.

In 1928 a significant change took place in the family's circumstances. They were able for the first time since leaving Persia to afford to rent a flat of their own and live together under one roof. Xenia, Olga and André moved into a modest apartment situated physically in Bois-Colombes; emotionally it was for the young teenager a return to paradise. At last he had somewhere to call home, with the stability of a loving family around him.

He had a room of his own, which became his particular haven and where he could retreat to read or simply be alone with himself. He rarely went to visit other boys or invited anyone back. In fact, he put up on his wall a quotation from the French writer Vauvenargues: 'He who comes to visit me will do me honour; he who does not come will give me pleasure.' On the only occasion when he did invite a boy home, the lad took one look at the quotation and left.

As a working mother Xenia made sure all the members of the family did their share of the chores. 'My mother brought me up to be a daughter as well as a son, which is just as well as things have turned out,' Metropolitan Anthony would explain to parishioners who were concerned about his having to fend for himself. The two chores he baulked at, for many years, were cleaning his shoes and dusting. In later life he claimed to enjoy washing up, finding it 'restful'.

Before he went to bed he would prepare things ready for the next day, a discipline that came from his father. Boris described his reasoning: 'Each night I have a servant Boris who does everything – cleans my shoes, gets my clothes ready – and the next morning Boris Edwardovich the gentleman can get up and have nothing to do.'

Boris Bloom did not feature in André's blissful domestic scene. His economically enforced separation from Xenia had become voluntary and permanent; they divorced, and Xenia reverted to using the surname Scriabine. Variously described as a stern and disappointed man or as ultra-sensitive, Boris's penitential search after truth had finally led him to God and he determined to retreat into an ascetic existence apart from his family.

As time went on this began to bear fruit and people were to see a more charismatic side to his nature, seeking him out for spiritual advice. Meanwhile, he lived in utter poverty in a tiny room at the top of a tall house, to which he returned after work to spend his free time in prayer, spiritual reading and silence, only allowing himself any social contact at weekends. For him paradise was no longer attainable in this world.

In order not to be disturbed he would often pin to the door a notice: 'Please do not bother to knock. I am at home but I shall not open the door.' In retrospect Metropolitan Anthony praised this move as a much more positive attitude than coming up with a series of excuses for not seeing people. At the time, however, it was unpleasant for the young André to knock and call out, 'Daddy, it's me!' and still be refused an answer.

His parents' divorce was yet another emotional blow for André. One of its results was to make him feel the total weight of responsibility for his mother and grandmother. He was now, and permanently, the man of the house, a situation he took very seriously, determined that he should not let them down. They in turn came to rely increasingly on him, with a closeness that at times he found stifling.

Meanwhile, for a few months André continued to delight in the luxury of having a home again. Years later he said in a broadcast, 'Even now, when I have dreams of perfect happiness, they happen in that flat.' Yet it was not a state destined to last. In the protective atmosphere of his mother's apartment, paradise once attained soon palled unexpectedly. Many of the fundamental concerns that had ruled his day-to-day life for years – where to find a bed for the night, where the next meal was coming from – had simply ceased to exist. Instead of an interminable struggle there was suddenly nothing in front of him but a future that was cosy but lacking in any purpose or meaning. With nothing to fight for, even the prospect of studying for a career now seemed an empty promise. Outside the walls of his *pairidaeza* the world was still a hostile place peopled with enemies. If that was all it could offer him it was not worth enduring.

He was nearly fifteen. In characteristically determined fashion he decided that he would give himself a year to try to find a way out of this 'endless meaninglessness' as he called it. If he could not, he would resolve the situation with the same reasoning of the nine-year-old who had tried to seek oblivion under a passing car: he would commit suicide.

PART TWO

NEW LIFE

CHAPTER FOUR

⟳ ⟲

CONVERSION

(1929–1932)

André's dramatic decision to find a meaning for his life or put an end to it was followed by months of barren existence, without any revellation that might deflect him from his suicidal intentions. He was to suffer from lifelong bouts of depression and a recurrent penchant for death. He claimed in his old age, 'I have been wanting to die ever since I was born' – but this particular early occurrence threatened to be his last. As the spring of 1929 approached, the schoolboy who should have been emerging into manhood seemed destined for eternal winter. He could not find an answer to his vain searching. No amount of concentration on school work or dedication to his Russian youth organisation convinced him that the world had anything worthwhile to offer. Nor did the example of his father apparently make any impression on him. How could a life of prayer and spirituality have any meaning if one were convinced there was no God?

One evening he arrived at his youth group to find that the leader had rearranged the usual programme of activities. André learnt that the volleyball was to be preceded by a talk from a priest. This immediately antagonised him, first because he was passionate about volleyball, and rescheduling the game was little short of treachery. Even more, despite the leader's protestations that the group was part of the Student Christian Movement and it was, after all, Lent, he was angry at what he felt to be an underhand attempt at enforced religious indoctrination. He expressed his opinion vehemently: he did not believe in God. Volleyball was what mattered to him. The leader, however, reasoned with them that no matter what their feelings on religion were, they owed a certain loyalty to their youth group, which would be disgraced if no one turned up for the talk.

'The least you can do,' he said, 'is to come along to make up the numbers. Sit quietly and shut your ears to the priest's words if you like; just be a physical presence.' Grudgingly André agreed and took his place at the end of a sofa where he thought he could, unnoticed, let his mind wander to more profitable things.

The speaker was Father Sergei Bulgakov, the Rector of the Russian Theological Institute of St Sergius, which had been founded in Paris in 1925. Despite being a distinguished theologian and an inspiration to many adults he was, in André's opinion, inept when it came to speaking to young people. His fatal tactic was to treat them as if they were scarcely out of kindergarten, and a kindergarten for the deaf at that; for he spoke in such a loud voice that André found it impossible not to listen to what he was saying. And the more the lad heard, the more horrified and angry he became.

Nothing the priest said could have been more designed to alienate a group of teenaged boys. He spoke down to them, as if he were enticing little animals: 'pussy pussy, come here' Metropolitan Anthony described this approach. He painted a sentimental picture of Christianity such as one might find in debased icons of the nineteenth century: a 'gentle Jesus meek and mild', offering the gullible what appeared to be nothing short of slavery. It was the very last thing youngsters training to be liberators of their subjugated country wanted to hear. André's indignation grew with every word.

By the end of the talk he was so incensed that instead of continuing to the volleyball game he rushed straight home, with the intention of verifying the authority of what the priest had said in order to leave himself in no doubt of Christianity's worthlessness. Absolutely confident that what he would find in the Bible would support the priest's point of view – he was obviously very knowledgeable – André resolved to see this despicable religion, with its cloying sentiments and its unsavoury influence, condemned once and for all.

He asked his mother for a book of the gospels and took it into his room. Sitting down at his desk he opened the book and was disconcerted to discover that there were four gospels. In order not to waste any more time than was absolutely necessary on what he was convinced would be a totally negative exercise, he quickly ascertained which was the shortest. Later he reflected that the choice of St Mark was significant. Mark had aimed his concise words at the impulsive and cynical youth of ancient Rome, just the sort of people André and his contemporaries were.

He began to read, and what happened next was something he was to spend a lifetime repeating.

> The feeling I had occurs sometimes when you are walking along in the street, and suddenly you turn round because you feel someone is looking at you. While I was reading, before I reached the beginning of the third chapter, I suddenly became aware that on the other side of my desk there was a Presence.
>
> This was so striking that I had to stop reading and look up. I looked for a long time. I saw nothing, heard nothing, felt nothing with the senses. But even when I looked straight in front of me at the place where there was no one visible, I had the same intense knowledge: Christ is standing here, without doubt.
>
> I realised immediately: if Christ is standing here alive, that means he is the risen Christ. I know from my own personal experience that Christ has risen and that therefore everything that is said about him in the Gospel is true.

He would later emphasise his remark that he heard no voice and saw no vision. This was not a sensory hallucination such as he would encounter in mentally ill patients when he became a doctor. Neither was it a mystical trance-like state or the product of the emotions, things he was always slow to trust. It was a totally convincing, direct experience of the presence of the risen Christ, but encountered with complete sobriety and equilibrium. 'God for me is a fact' was one of the phrases he was in the habit of using, and he counted the resurrection not as a matter of faith to be believed or not, but as a certainty he had experienced.

His encounter with Christ meant something else. There was now reason to go on living and a purpose for his life: to share his discovery with others. But again, these were not thoughts of mere elation. With chilling earnestness he perceived not only the joy but also the responsibility with which Christ had blessed him.

'I could see at once', he said many years later, 'that I had to spend the whole of my life telling people about God, and that it would be impossible for me to have any personal life whatsoever.' That resolution was to shape his future.

With new eyes André turned back to the gospel to continue reading, within the sure knowledge that he could trust every word. What he discovered there completely shattered his preconceptions. God was not at all as Father Sergei Bulgakov had painted him, a God who enticed people into slavish obedience; he was a God who had infinite respect and care for humanity. For instance, in the parable of the prodigal son the father did not let the son utter the words, 'I am no longer worthy to be called your son' that the young man had rehearsed. Christianity was not after all a religion of slavery but of adopted sonship, and that filial status was something which could never be taken away.

Another thing that struck him from his first reading of the gospels was that God's love was so limitless that in Christ he was prepared to share every part of the human condition in order to redeem it – even that most terrible consequence of human sin: the loss of God from which humanity dies. In his cry from the cross, 'My God my God, why hast thou forsaken me?' Christ himself had experienced the terrifying separation from the divine presence that is the common lot of fallen humanity, and he had descended into hell.

This touched André profoundly because he had truly been living in what with hindsight he had no hesitation in describing as hell, and with no prospect of finding his own way out. 'When we read in the Apostles' Creed the words: he descended into hell, we tend to think glibly, that's just one of those phrases,' he would explain to people. 'But I know from experience that it's true. He descended into my hell.'

Towards the end of his life he summed up all these thoughts as the discovery of a God whom he could venerate, respect, fear and love. In particular, he singled out respect as important, perhaps because it was the opposite of what he had felt for the false god conjured up by Father Sergei's talk.

'If God is all-powerful, if he is the Lord of all, I can indeed worship him. I can fear him. Perhaps I can even love him. But can I respect him, can I see in him someone who is worthy of being respected?' he had asked himself. And the answer he had found in his reading of the gospel was 'Yes, I can respect a God who has not created us irresponsibly. This God, having created a world that it might be in glory and partake in his own life, such that one day all creatures should be united to him and he should be all in all, has not created us with the dread gift of freedom and then left us to perish and to come one day to be judged. But he has entered into history and carried in his human life the cross of the whole created world that had fallen away, and he has paid the cost of his act of creation and the cost of his giving us freedom. And I felt therefore that I could love him with

veneration and respect, and not simply because of an impulsive movement of my heart.'

It was not only his opinions on religion that André now had to revise.
Everything he had previously thought about other people was also
untrue. In later life he described this change of heart in the third person,
so distant had he come to feel from his former self.

'I knew a young man whose life had been hard and cruel. Suddenly, discovering God, he also discovered that God had not only created everybody, but he loved everybody unto death and beyond.' The realisation that
God loved all people indiscriminately meant that André's own attitude to
them had to undergo a fundamental change. If he wished to be at one
with God and do his will then he too had to learn to love them, whatever
the consequences. He could no longer think in terms of enmity.

The next morning he emerged into what he described as a transfigured
world, in which he saw everything with new eyes. A whole period of his
life was now at an end and a new life beginning. It would be unswervingly
centred on God: the certainty of his existence and the desire, indeed the
compulsion, to tell others of that certainty. He felt so enraptured and so
grateful for what had happened that he was bursting to tell everyone.

'I went berserk! Travelling to school on the Paris Metro I would accost
my fellow passengers: Have you discovered God? Have you read the
gospels? I drove my friends at school mad.' And over sixty years after his
conversion he would add, with a gleam in his eye, 'Well, I am still berserk!'

His 'madness', as he put it, had other effects. Obvious outward changes
occurred in his life. His family and friends could see that something
dramatic had happened to him. But just what had happened he did not
say.

'I kept it an absolute secret within myself,' he explained later. 'I never
told anyone what had happened. People saw that I had changed in one
way or another. I believed in God, whereas I hadn't before; I believed in
Christ. I read the gospel, I began to go to church and I changed my ways –
well, I was just a boy so it was not a great change, but I changed within the
limits of my age. And I never said to anyone what had happened, because
I felt it was a thing so holy that I had to keep it undefiled, and I was afraid
to let people poke into it. I wanted to keep the experience safe in the
walled garden of my soul.' He had rediscovered his own *pairidaeza*, into
which he could retreat in prayer and encounter God in total seclusion.

André's prayers were, initially, the product of self-teaching. He simply
got down on his knees and poured out his heart, placing himself in the
presence of God whom he had discovered in the intimacy of personhood,

not as an almighty but distant Creator. He remained insistent on this personal relationship with God all his life, and it was to become one of the points of contact between him and the Evangelicals. Like them he was also insistent on joy. He was overflowing with the joy and gratitude of God's infinite mercy to him, and he responded readily to other Christians of all denominations whenever he met the same qualities.

To be in God's presence, he discovered, was life to the full. He quickly came to feel that when he was not praying, something was lacking. Consequently he began to spend as long as possible – up to eight hours or so a day, he claimed – in prayer, delighting in the wonder of his relationship with Christ.

After a while he obtained a prayer book. To read it entailed learning Church Slavonic, which was no great hardship for a natural linguist. Knowledge of Slavonic was also important for following the Liturgy. A baptised Russian Orthodox, his initial reaction had been to attend the Russian church. However, knowing nothing of theology and aware, albeit in hitherto negative terms, of the Roman Catholic and Protestant churches around him, he was anxious to discover which church was the most faithful to the Gospel message that he had discovered.

Over a period of time he investigated the differences between the churches, and his study confirmed Orthodoxy as the one whose teaching and experience accorded most closely with the truth and beauty of the Gospel as he understood it. Divine love, totally self-offering, limitless, unwavering, was something André had experienced irrefutably in his personal encounter with Christ. He was to go on experiencing it in the faith and expression of Orthodoxy for the rest of his life. 'I am passionate about Orthodoxy' was one of the phrases that readily fell from his lips.

Thirsty for the religious knowledge to complement his faith, he began to read avidly. However, he was also aware that knowledge was only part of his needs. Above all he had to learn how to live the Christian life. In Orthodox terms, he realised he was made in the divine image, a human icon. But like so many icons he had lost his pristine appearance. Damaged by the events of his hard life, he needed to peel away the cruel layers which distorted and masked the image of God at the core of his being, in order to become a recognisable icon which would in turn lead other people to Christ. Only then, he realised, would his hearers accept as plausible the message he was dedicated to proclaiming.

That was not something he had the experience or strength to do on his own. He decided he needed help in the traditional Orthodox form of a trusted spiritual director who could guide him towards the fullness of the

Christian life. It was with this purpose in mind that he set about looking for a spiritual father.

In 1931 the name of a certain monk was suggested to him: Archimandrite Afanasy (Nechaev). In discussing the relative merits of Father Afanasy and another possible candidate André was told, 'So-and-so is a monk first and then a Christian; Father Afanasy is a Christian first and then a monk.' The choice was obvious.

Formerly a monk of the renowned monastery of Valaamo, Father Afanasy had an unusual background. He had been born in the 1890s to a devout but very poor Russian peasant family who had sent him to the local seminary because it offered free education, but by the time he left school he had lost his faith and refused to become either a priest or a teacher. For some years he worked as a labourer and then a railwayman. When the Revolution came he took no part in it but he was, like everyone else, caught up in its cruel consequences.

A chance meeting with a member of the Salvation Army changed his life. The man showed him not only the futility of his godless existence, but also that it was unworthy of what he could be. How could he continue to live with an empty soul? Gradually, under the Salvationist's influence, he recovered his Christian faith – but as an Orthodox – and with it a deep and abiding joy. This, together with humility, was a quality that was to mark him out for the rest of his life.

In the 1970s Metropolitan Anthony met an old woman in Russia who had known Father Afanasy at this time, when she was just a teenager. It was the sense of his joy that had remained with her ever since. He had, she said, the ability to enter a room, meet a person and dispel the darkness, inundating with joy the souls of everyone with whom he came into contact – and all this at a time when the Revolution had plunged the whole of life into dark, terrifying turmoil.

Despite the beginnings of religious persecution in Russia he began to speak about his faith openly and fearlessly, and to put it into practice among the dispossessed and the hopeless. However, after several years he joined the numbers of people who escaped into Finland, where eventually he made his way to the Russian Orthodox monastery of Valaamo. There he became one of the many workmen employed by the monastery, living beside the monks and absorbing something of their way of life and their prayer. 'The main principle of penance at Valaamo is doing everything with one's own hands,' he wrote later, 'but the highest goal is spiritual growth; labour is but a means.' He wrote this as he documented the many tasks that the monks and workers were employed with: not only tending the farm but also cottage industries and icon-painting.

He did not immediately decide to become a monk but rather sought to deepen his spiritual life and try to find his way towards renunciation of self and the world so that, finding God's presence, his life could become totally Christ-centred. Yet he was plagued by guilt: that by finding peace in the monastery he was betraying the world outside, which was in such chaos and which so desperately needed Christ.

There were two encounters in particular that influenced his thoughts. The first was with one of the hermits there, who illustrated for him the severity of the monastic life by colourful example, in the manner of the Desert Fathers of Egypt. The second was another old man, still a novice after fifty years in the monastery. He explained his indecision: a monk was a man who wept out of compassion and who prayed for the whole world, yet after half a century he still felt he had a heart of stone. He could not make his vows until he had learnt to be compassionate.

This was a revelation. To become a monk did not mean leaving the world after all, but continuing to bring it to God through the mystery of prayer. On those terms the young man was ready to make his own vows. In time Father Afanasy was ordained and several years later sent to France, where by 1931 he was acting as parish priest of a small Russian congregation in Paris and gaining a reputation as a spiritual father.

However, there was more than spirituality to take into account as André made his decision to seek out Father Afanasy. The Church of the Three Hierarchs at 5 Rue Pétel was at that time the only Russian church in Western Europe to belong to the Patriarchate of Moscow, and its history was inevitably bound up with the Russian politics of the day.

Since the 1917 Revolution the position of the Russian parishes outside the borders of the Soviet Union had been problematic. In June 1930 Metropolitan Evlogy, the Russian bishop in Paris, together with almost all of his flock, had decided to leave the jurisdiction of the Moscow Patriarchate. He had gone to London to take part in public prayers with the Anglican Church for the suffering Church in Russia, and the Soviet authorities construed this as an attack on their government. They forced the ruling bishop in Moscow, Metropolitan (later Patriarch) Sergius, to issue a condemnation of Metropolitan Evlogy's actions and to demand from him a promise not to do any such thing again.

In all conscience Metropolitan Evlogy could not comply; and in consultation with and the approval of his diocese he joined the jurisdiction of the Ecumenical Patriarchate (Constantinople). (In 1945 Metropolitan

Evlogy was to return to the Moscow Patriarchate with part of his flock, although the majority remained under Constantinople.)

In 1930 only a handful of people had remained faithful to Moscow when Metropolitan Evlogy left, not because they had any sympathy for the Bolsheviks but because they wished to give moral support to their captive, persecuted Mother Church. Metropolitan Anthony was later to describe the situation as one in which they knew that the Church was a prisoner to the Soviet system, unable to say and do what she wanted; but at her heart, so they believed, she remained true to the Faith. In their eyes, Metropolitan Evlogy and his followers had betrayed the martyrs who were giving their lives daily in Russia. There must be, they reasoned, a middle way between political exile and spiritual fidelity; and they were determined to find it.

Most of the members of this small Patriarchal group belonged to the Brotherhood of St Photius, which had been founded five years earlier by a group of young people, mainly students from the St Sergius Institute. They saw the Russian diaspora as a providential scattering of Orthodox seeds whose God-given purpose was to reawaken Western Europe to Orthodoxy. Its manifesto stated unambiguously that they saw the Orthodox Church as the one true Church of Christ, to which every person and country had a right to belong, regardless of geography or nationality. The Church could not be limited by human considerations such as being born to Greek or Slav parents. The theologian Vladimir Lossky, a prominent member of the Brotherhood, was adamant that Christian unity could only be achieved through the truth of the Orthodox faith, and by the rekindling of that faith in the West, first in the hearts of the émigrés themselves and then among the local populations. For exile had taught the Russian community in Paris one important thing. Just as Christ on earth had himself been an exile, born as an outcast in a stable and dying outside the walls of Jerusalem, so the vocation of every Christian was nothing less than understanding life as exile from the Kingdom of God, which could only be regained by treading the Way of the Cross.

It was surely possible to remain part of the Patriarchate of Moscow while becoming also a church for the local population, and French-speaking where necessary. Already, under Metropolitan Evlogy and with the blessing of some of the more forward-thinking professors from the St Sergius Institute, the Liturgy had been celebrated in French. When Father Lev Gillet, a French Roman Catholic priest, became an Orthodox he was appointed rector of the francophone parish of the Transfiguration and St Genevieve.

There were plenty of Russians who were opposed to the Brotherhood's thinking, seeing their Church as the guardian of Russian culture. Against this attitude the small band loyal to Moscow soldiered on, determined to maintain its fidelity both to the Russian Church and to the mission of spreading Orthodoxy in the West. Of various shades of political opinion, its members were all united in their conviction that the Mother Church, persecuted by the atheist Soviet regime, needed their prayers, their affection and their unflinching support.

Some of them were to become revered names in Orthodox circles: as well as the theologian Vladimir Lossky there were the icon-painters Leonid Ouspensky and Gregory Krug; Evgraf Kovalevsky and his brothers; the future Archbishop Seraphim of Switzerland; and Maria Kolash, who had been a friend of Chekhov's wife and who was to produce an excellent biography of the writer.

With Metropolitan Evlogy's departure, and with him the francophone parish under Father Lev Gillet, the group concentrated their immediate efforts on re-establishing the Patriarchal presence in Paris and finding a place for worship. By Easter 1931 they had found and consecrated very basic premises in a basement in the Rue Pétel in the 15th arondissement. In the conditions of poverty that prevailed among the Russian community, parishes used whatever buildings they could, setting to work with their own hands to turn disused workshops and garages into little churches, humble outposts of paradise. The one in the Rue Pétel had once been part of a bicycle factory. The parishioners each brought what they could to help furnish the church.

In accordance with the Brotherhood's theological vision the church was given a double dedication: to the Three Holy Hierarchs – St Basil the Great, Gregory the Theologian and St John Chrysostom – representing the universality of Orthodoxy; and to St Tikhon of Zadonsk, a saint of the Russian spiritual tradition. The church was dimly lit entirely by candles, and with the choir directed by the talented musician Rodionov an atmosphere of reverent worship was soon established.

In 1933 Ouspensky and Krug were to decorate the church. To the latter Father Afanasy gave the task of painting the two iconostases and to Ouspensky that of painting individual icons such as the dedication icon of the Three Hierarchs, and the major feasts of the Church. The fact that both men were gifted painters was only a part of their iconographic skills. Both espoused the ideas and theology of the Brotherhood of St Photius, going deep into the relation between the Universal Church and the local church, stripping away the folkloric aspects of Orthodoxy and returning to a true inner spirituality whose foundation was the Trinity. They understood the icon to be a witness of theosis – the deification of the human person – and an expression of how humanity in a state of prayer is sanctified by grace.

Father Gregory Krug's icons went on to be well known through reproductions which are still popular today, while Ouspensky became an inspiring teacher of future iconographers and is perhaps best remembered for his book *The Meaning of Icons.*

For twelve years Father Afanasy was the person who carried the small parish spiritually. He gathered around himself a number of monks but did not live in community, choosing instead the solitary, eremitic life more common in modern Orthodoxy than it is in the West: the life of individual prayer and the silence of the hesychast.

It was to this church that the young André set out one Sunday morning to attend the Liturgy and size up Father Afanasy as a possible spiritual father. He had difficulty finding it, so that by the time he arrived the Liturgy had already finished and Father Afanasy was just leaving. Watching him as he came up the wooden staircase leading from the basement, André was so struck by the light of eternity he saw shining in the monk's eyes that without hesitation he went straight up to him and said, 'Will you be my spiritual father?'

This experience was one that Metropolitan Anthony considered crucial, and he would often repeat the saying, 'No one will find eternity unless they see it shining in the eyes of Christians.'

Father Afanasy's influence on André's spiritual development was to be considerable. He was not impressive by worldly standards. He did not have superior education or outward holiness but he was, as the Metropolitan would say, stretching wide his arms, 'big', not only in physical size – he was a tall, broad-shouldered man – but more importantly big of heart. His compassion lacked any sentimentality; his thoughts, words and ways were always uncompromising, because he would not compromise the Gospel.

'He was luminous, reflecting the glory of God; a profound yet very simple man, not a saint, just a man of our times – but a man who was free, with that incomparable, sovereign freedom of which Christ speaks,' was how Metropolitan Anthony described him. By 'simple' he meant open and direct, free of complicated intellectualism. There were, however, people who thought Father Afanasy simple in a less complimentary sense, confusing his humility with foolishness. On one occasion at a meeting someone was very rude to him, but he sat still, making no attempt to justify himself. Afterwards he said to André, 'What a wonderful and loving person, to be so honest in telling me the truth to my face.'

The relationship which developed between Father Afanasy and André was the typical spiritual father/son of Orthodoxy. From the beginning it was assumed on André's part that Father Afanasy was training him for eventual life as a monk, although Father Afanasy initially sought to discourage this. Either way, an important part of Father Afanasy's work was to act as a confessor to his young disciple. Nevertheless, when an old and experienced confessor himself, Metropolitan Anthony would admit that his first confession with his new spiritual father was a disappointment. Seeing it as a significant moment in his religious development he was expecting something dramatic: perhaps, after a lifetime's confession, he would receive advice of such breadth and proportion that his world would change. What he actually heard from Father Afanasy were words small enough to meet him where he really was rather than on the heroic stage of his imagination.

'You are surrounded by so many sins and weaknesses that you cannot possibly conquer them all at once. If you tried you would be defeated before you had hardly begun. Instead you must learn to be like a little mouse and nibble away at them bit by bit.' And in recounting this in later years Metropolitan Anthony would make little nibbling movements with his jaw. Although at the time it was far less than what he was hoping to hear, he came to see its value, because it was advice that actually worked, and he began to nibble away at his sins and faults in obedience to Father Afanasy.

He was attracted to his spiritual father's particular brand of monasticism. The solitary prayer of the hermit suited his lonely temperament and, leaving aside his prayer manual, it was in stillness that he came increasingly to find God. He would in turn explain this to his own spiritual children: 'As long as the soul is not still, there can be no vision, but when stillness has brought us into the presence of God, then another sort of silence, much more absolute, intervenes: the silence of the soul that is not only still and collected but which is overawed in an act of worship by God's own presence.'

However much André's life began to be enriched on the spiritual level, it remained materially poor to an extent rarely encountered in the West today. The vegan rigours of Lent were scarcely bettered during the non-fasting seasons. One year his family had to save hard all through Lent in order to be able to afford a tin of corned beef for the Easter breakfast, the most lavish meal of the Orthodox calendar.

They were not alone. Only the degree of poverty varied from one Russian household to another. One year André and a friend spent Good Friday with a family whose efforts at saving had enabled them to buy a small, scrawny chicken ready for Easter. Faced with two young guests, they felt obliged to cook it there and then. Unfortunately their generous intentions were wasted on André. On the very day when his seven weeks of dutiful asceticism were meant to reach their culmination in a total fast he was horrified to be given meat. He ate it gracelessly, and on leaving the house he erupted in anger, 'They made me break my fast!'

'Well,' said his friend, 'if that's all there was to your fast . . .'

He would tell this story as a cautionary tale to his parishioners, and point them towards the true significance of fasting described in the fifty-eighth chapter of Isaiah.

A similar episode he would relate was of a visit he made to a family whose son brought the mother a bunch of flowers. Again, André's anger flared as he judged the situation only in the crudest terms.

'How can you waste money on flowers when there's no food in this house?' The mother chided him gently. 'I can live without food but I can't live without flowers,' was her wise reply. Relentless, loveless asceticism was not the essence of the Christian life.

André's involvement in the Russian youth organisations continued, with two differences. Firstly, his focus was now on bringing his faith into the situation. Secondly, as he moved in age through the camps he began to take on roles of responsibility, eventually becoming a youth leader.

One year the camp was held on a hilltop where a village had once stood with its church. Over a long period the houses had spread down the hillside until the community had established itself, with a new church, in the valley, and the church at the top had been abandoned. The Russians had been given permission to pitch their camp there, and to erect their chapel tent on the spot where the Catholic church had once stood.

They received a request from a very old lady from the village who could remember worshipping in the old church many decades previously and who was intrigued to hear that services, albeit foreign ones, were being held on the same ground: could she come to the Liturgy and pray where she had prayed as a young girl?

'Of course we said yes; and on Sunday morning we looked out and saw a strange procession coming up the hill. There were four stout men carrying two poles on which was slung an armchair, and sitting in it was the old granny.' She was carried into the chapel and sat majestically in her chair while the service carried on around her.

The Liturgy was in Slavonic, and at its close André went up to the old lady and said, 'Oh Gran, it must have been very boring for you, you couldn't have understood one word!' The old lady replied scornfully, 'How can anyone who is as big as you be so stupid? Of course I understood. I have eyes.' She went on to give an account of the service to him, explaining how, although she couldn't understand the language, she had been able, through all the visual symbolism of the Russian Eucharist, to relate it to her familiar Roman Mass and so follow everything that was happening.

This visual impact of Orthodox services was something Metropolitan Anthony came to recognise as very important. During his ministry in London he was to come across another striking example when a deaf man, previously used only to the undemonstrative and word-focused services of Methodism, discovered in the Liturgy a form of worship where, to his delight, words were not essential to his participation and meaning was conveyed through actions and visual symbolism.

In his work as a youth leader André discovered that words could sometimes do more harm than good. One day a renowned preacher was invited to give a lesson to the Sunday school pupils. André and the other leaders arranged themselves round the walls, listening with admiration to this man who spoke so magnificently. However, when the lesson was over one of the teachers asked a seven-year-old what he thought of the talk and the child replied, 'It was good entertainment; but what a pity Father doesn't believe what he says.'

André realised that the child had reacted negatively because the priest's words had come from the intellect – and the children were left cold by his reasoned arguments, when they would have responded to a message from the heart. This was a point he was to keep in mind when he began to preach. He always spoke 'from the heart', because he knew that what convinced people of the truth of the Gospel was not a matter of words but of life.

He knew, too, that there was a need for believers, even children, to have their own experience of the things of God, as another anecdote from the camps showed. A little boy came out of the chapel tent, his face shining with joy, and the leader said, 'What's up with you?'

'Oh, I went into the chapel and suddenly there was an angel there,' replied the boy. He was not a mystical child and he did not develop into a mystic, but he had perceived something. Metropolitan Anthony was quick to explain the boy's experience to people to whom he told this story. 'When he said an angel was there he did not mean, "I saw it with my eyes," but "I knew that it was present," which is very different, because what you see with your eyes may call for an interrogation mark. What you know for sure, without any kind of visual or auditory or other phenomenon, is another thing.' It was reminiscent of his own conversion experience.

By this time André was approaching the moment at school when he had to make serious choices about a future career. The intention to teach foreign languages had been superseded by the desire to dedicate his life wholly to God. His first thought in that direction was to become a desert hermit like those about whom he had read with such enthusiasm in the lives of the Desert Fathers. For several reasons, as he later explained with his dry sense of humour, that was entirely impracticable. Firstly, deserts were few and far between, and in any case not accessible to people like himself who were stateless.

Secondly, he was aware of his growing responsibility as the man of the house for the material support of his mother and grandmother. That also ruled out another option he considered: to become a monk at Valaamo.

He would have to find a solution closer to hand. He was ordained to the minor order of Reader, potentially the first step on the road to the priesthood. It particularly pleased him that the bishop also blessed him to preach. 'And my first sermon was not worthy,' he had to admit, shaking his head.

He decided to talk over training for the priesthood with Father Georges Florovsky at the St Sergius Institute. He knew without doubt that his whole life had to be centred on God's work. Anything less would be a compromise, and that was a notion not only totally foreign to his nature but also, as he saw it, to Christianity. This unflinching dedication must have communicated itself to Father Georges, who tailored his reply accordingly.

'Go away and read the lives of the saints and the Fathers – and come back in fifteen years' time.' To a fervent young man of only seventeen it was a devastating answer. He would have to wait almost his whole life over again before his vocation could even begin to be realised. When, in old age, he admitted to having once suffered a fifteen-year bout of depression it was not difficult to identify which years they were. This was to be the first of several knock-backs he was to receive on his journey to the priesthood. However, despite his pain he accepted Father Georges' judgement, and came to consider him someone for whom he could have the greatest respect both as a person and as a theologian.

With the doors of St Sergius closed against him André had to reassess his position. He talked it over with his father. In what he described, in the sermon he gave on the fortieth anniversary of his consecration as a bishop (30 November 1997), as a sad moment, Boris asked him: 'What is the dream of your life?' Andre had no hesitation in replying, 'To be with God alone.' Then his father looked at him with sadness in his eyes and said, 'You have not even begun to be a Christian.'

As he later came to realise, to love God did not mean retreating into a private realm away from society, but sharing with him all his concerns for the world and for each person. It was not enough to have in one's heart a warmth for God. The test of one's love was to share God's own love for one's neighbours. Boris, understanding this, made a suggestion: to seek a profession which would not only be satisfying intellectually but which would also enable him to put God's love and compassion for the world into practice.

Gradually this began to fuse with his earlier thoughts of monasticism and priesthood and to crystallise into a possible way forward. After much thought and prayer he decided to study medicine with the intention, once he qualified, of taking monastic vows and becoming a worker priest serving one of the impoverished Russian communities in rural France. In that way he could act as both physical and spiritual healer.

He now had to adapt his schoolwork to his new choice of career. Up till that point it had revolved around Classics and modern languages. With his change of direction his lack of physics became a matter of desperate concern. After intensive study he successfully completed his baccalaureat and enrolled at the Sorbonne to read physics, chemistry and biology in the autumn of 1932.

∽ ～

CHAPTER FIVE

STUDENT YEARS

(1932—1939)

The Sorbonne School of Science was to open up a new dimension of spiritual as well as scientific understanding for André. Taking Georges Florovsky at his word he began to read the Fathers, and discovered in particular the writings of Theophan the Recluse, a Russian saint of the nineteenth century. He also discovered secular writers such as Dostoevsky. Parallel with this, under the guidance of Maurice Curie, nephew of Marie Curie, he learned to see physics as 'deep and vast, a harmony full of meaning and beauty' as he put it. The same was true of biology and chemistry. The marvels of the natural world, God's creation, unfolded as a complement to his spiritual reading.

The Orthodox understanding of matter and creation differs from that of Western Christianity. The Fall is seen in less disastrous terms than the Augustinian view; the fallen world is still seen as 'very good'; and the human person not as a superior soul lodging in a tainted body but a unique creature of body and soul together, both destined for eternity. This theology came to life for André as his studies continued. 'Suddenly, under these various influences that happened to be interwoven, the whole world became full of meaning. In that sense my training in science was part of a revelation about God and the created world.'

In later years he would talk often of creation and the Fall. One aspect was his understanding of the two ways in which knowledge could be acquired: by the Tree of Life – experiential communion with God, by feeding on what God communicated to humanity, which would transfigure humanity to become ultimately partakers of the divine nature; or by the Tree of the Knowledge of Good and Evil – acquiring knowledge apart from God, through the created world which was still imperfect and immature. As a part of the fallen world himself André strove to deepen his communion with God at the same time as studying it by human means.

The second thing that played a great role in his experience was, three years later when he began his medical training, his first contacts with patients in hospital, in which the Orthodox understanding of the human person came to the fore in the most practical way.

'You know, we usually don't think about our bodies,' he would say. 'We tend to feel we are a spirit, a soul, moving about in a body which we don't perceive very deeply. And here I discovered people who did not say, "My body is in pain." They would say, "I am in pain"; they had become aware that body, soul and spirit are one. Furthermore, something that amazed me is that a person can so trust another human being as to say: "I trust your integrity and I will allow you to look at my body, to touch my body, because I trust that everything you do will be for my good."'

This understanding of the unity of the body and soul he found summed up by St Isaac of Syria, who wrote regarding the Last Judgement that God could take no final decision about a person before the resurrection of the body because the body had its part to play in a person's eternal destiny.

'It's the total human being that can enter the Kingdom of God, not a body dragged into it as though it had no ultimate significance,' Metropolitan Anthony would explain:

> When we think of Christ, his body has absolute significance. When we think of saints and all they did, beginning with writing, with speaking, with looking, with hearing, with touching – not to speak of miracles or anything greater than this – everything was done through their bodies. How wonderful! One can really see the body, as St Maximus the Confessor describes the body of Christ in the Incarnation, as human flesh filled with divinity in the way in which a sword of iron plunged into a furnace is filled with heat and glows with fire so that one can now cut with fire and burn with iron. That is what we are in our bodies and souls.

It was a vision that was to inspire him all his life.

André continued to support himself financially in the same way he had done at school: by tutoring in Latin, maths and science during the evenings. His work schedule was unremitting. Each weekday evening he spent several hours teaching, cramming his own study into the weekends, which would often entail working all through the night. At eight o'clock on Saturday morning he would snatch a few hours' sleep, rising at noon to begin work again.

One of the pupils to whom he gave lessons was a Russian teenager whom he had met at the camps. Her name was Tatiana Zakharova, known as Tatisha, the daughter of the Russian concert violinist Cecilia Hansen. She was a tall, attractive girl with a lively personality and a sense of humour that sometimes propelled her into mischief.

A couple of years earlier, when both boys and girls were camping separately in the South of France, ten of the girls were invited to the boys' camp near Cannes for the feast day of St Alexander Nevsky. This entailed a forty-mile train journey for the girls, accompanied by their elderly and saintly priest, Father Sergei, and a stay overnight at the boys' camp where André was a leader.

The boys entertained their guests splendidly and everyone had a great time. The next day there was a parade reviewed by a Grand Duke, and Tatisha was already in sufficiently high spirits to say only, 'Good morning' to the Grand Duke instead of the prescribed, 'Greetings, your Imperial Highness'. Spurred on by this misdemeanour, Tatisha decided it would be a pity to spoil the fun by going home.

When the group of girls set off for the station, she and three friends lagged behind. They had been put in charge of Father Sergei's vestments but had deliberately 'forgotten' them and had to return to the camp, thus missing the train. While the four girls giggled about having to spend another night in the boys' camp, André, with his strong sense of responsibility, took the situation very seriously. He made sure the girls were at the station first thing the following morning and was relieved to see them safely on to the train.

But he had not seen the last of Tatisha. Back in Paris and faced with having to coach her in maths and science so that she could pass her exams, he again adopted a serious demeanour, particularly since Tatisha's grandmother had engaged him not only on account of his teaching skills; she also hoped he would be a sobering influence on her effervescent granddaughter.

By the end of the lessons he was usually in despair of ever getting Tatisha to understand even the basics of physics and chemistry, and she found the lessons just as painful.

One evening when André was invited to stay for supper he sat down at the table and began helping himself to some sugar lumps to put into his cocoa, gingerly trying out some new tongs. Suddenly he accidentally dropped a lump into his cup with a splash, sending the cocoa flying all over the immaculately starched tablecloth. To make matters worse his wretched pupil, pleased at getting her own back after her hour of torture, giggled at his embarrassment.

The last laugh went to André, or so he thought, when Tatisha failed her exams and was sent off to an English boarding school. Their paths would surely not cross again.

Another young woman on whom he made an impression at the camps was an Anglo-Russian, Anna Duddington. She found him suitably aloof from the girls, given his future monastic vocation, and extraordinarily conscientious, strict on discipline but also on himself.

The various activities included, one year, some drill to the tune of the Turkish March. Then an unusual situation arose: there was no one available to form a choir to sing at the Liturgy. The priest had no option but to ask André to sing alone.

This was not a prospect he relished, convinced as he was of his total inadequacy in all things musical. Certain parts were not too difficult; he could make a fair stab at the response of 'Lord have mercy' at the litanies. Much trickier, however, was the Cherubic Hymn, a solemn and, as a rule, complicated set piece that could be sung to a variety of melodies. André tackled it as best he could, but to his dismay the priest began glaring over his shoulder at him. At the end of the service he asked what had been the matter. The priest scowled. 'You sang the Cherubic Hymn to the Turkish March!' This was one more story André used to prove to himself and others how unmusical he was.

Despite André's youth work, studying and teaching commitments he did not skimp on prayer time. His daily long walk to and from the university provided the opportunity for reciting Matins and Vespers. Since his tutoring barely made him enough money to survive he often had to choose between buying food or textbooks. In his first year at university he became, in his own words, emaciated, and so weak that he was barely able to walk more than fifty yards without becoming exhausted. He would cross a road, rest, walk to the next corner and rest again; all the while deep in prayer despite his physical weakness. At one stage he was given a key to the church so that he could stop there on the way home to say Vespers.

Having completed his science degree André entered the Sorbonne's medical school. During his first year there he had to care for an elderly Russian who was dying alone. This was not just a matter of looking after a patient; there was a spiritual side to the relationship as the two men became friends. Eventually the old man passed away and left his body to medical science.

A year later in the anatomy theatre André was confronted by the man's corpse for dissection. 'It was one of the most tragic experiences of my life,' he described it, when he was himself an old man. 'I dissected him with veneration. His body was conveying something holy to me.'

At home his life continued to be austere. His family did not always appreciate the time he spent in prayer. One day when he was on his knees in his room his grandmother came in and asked him to come and help peel the carrots for dinner.

'Oh Gran, can't you see I'm praying?' he appealed to her.

'Well, I thought all this praying was supposed to make you a more loving person. So put your love into practice and help me with the carrots!' was Olga's response.

He came to realise that piety could be a source of real annoyance to people close to someone who was attempting to live an ascetic life. For instance, his room, at the front of the building on the top floor, easily became hot and stuffy, so he always left his window open in the morning when he went out; and grandmother always shut it when he had gone. At first he would beg her, 'Gran, please don't shut the window!' but she would inevitably find some excuse: it was a chilly day, it was raining, there was a draught. A battle of wills was developing. Something had to be done to preserve his own spiritual peace, if not the peace of the household.

Finally he hit on the idea of making a bet with himself every day that grandmother would indeed shut the window. As he rounded the corner of the street in the evening he would look up at the window, firmly secured, and be able to say to himself in triumph, 'I won!' and so in a totally unpious way avoid the anger which had threatened to undermine his inner stability.

As a spiritual father he would quote these two examples as ways in which people could learn to deal with the practical difficulties of living out their Christian piety within the tensions of family life. He was well aware that similar niggling incidents, some more trivial than others, could threaten a person's spiritual and emotional well-being.

For instance, when a young woman tried to explain her loss of faith which was the result of something she thought he would judge insignificant, she described it apologetically as, 'Something silly, but it was the last straw.'

'The last straw is always something silly,' he replied. With those few words of total understanding of the way small things could nibble away at a person's faith – the reverse of nibbling away at one's own faults – he revealed an empathy and sense of compassion that sowed the seeds for a renewal of faith.

But he was always conscious of the major sources of unhappiness that could blight someone's life. 'Suffering is important, but there are degrees of it. Misery that kills life within you is destructive and evil, and should not be allowed by the people who surround you,' were words he spoke both from his own experience and that of other people.

On the other hand, he could see the formative value of a certain level of struggle:

> Poverty, facing hardship, conquering is something that can be positive. You know there is a passage in the Bible in which it says, 'The people of Israel grew fat and forgot God.' Well, this is what happens to each of us. When life becomes comfortable, when we feel shielded from every problem, when we have all things in abundance, we simply go blind to other things. My childhood was hard; I know concretely what it is to be hungry, to be homeless, to be beaten up, and I thank God for all the hardships I ever had. I really feel profoundly grateful because they have taught me so much about life and about the necessity of facing up to things and conquering. And if we are beaten, we learn to be like the spider in the story of Robert the Bruce: start again, start again, start again until you conquer, because in each battle lost you learn something about winning a victory.

These words referred not only to individuals. He saw the same process at work in the Russian Church:

> The Church has suffered a great deal, much more than we can imagine. But I remember someone who had a right to express an opinion: Patriarch Alexis I, who was a bishop before the First World War, stayed in Russia and went through all the events of the Revolution and all the siege of Leningrad in the Second World War, and everything that happened to the Church, as a responsible member of it. He once said to me, when I asked him what he thought of the freedom of the Church, 'No one can take the freedom of the Church away, because our freedom is to be the Body of Christ crucified for the salvation of our persecutors.'

This was suffering and conquering on the grand scale. But he never lost sight of the everyday problems of life, and the need to find less heroic solutions to them. In private appointments he might offer a piece of totally practical, if perhaps less than pious, advice for dealing with a particular situation with the words, 'It will give you wicked satisfaction – but less emphasis on the wicked, and more on the satisfaction!' Such 'wicked' advice could, however, make all the difference between people finding the strength to endure their problems or succumbing to despair; and despair, he knew from reading the Fathers and from his own life, was a thoroughly negative and godless emotion that had to be rooted out by whatever means came to hand.

He understood how necessary was practicality in the spiritual life through his dealings with his own spiritual father. One day he went with Father Afanasy to a cemetery to tend some neglected Russian graves. The elderly monk looked at his eager young disciple and suggested that he could perhaps come and live there. He could pitch a tent in the corner by the compost heap, in the manner of Job, and so be on hand not only to keep the graves tidy but also to pray for the departed.

'I could see at once that it wasn't feasible for me to do as he said,' Metropolitan Anthony would recount to his own spiritual children. 'How could I possibly continue my studying if I were to live in such a way? I made up my mind at once not to obey him, but I didn't say anything.' He let Father Afanasy walk along continuing to make plans for André's new life in the cemetery, and it was only as they were leaving that, to André's relief, Father Afanasy admitted quietly to him, 'I suppose it wouldn't really be practicable.' Metropolitan Anthony gave this as an example of an occasion when one could not necessarily follow one's spiritual father's advice blindly if he were speaking out of a certain ignorance and practical circumstances dictated otherwise.

However, to someone who saw his future as a monk, he understood that the guidance of a spiritual father was an integral part of life. There were occasions when obedience was paramount, because there was a great difference between common sense practicality and easygoing sentimentality. This could be a painful experience.

One day, André had a violent disagreement with someone: 'We quarrelled unto death,' as he put it. When he told Father Afanasy of this the monk gave him a candid reply based on the Sermon on the Mount.

'If you are not prepared to forgive this man you cannot expect God to forgive you. So in future, when you recite the Lord's Prayer, you must say, "Do not forgive me, as I do not forgive those who trespass against me."'

André found that very hard to do. He did not like to think of himself bereft of God's forgiveness.

'Well,' said Father Afanasy after André had tried this for a while, 'if my advice is too difficult, just miss that petition out completely. But I still forbid you to ask for forgiveness while you yourself cannot forgive.'

André battled with that for some time before he eventually admitted the impossibility of his situation. There was no alternative to finding forgiveness in his own heart. In the most painful way he had learnt that words of prayer could not be recited glibly like some madrigal performed for God's benefit. They had to be meant, and they had to be lived, at whatever the cost.

Despite André's close relationship with Father Afanasy it was inevitable that circumstances arose when he had to make his confession to another priest. One day he arrived at church to find that the only one available was the very last he would have chosen.

It was no secret that this man was an alcoholic; he sometimes drank so much that he was incapable of celebrating, or got into brawls, and André felt little sympathy or respect for him. It was therefore with reluctance that he approached him. Yet the priest was so pierced by the young man's confession that he was reduced to tears.

'And it wasn't as if I had done anything terrible,' Metropolitan Anthony would say. It was the man's sensitivity and compassion rather than the penitent's sins which were so great, as he offered words of advice intended to keep André from falling into the same sins as himself.

He would quote this as an example of how his own sensitivity to other people began to grow. Afterwards he learnt that this particular priest, who was outwardly so unsatisfactory, had a tragic history. Following the Revolution he had attempted to leave Russia with his family. In Odessa they were in the process of boarding a boat for escape when his wife and children were hit by Bolshevik fire and perished before his eyes. André discovered that not being judgemental was as important as forgiveness.

Life among the Russian clergy in Paris was hard in the extreme. They had to be supported entirely by their largely penniless parishioners. Since there was very little cash available people would leave food for them outside the church doors; otherwise they starved. It was hardly surprising that more than one sought consolation in alcohol.

There was an old hieromonk (a priest-monk) who had, in Metropolitan Anthony's words, 'lost his teeth and his voice – the one through age, the other through drink', for whom André was one day called to serve at Vespers. The old man rattled off the service at such a rate that it was barely comprehensible, and at the end André, with the self-righteous certainty of youth, went up to him and said, 'You know, Father Efimy, you gabbled away so fast that you have robbed me of the entire service. But what is worse, you have also robbed yourself of it.'

At that the old priest began to cry. He explained that when he was a young child in Russia his parents had given him to a monastery because they were too poor to feed another mouth. For almost the whole of his life he had been surrounded by the services.

'The words,' he said, 'are now so deeply written upon my heart that it is enough for me to begin the opening blessing and they come gushing out in a torrent of love and joy.'

André was duly chastened for his hasty judgement, and when himself a bishop he would never pass over an opportunity to repeat this story against himself.

There was another incident where he witnessed a priest being moved to tears. It was Good Friday. Everyone was gathered round the tomb of Christ in the centre of the little church. Instead of giving a homily, the old priest simply knelt down with the words, 'And now, let us cry together.'

The poverty of the clergy was reflected in those around them. A certain priest who had the reputation of being something of a fool for Christ arrived one morning to serve the Liturgy not only minus his cassock but also minus shoes and socks. 'Has he gone mad?' people asked themselves. Then he explained that on his way to the church he had passed a number of beggars. One possessed no shoes, so he had given him his; to another he gave his socks; to a third, who had no covering, he gave his cassock.

Surrounded by such conditions and struggling with them himself, André's student life progressed, in rather more sober fashion than that of his contemporaries. Not for him the antics for which medical students are renowned. He had neither the time nor the money for much of a social life, nor even the inclination. He claimed he could count on one hand the number of times he went to the cinema, and even fewer to the theatre. His focus remained on monasticism, although people around him did not always appreciate this. He had matured into an extremely personable and handsome young man, with the intense brown eyes and dark hair of his Italian ancestry. He was good-mannered to the point of excess. 'He was too charming for words,' Nicholas Lossky recalled. And he was continually surrounded by a bevy of admiring young ladies, a situation that was to dog him all his life.

One day he was confronted by one of the nurses who, despite being a devout Roman Catholic, fancied herself as a reader of palms. When she had read those of all the other students she approached André, and he reluctantly held out his hand. She took one look and shrank back from him in horror.

'What is it?' André asked her. 'What can you see?'

'You will never marry.' She looked up at him and hesitated. 'But – you will have lots of children!'

'Who, me?' He stared back at her with innocent disbelief; but no amount of protestation could convince her of his integrity.

'And do you know,' he would say in amazement to his parishioners years later, 'after that she refused to have anything to do with me!'

It was only when he was a famous and middle-aged bishop that the nurse came to see him at his cathedral in London. After the service he said to her, pointing to his congregation, 'Well, Marguerite, you were right. I have never married – and yet here are all my children!'

What did take up André's limited leisure time was his continuing work with young people in the Russian Student Christian Movement, in youth clubs and at the summer camps. His enthusiasm and popularity were such that Father Afanasy feared the success would go to his head, and told him to give it up for a while.

This was another situation which called for obedience. 'All right,' André replied, 'but what reason shall I give? It will sound silly if I say I can't continue my youth work because it is spoiling my chances of sainthood.'

'No,' said Father Afanasy, 'just tell the other leaders that you are leaving because your medical work is taking up more of your time and is the main focus of your interest. If they get angry, shrug your shoulders and say, "Well, I live my life one way and you live yours another" and leave it at that. No one must suspect you have higher motives.' So for a time André gave up all his youth work, and had to learn not to regret the loss.

It was not only exterior things that Father Afanasy called his disciple to forego. He insisted on restraining his piety, too, when it became excessive. One day he asked André how long he spent in prayer each day, and instead of approving the zealous reply he commanded him, 'Well, for the next six months I forbid you to pray at all. Just say, the last thing at night before you fall asleep, "At the prayers of all those who love me, O Lord, save me." And we will do your praying for you.'

In later life Metropolitan Anthony recognised in others the same condition he termed 'spiritual indigestion' which too much prayer could bring. He also saw the value in using Father Afanasy's beautiful formula for closing the day, even when allowed to pray, and he would sometimes counsel his own spiritual children to use the same words, adding: 'Then recall one by one all the people who do love you – the Mother of God, your patron saint, your guardian angel, your family, your friends – and before you reach the end of the list you will be asleep.'

In 1937, two years before André was to qualify as a doctor, his father died, worn out at the age of fifty-three by the hard life he had endured in exile. Up till then André had come face to face with death in two ways: as a medical student and in church, since it is the Orthodox tradition to bring the dead into church to await the funeral which is conducted around an open coffin. This, however, was to be his first really close personal encounter with it, and it had a profound effect on him.

Boris had summed up his own attitude to death by telling his son, 'You should await your death as a young man awaits his bride.' In his reclusive, almost monastic life of prayer and asceticism he had put those words into practice.

It was Easter Day, 2 May, and, after the exuberance of the midnight service celebrating Christ's triumph over death, the Easter party was in progress. For André it was a particularly joyful occasion because for once both his parents were together. Suddenly Boris began to feel unwell, and his son went to sit with him for a while. As they started talking the years of shyness and reticence began to fall away.

'The doors were open,' was how Metropolitan Anthony described this inner meeting. It was such a profound experience that when the time came for André to leave for the hospital he went round the room saying goodbye to everybody – except to his father. He felt there was no need; having met as they had done, they could never in any way be parted.

Boris died that night. When André arrived back the next morning to be met with the unexpected news, he went up to his father's room. He was conscious of closing the door and standing before his father's body, enveloped in a deep silence that had such an intense and substantial quality that he perceived it as a presence.

'I heard myself say, "And people dare to say death exists. What a lie!"'

In his later years Boris had developed a certain following among people seeking spiritual advice. Among them had been a young Jewish girl who had come to rely on his counselling, and she turned to André to ask what she should do now. His reply was: be baptised. She was doubtful. There were still so many unanswered questions. André advised her to accept baptism and deal with the questions later. When, some time afterwards, he asked her what her questions were, she replied, 'There's nothing to ask any more.'

In 1939, after seven years of study, André was nearing the end of his medical training. A competition was to be held which would enable the winner to embark on the first rungs of the academic ladder. André studied hard for it, hoping to do well. As he put it later, 'I had begun to fancy myself as a Professor of Medicine.' He told Father Afanasy about the competition and described the feelings it aroused in him. The old monk looked at him and said, 'Do they include vanity?'

André had to admit that a certain amount of vanity was involved. It was obvious something would have to be done about that. He offered to withdraw, just as he had previously withdrawn from his youth work. This time the answer was even more challenging.

'On the contrary,' replied Father Afanasy, 'do enter. But I want you to do badly so that everyone will think you are hopeless.'

It was shattering advice after so much hard work and from the point of view of his career it made no sense at all. As Metropolitan Anthony admitted when he himself was a mature spiritual father, it was not the sort of crushing counsel that should be given to everybody. He was the first to see that there were times when, like the nibbling mouse, one should only tackle certain spiritual faults, and perhaps for a while leave the others as a prop which could be dealt with later.

Nevertheless, despite feeling dispirited he entered the competition, deliberately wrote rubbish, and came eighty-fourth out of eighty-six candidates. Not only did he have to endure derisory comments, his immediate prospects of an academic career were destroyed. Yet Father Afanasy's concern was not his disciple's medical achievements but his spiritual growth. 'Everything is of secondary importance to building up your soul' was the supreme lesson for a prospective monk to learn, and the most effective way to learn it was by real experience and not theoretical lessons in piety. Instead of listening to a speech on humility, doing brilliantly and then uttering platitudes about attributing his success to God's grace, André had had to encounter humiliation from the inside. But it taught him more than a thousand sermons. Whenever, over his long life, he repeated this story, the real pain he had felt was evident; but so was his conviction that Father Afanasy had ultimately been right.

As it happened, any effect the competition might have had on André's career was about to disappear. By the time he qualified as a doctor in the summer of 1939 the world was on the brink of war. Having taken French nationality in 1937 he realised he would be called up to serve in the

Medical Corps of the French army, where his potential skills in surgery would be in demand. His boyhood military interest, in which he had envisaged the Soviet regime as the enemy, was now to be turned to the fight against Hitler. But was that compatible with the Christian life? For a moment he hesitated, unsure whether the army was a fit place for a disciple of the Prince of Peace.

He consulted a priest who had fought in the Russian Imperial Army in the First World War. The priest explained how he had at first thought of the soldiers as killers; but when he reached the front he realised that the men were, as he put it, martyrs.

Another way in which André sought an answer was through prayer and reading the Bible. Eventually his mind was made up by a verse from the Book of Ezekiel, which he took as a personal word from God. He would accept to fight. His decision was later reinforced as the right one, when, in occupied Paris, he experienced at first hand the brutality and evil of the Nazi regime.

Nothing ever changed his mind over the rightness of his decision and he developed a forceful way of putting across his justification for a Christian's engagement in war. Experience had shown him that no one could escape from contributing to the war effort of a country under attack, even if they refused to fight and stayed at home to bake bread instead. The difference was, he would argue, that such people were acting dishonourably in refusing to 'soil their dainty hands with another man's blood'. Many years later, confronted with a catechumen who was a pacifist, he made his own position quite clear.

'I want you to realise you are being received at bloodstained hands,' were his uncompromising words. He could produce ready arguments against pacifism with which to silence people who disagreed with him, confronting them with hypothetical situations such as what they would do if they came across their girlfriend or daughter being raped. Would they not defend her, by force if necessary? He once put this argument to an earnest young man who replied: no, he would not commit violence to save his girlfriend. 'Well, if I were your girlfriend,' retorted Metropolitan Anthony, 'I'd get myself another boyfriend!' He went so far as to say that killing in battle was justified whereas abortion was not.

During the era of the Cold War he upheld the majority opinion that the West's defence against communism justified the retention of nuclear weapons, despite the risk of catastrophe, and even though they were trained on his beloved Russia.

As the end of August 1939 approached André realised it was time to make another decision. He had long been preparing to answer the unequivocal call to the monastic life, and his impending army call-up pre-cipitated his profession. At the commemoration of the Beheading of St John the Baptist he asked Father Afanasy to accept his monastic vows. Five days later he was drafted.

CHAPTER SIX

꘎ ꘎

DOCTOR, SOLDIER AND MONK

(1939–1949)

O rthodox monasticism is more fluid than that of Western
Christianity. There are no distinctive Orders, and monks may
still follow the ancient idiorhythmic way of the solitary monastic, with prayer and obedience to their spiritual father as the
basis for a simple life of stability before God. This was to be André's way,
which he had long accepted as being the one for him; but it also had to
be done in secret, since being either a doctor or a soldier would not be
compatible with the monastic profession.

It was not so difficult to see how he could live the life in Christ as a doctor, but fulfilling his monastic vows in the French army was another
matter. He put to Father Afanasy two questions. The first was how often
he should pray, to which the unhesitating answer came, 'All the time, dear
boy, all the time!' The Orthodox Jesus Prayer could be used in any situation. The second question concerned his vow of obedience. Father
Afanasy saw no problem. His army superiors and his patients would be his
new masters.

At the outbreak of war he was sent to a large military hospital close to
the front. He was to be commissioned and serve as an army surgeon with
the rank of captain, but his basic military training became, like the rest of
his army career, an excellent school for monasticism. He likened it to the
life of the Desert Fathers, in which the simplest incident had spiritual
value.

For instance, one day a corporal nominated André as an 'army volun-
teer', thrust a spade into his hands and told him to dig a trench from north
to south. He accepted the task on Father Afanasy's terms as an absolute

obedience, even though he had overheard an officer telling the corporal the trench should run from east to west. But that was not André's business. He dug with an inner freedom, and after three hours' hard but gratifying work he was proud of his trench. The corporal came up, swore profusely at him and said, 'Idiot, you were supposed to dig from east to west,' and ordered André to fill in the trench. His inner freedom had prevented him from trying to prove to the corporal that he was mistaken and he was able to accept the result as God's will expressed through human error.

This was not the only occasion when army life taught him to accept unjustified blame. In the military hospital the boiler had broken down in the ward where his patients were; it was in such a state that the orderlies refused to touch it. Concerned for the welfare of his patients, André had no hesitation in taking off his uniform, cleaning out the stove and stoking it with coal. His fellow officers disagreed, accusing him of 'degrading the dignity of an officer'. He was adamant that the functioning of the stove was far more important than matters of rank, but he was nevertheless banned from the officers' mess. A socially awkward animal, he was not unhappy to have additional time to himself in which to read or to pray.

Despite Father Afanasy's exhortations he was aware that the mechanical disciplines imposed by the army, like those of school or his youth organisations, were not the same as Christian discipline, which was the condition of the disciple, born of a freedom rooted in love, loyalty and responsibility. To be a soldier blindly obeying a corporal was a far cry from being the disciple of Christ, who was ultimately his only Lord, master, guide and teacher; and monastic vows were harder to live by than outward orders.

Although Orthodox monks not living in community are allowed for practical reasons to own personal property, they are still bound by the rule of inner poverty. An incident provided an unexpected insight into that. It was Christmas 1939, André's first away from home as a soldier. Sitting in the barracks reading, his attention was attracted by a pencil. It was hardly a source of temptation, but he suddenly thought: you will never again be able to say, 'This is my pencil'; you have given up everything you might have owned. It took him several hours to free himself from the desire for possession that the pencil – little more than a chewed stub – aroused. In purely practical terms it remained his, complete with his own teeth marks; but what he had to achieve was freedom from the acquisitiveness that he was later to find so destructive in post-war society.

As a monk who was destined to spend his life 'in the world', salaried as both a doctor and a parish priest, this was a necessary lesson. He was acutely aware of the extent to which people could unwittingly become the possessed rather than the possessors. In later life he would demonstrate this by picking up his pocket watch, which to all intents and purposes he owned, with the words that as soon as he closed his hand around it he gained a watch but lost the use of a hand. 'Never become enslaved by things, remain inwardly free,' he would tell any of his spiritual children who were concerned at their level of material prosperity.

The sense of danger pervading army life heightened his awareness of being in the hands of God. He readily admitted to experiencing fear, which he found entirely natural in the war situation. But he was always anxious to distinguish it from cowardice, that giving way to fear which leads to acting dishonourably.

He also began to see the world in perspectives other than his own. Above him was the will of God and below him the rest of creation, ignorant of his very existence. One day when he was lying in the grass under gunfire he caught sight of two ants dragging along a piece of straw, completely oblivious either to his fear for his own skin or the war going on around them. Between the extremes, his personal destiny, he discovered, was of no great consequence.

Another lesson he learnt from his army service was the importance of putting people's needs first. Early on he made the decision that he would treat every patient equally, with no discrimination between a Frenchman or a captured German, because he felt that once an enemy soldier was wounded and out of the battle arena he was simply a child of God who needed the same care as any other patient. When a German soldier was brought in with a smashed forefinger, the consultant took one look and said to André, 'Take it off.' The soldier turned with plaintive eyes to the medical staff and asked whether anyone could speak German. André talked to him and learnt that he was a Black Forest watchmaker. To the consultant, amputating one enemy soldier's finger in the middle of a battle might mean nothing, but to this particular man it would mean never working again. Much to the consultant's displeasure, André insisted on treating the man's finger in his own time, and instead of a five-minute amputation spent several weeks making sure the German could leave the hospital with all five fingers intact.

Inevitably, some patients were destined not to recover. One was an Alsatian soldier, whose pastor was called to his bedside. Once the man slipped into unconsciousness the pastor left the room saying, 'Now I can do nothing for him.' André, enraged, told him that was nonsense and sent him back with the order to read the Gospel out loud to the man, beginning with the raising of Lazarus. After two days the pastor said to André that the man had regained consciousness and had said he had heard every word.

'My past came back,' he had said. 'Now I can die in peace.'

During his ministry Metropolitan Anthony would experience similar occasions when he would read or sing to dying parishioners, bringing them back to consciousness so that they could make their peace with God or relatives before death. In a similar way he urged pregnant women to pray and sing hymns aloud to their unborn babies.

When France fell to the Germans André was demobbed and sent to Pau, close to the Pyrenees. His first concern was to find his mother and grandmother. The last he had heard was that they had been evacuated to the Limoges area, although the letter with this information was three months old before it reached him. He eventually tracked them down to a small village where he found them in a sorry state. Xenia was ill and Olga, by this time in her late seventies, had aged alarmingly. An admirer of de Gaulle, André considered joining his hero but it was not physically possible, so he decided the best thing would be for all three of them to return to occupied Paris.

The way he achieved it he described as 'partly legally and partly illegally': legally in the sense that they had all the right papers, and illegally, he would admit cheekily, because he had written the papers himself.

Still in uniform, he could spare just enough money to buy a civilian jacket. Then he, his mother and grandmother set out northwards towards the demarcation line with occupied France. When they arrived at the nearest town to the border, André went to the Mairie to obtain the requisite papers for entering the Nazi-held zone.

'Impossible,' said the mayor 'I'd be shot for giving you a pass.'

André set about trying to persuade him with all the charm and wiles he possessed. Finally the mayor agreed to put out the necessary papers and the official stamp and leave the room. 'You stamp the forms, take the papers and fill them in yourself,' he said. 'If you are arrested at the border I shall denounce you for stealing them.' That was all André needed. He stamped the forms, filled them in and set off for the station with Xenia and Olga.

André knew that if the German border guard saw his uniform he would be arrested immediately; French soldiers crossed into the occupied zone on pain of death. Since his new jacket could not completely conceal his army trousers he decided the best plan would be to stand as close to the official as possible so that the lower half of his body was hidden from view. He persuaded the other occupants of the carriage to hand over their papers to him, explaining that with his knowledge of German he would be the best person to deal with the formalities, and awaited the border.

When the guard reached their compartment André went over to him, pressing up against him as close as was decently possible, and handed over everyone's papers. The man was surprised at his excellent German, at which André explained his childhood in Vienna and his love of German literature. His Teutonic ego suitably flattered, the guard failed to notice the irregularities of either André's trousers or his papers, and the border was safely negotiated.

Back in Paris he took up his medical work again. One of his acquaintances was an old French doctor, a member of the Medical Resistance, who offered to enlist him. This, André realised, might have serious implications for the safety of his family. He discussed it with his mother, and they made a pact that if either were arrested by the Gestapo and tortured in each other's presence they would not divulge any secrets, even if they were forced to witness the other tortured to death.

André's role was to give medical aid to injured Resistance workers, for whom he spent many hours performing minor surgery in the basement of the Hotel Dieu hospital. His work there gave him the opportunity to pass on medicines and surgical supplies to Resistance units; and when he was put in charge of an ambulance he used it to ferry Resistance members around.

He also worked for a time at the Hospital Broca. A member of his church, the celebrated icon painter Gregory Krug, began to suffer olfactory hallucinations, which alarmed his family. Unfortunately his sisters did not help matters. When Father Gregory complained that he could smell sulphur, they would say, 'So can we,' in an effort to shield him from the truth of his delusions. Finally they came to André, for advice they imagined would be of a spiritual as well as medical nature. Instead he recommended electric shock treatment, which in his words 'was the best we had in those days'. He was never slow to look at a person's physical needs rather than seeing everything in religious terms. In this case Father Gregory responded to treatment and eventually returned to health.

Others did not. A young girl, who was his patient as well as being the daughter of a friend, contracted an incurable disease, from which she was to die during André's early years in London. Her courage in the face of spiritual as well as physical distress remained with him all his life.

He came to see that the recovery or otherwise of his patients did not necessarily depend on medical skills. On one particular night he treated two men: the first had been riddled with machine gun fire without one vital organ being hit, and made a full recovery. The second, merely involved in a brawl in a bar, had been stabbed with nothing more than a penknife; yet by the time he reached the hospital he had already lost so much blood that he was at the point of death. André had to come to terms with such apparent victims of circumstance, reconciling these strange twists of fate with his faith.

There was one event, however, which disturbed him on a spiritual level. A friend of his, a brilliant and brave young man, had spent three periods as a prisoner of war, and three times he had made a daring escape. Once more back in Paris he slipped and fell while running for a bus; and the fall killed him. André could make no sense of it. How could this hero, who had outwitted the Germans so magnificently and overcome so many dangers, come to such a pointless and ignominious end? On his own admission he thought long and hard to see anything of the divine purpose in it. It was a lesson in the truth of the biblical words: my thoughts are not your thoughts and my ways are not your ways. However near he drew to God, he would always have to accept that some things could never be explained satisfactorily in human terms. The monastic surrender involved obedience not only to a fallible army corporal but also to the unsearchable divine will.

In 1942 André's work at the Hospital Broca took a sinister turn. The Nazis earmarked the patients in his department to be despatched, on recovery, to labour camps or for experimentation in Germany. Although he was powerless to refuse outright to comply with the order, he was determined that something should be done to save his patients.

André and his colleagues soon discovered a chink in the armour of the Gestapo. The apparently fearless Germans were terrified of infectious diseases. So the department devised a simple system to outwit them. Each patient admitted to the ward was sent for an X-ray. André and the physician would position him at the X-ray machine, and then he would draw signs of TB on the plate. The patient was then diagnosed as suitably infected. In this way they avoided handing over anyone to the Germans for a whole year. Eventually, however, even the paranoid authorities began to suspect some trickery, and André decided it would be wise to leave the hospital to save his colleagues from further suspicion.

The Russian Grammar School offered him a job as – he was given to understand at first – a natural history teacher. This was almost entirely within his capabilities and his response to the headmaster was to say, 'I'll accept as long as I don't have to teach botany, as I've never learnt to tell one flower from another.' The headmaster appeared to agree; then added peremptorily, 'You will also teach history.'

'History?' André was astonished. 'Whatever makes you think I know any history?' The man was not to be put off. 'You did Classics at school, didn't you? You can't deny you know ancient history.' Indeed, André could not deny it.

'And you have no right to call yourself a Russian if you don't know Russian history; you must have learnt some in your youth group.' There was no point in arguing further. He would have to teach history. The headmaster paused. 'You will also teach languages.' As a linguist André could hardly argue with that, either. Another pause. 'You will also teach geography.' Against geography André thought he could muster a good argument. He had never been in the least interested in the subject and reckoned his knowledge of it to be minimal. The headmaster had no sympathy at all. 'If these twelve-year-olds can learn geography on Wednesdays and Thursdays, surely you are capable of learning it on Mondays and Tuesdays!'

André ended up teaching for twenty-five hours a week, with an additional two hours a day of pastoral supervision, for the sum of £1. The list of subjects he was called upon to teach 'as the need arose' was stretched to include gym and games, as well as the other sciences and maths. This apparent mastery of so much of the school curriculum provoked what he felt was a totally justified response from one of the parents.

'You are either an incredibly well-educated young man to be qualified in so many subjects, or else you hardly know anything about any of them!' said a bemused mother.

'Of course,' he admitted years later, 'I humbly said it was the latter.'

This was, at any rate, the story he recounted about himself. After his death Veronique Lossky, one of his former pupils, remembered him only as a maths teacher and pastoral supervisor. In the latter capacity his year at the Russian Grammar School offered him further insights into relationships with people, and the importance of even the most insignificant word or action. In one of the classes he taught was a girl who was particularly difficult. André knew she came from a problem home. One day he noticed that she had put up her desk lid and was crying behind it. He carried on as if he had not noticed, but when the bell rang he positioned himself by the door while the children filed out of the classroom. As the girl passed him he said quietly to her, 'Never lose heart.' These few words of compassion struck a chord. Twenty-five years later, when he was a bishop in London, he received a letter from the girl explaining that his words, and the genuine care with which he had spoken them, had been a turning point for her in her moment of despair, giving her the strength to endure what had seemed impossible. He would later repeat this story in order to illustrate how the smallest remark could have a deep effect on people, and how even the most unassuming person could make an impact on others.

Another story he recounted of his time at the school concerned an elderly member of staff who had once been André's scoutmaster. He was a gaunt man in every sense, emaciated, distant and unbending. One morning when André and a group of children were in the school yard they saw this master arrive. There was a down-and-out sitting on the pavement by the gate, and the master came up to him, exchanged a few words and raised his hat. Puzzled by this gesture, André asked him about it later. The master explained: 'Walking here from my home on the other side of Paris I had already given away the last of my money to other beggars so that by the time I reached the school I had nothing left to give this poor man. But I did not want him to think I passed him by through lack of concern. So I stopped and told him that I had nothing to give him but my respect. And that was why I raised my hat to him.' Not long afterwards this noble man died, worn out by a life of self-sacrifice, hard work and malnutrition.

An even nobler person was a pupil whose house had been firebombed. Everyone had managed to escape except for an old lady. On hearing she was trapped in the house the pupil went back in to die with her. This impressed itself on André's mind as an example of sacrifice, which, like Christ's, did not stop short of the ultimate. And to stop short was no sacrifice at all.

André continued his secret work with the Resistance while he was at the school. Plenty of other members of the Russian community were also engaged in anti-Nazi work, in particular Mother Maria Skobtsova, now canonised, whose charitable organisation Orthodox Action was instrumental in helping Jews escape from occupied Paris. A number of priests, including Father Afanasy, were involved in 'mercy baptisms' to give them a Christian identity. Mother Maria had become a nun after a bohemian life and two marriages, and on first acquaintance André had found her distinctly uncongenial. 'I was walking past a café in the Champs Elysees,' he said, 'when I spotted a glass of beer on a table, and behind it a Russian nun smoking a cigarette.' His youthful piety had been outraged and for a long time he had nothing to do with her. Eventually he came to recognise what he described as her 'inner change', and after her death in a

Ravensbruck gas oven he was more than ready to acknowledge the martyrdom of this unconventional monastic.

André's own pursuit of the monastic life continued in secret. It was by this time over three years since he had made his vows as a novice but he was still not tonsured, and he began to badger Father Afanasy to tonsure him and bestow on him the monastic habit. But his spiritual father's uncompromising spirit, born of living according to the absolute commandment of the Gospel to renounce everything in order to follow Christ, would not allow him to accept anything less in his disciple. His answer to André's pestering was always the same: 'No! You are not yet ready to give yourself completely.'

This total giving of self was how both men understood the word 'sacrifice'. For them it was not, as so many people see it, a grudging relinquishing of something cherished but, as the Latin root of the word implies, the joyful dedication of self as a holy offering to God. André thought he was ready to make such an offering. Father Afanasy knew otherwise.

'Only when you can say to me, "I have come in total obedience; do with me whatever you will," can we talk about your tonsure. So long as you are concerned about your mother and grandmother you are not ready, because you have still not learnt to put your trust wholly in God and to rely completely on obedience.'

Six months of desperate spiritual struggle followed, in which André came face to face not only with his conflicting loyalties but also with his own deficiencies. It was a dejecting revelation. His father had given him an example, in leaving his family to live in a solitude close to monasticism, but in doing so Boris had thrown the charge of caring for them on to André, who felt it acutely. If he in turn were to abandon them, they would be totally at the mercy of a hostile world.

Or in the mercy of a loving God, according to the measure of André's faith. For a long time he alternated between these two poles. In his prayers he argued with God, he sought assurances, even compromises. Slowly, painfully, he learnt that God did not strike bargains. He learnt afresh that his call was absolute. Of that he had been made dramatically aware at the moment of his conversion. Now he was being asked to take a further, final step: even to lay aside the filial duty which he considered selfless, to lay aside everything but total trust in the divine will. However much he repeatedly questioned God, he always received the same reply: 'I have called you; it is up to you to answer unconditionally.' As he entered the concentrated endeavour of Orthodox Lent he came to the stark realisation that there was more than his monastic vocation at stake.

'Either I had to say yes or I had to cease regarding myself as a member of the Church; I had to stop going to church, stop receiving Communion, because there is no point in receiving Communion and then saying to God "no"; and there is no point in being a member of Christ's Body if you refuse to do his will.'

The moment finally came, as Holy Week 1943 approached, when André felt he could struggle no more. He left the house one morning unaware of what the day ahead would bring and made his way as usual to the school; but suddenly, during one of his lessons, he was overcome by the feeling that he could vacillate no longer; he had to make his decision that very day. By the time school finished he had made up his mind. Without even returning home for a last word with his family, whom he presumed he would never see again, he went straight to Father Afanasy and said, with all the intensity he could muster, 'I have come.'

'To be a monk?'

'Yes.'

'All right, sit down.' Father Afanasy immediately proceeded to puncture André's lofty intensity with a series of the most mundane questions: he needed to acquire sandals, a belt, other things necessary for the rite. Then, he promised, he would tonsure André a week later. They both fell silent for a while. Then André asked the old monk: 'What shall I do now?' He expected to be told, 'Sleep here on the floor; the rest is not your concern.' That was how his bishop lived – in total poverty, often sleeping wrapped in his bishop's mantle on the floor of his church when a beggar needed his room. Instead he heard words that were, in their way, just as uncompromising and just as difficult to accept. 'Now? You can go home.'

'What do you mean, home? I've just renounced my home and my family.'

'Yes,' replied the wise monk, 'you have indeed renounced them. But as your spiritual father I am ordering you to return to them on obedience.' André was dumbstruck, but Father Afanasy was adamant.

He was tonsured during Holy Week, in the presence of his family, a circumstance he had just a few days earlier thought impossible. It made a profound impact on his mother and on her appreciation of the Passion events, so that during Bright (Easter) Week she said to him, 'No one who has lived through our Holy Week and Easter can ever be the same again.' He repeated her words in his Easter night sermon in 1995, without naming her but merely imputing them to 'a deeply, genuinely believing woman'.

André had made the decision to continue keeping his monasticism a secret. However, the secret was not easily kept. 'Everyone knew about it,' commented Nicholas Lossky after Metropolitan Anthony's death. His outward life continued as before, as far as his official work at the school and his secret work for the Resistance were concerned. At home, André's endeavours to lead a monastic life were creating difficulties. For instance, he ate strictly according to monastic rules, insisting that his vegetables always be boiled, not cooked in oil. He also refused all physical contact with his family, and would not so much as give his grandmother a good-night kiss on the forehead. Russians, like Olga's native Italians, are renowned for their social kissing and hugging, and the old lady found this very hurtful. Whatever benefits André's over-zealous asceticism might have had for him, it was nothing but a trial for the rest of the household.

Eventually he began to realise how his apparently 'religious' conduct was at odds with the supreme Christian principle of love. That was a valuable lesson for him to learn, and as a bishop he would warn against such excess of piety. He was said to have come very suddenly to the awareness of his folly in refusing to kiss his family – while travelling on a Paris bus. In fact, the incident was of a far deeper nature. Metropolitan Anthony admitted towards the end of his life that while he had had a revelation of Christ at his conversion, he had been given no understanding of the Holy Spirit. As the bus rounded a corner and he was saying to himself, 'How can I know I've made some sort of contact with the Holy Spirit?' he was unexpectedly filled with an amazing, burning love: not only for his family, not only for the human beings surrounding him, but for the whole of creation. This, he came to realise, was the gift and experience of the Holy Spirit who had, as he put it, communicated himself to him and made him partake of love divine.

When in 1999 he spoke of this moment at his Diocesan Conference, he referred to himself in the third person as 'a young man, a contemporary of mine', so remote had that erstwhile lack of understanding become.

From then on he began to unbend, much to the relief of his mother and grandmother, and to the benefit of all those who were to encounter him in his future ministry. Indeed, later in his life his insistence on physical contact was to become something which marked him out. The England to which he was to come in 1949 was still very much in the grip of a puritanical stiff upper lip attitude. 'Oh, the English! They hate to touch each other!' he would say in horror. Eventually he became insistent on the use of bodily contact in his pastoral work. He hugged people; he gave them his shoulder to cry on. And he taught his priests to do the same. This warmth was not always seen or appreciated by outsiders, to whom he could give the appearance of being rather cold in his later years. 'He was not a cuddly person,' Richard Chartres, the Anglican Bishop of London, said – mistakenly – after his death.

But the indwelling love of the Holy Spirit was about more than a hug. There were times when Metropolitan Anthony was pervaded by it, so that people who came to him were overwhelmed at being enfolded in divine love. It was an experience that was totally 'other', something that they felt did not originate in him, and this experience changed people's lives and converted them. He sometimes exhorted his own flock with the words: 'Does anyone meeting us say, "This person is something I've never seen before?"' They could truly reply, with respect to him, 'Yes'.

He had seen the same thing in other people – people filled with the Spirit who reached out to others and brought to life a knowledge of the divine that was lying dormant within them. The power of such an inner life filled with the Spirit was, he said, akin to the words of Christ, 'Lazarus, come forth!' – the power that could transfigure another person. This was indeed what had drawn him to his own spiritual father.

André was to enjoy only three months of monasticism under the direction of Father Afanasy. One day he sent André a note in which he said, 'I have experienced the mystery of contemplative silence.' Three days later he died.

André's sense of bereavement was compounded by his need as a monk to be subject to the obedience of a spiritual father. It seemed unthinkable that after his experience of finding Father Afanasy he could start again, assessing the relative merits of potential candidates among the other clergy. Sitting in his room one day he asked himself, 'What shall I do?' He heard a voice within himself: 'Why are you looking for a spiritual father? I am still alive.'

That experience was, he claimed, uncharacteristic. He was not, and was never drawn to be, a mystic. 'I do not have thoughts like that at every corner,' was his comment on another rare occasion when he felt 'spoken' to in this way. When such a thing did happen he had to apply his sense of spiritual discernment in trusting the experience was right.

In this instance he was sure that it was. His search for another spiritual father was at an end. He would in the future meet many distinguished and spiritually mature men who gave him advice, but no one ever replaced

Father Afanasy. Their spiritual relationship would continue through prayer into eternity, according to Orthodox tradition.

Metropolitan Anthony would speak of Father Afanasy with great affection and reverence throughout his life, and it was undoubtedly thanks to this man's rigorous and committed schooling that he became the person he did. Father Afanasy had taken to heart, and transmitted to his pupil, the saying of the Russian St Theophan the Recluse, 'God and the soul – that is all there is to a monk.' André had discovered that externals were one thing: in uniform he was expected to behave as a soldier, in a white coat he was a doctor – and later in vestments he was expected to behave as a priest. But underneath it all, the structure of his inner life could remain free, subject only to his spiritual father and to God.

In the same year that Father Afanasy died André gained his M.D. The war was turning the corner. It was in this more promising outward situation that André suddenly found himself arrested by the Gestapo. He was hurrying down the steps of Metro Étoile when a hand came down on his shoulder. 'Show me your papers,' said a voice. André handed them over and found himself under arrest. He was taken in for questioning. The interrogator, a Frenchman employed by the Germans, recognised him as a foreigner despite his French citizenship and accused him of being an English spy. André demanded to know why.

'Your surname 'Bloom' is spelt with double 'o', in the English manner.' André laughed in his face. 'Don't be ridiculous. If I were an English spy I'd be sure to have given myself a typically French name. The last thing I would be called would be Bloom, to give myself away.' The man was not to be put off. 'Well, you're obviously a foreigner of some sort. What are you?'

'I'm a Russian,' André announced with pride.

'No, you can't be,' the man replied. 'We have been told all about Russians. They don't look like Aryans. They have slanting eyes and protruding cheekbones.'

'I'm afraid you're confusing us with the Chinese.' André had subtly taken command of the conversation with a calculated and fearless courtesy. The interrogator felt obliged to justify himself, and called in five other officers from the next room.

'This man says he's a Russian.'

'He's a liar!' the five answered in chorus. 'Russians have slanting eyes and protruding cheekbones.' The interrogator dismissed his witnesses and sat back, not without some sympathy for his captive. 'Wherever you come from, what do you think of the war?' he asked. Still very much in command, André replied with an apparently naive honesty. 'It's going wonderfully. We're beating you on all sides.'

His questioner was taken aback. 'Is that really your opinion? You admit you're not a Nazi sympathiser?'

'No, I'm resolutely against you.'

The man caved in. 'In that case, you'd better get out of here as quick as you can. This door here is unguarded; run!'

'So I ran,' Metropolitan would recount years later. 'Or rather, I didn't even run, I just trotted off quietly so as not to attract the attention of the other five officers.'

The technique he had used in this interrogation – of making sure he held the initiative in a conversation, even when circumstances might have suggested otherwise – was one he was to cultivate not only as a doctor and Resistance worker but also as a priest and bishop. What he also learned from his brief arrest was the value of living in the present moment. Under interrogation he suddenly became aware that his past – such as his Resistance work, for which he would be shot – no longer existed. Neither, in his precarious circumstances, did any anticipatory future. All his attention was forced into the present moment, and it was this intensity of concentration that, he claimed, allowed him to think quickly enough to outwit his captors. He was to use the same techniques throughout his life. He would always listen patiently to people who came to see him, with a concentration that made them feel as if they were the only person who existed; even more, as if at times he could read their thoughts. He would then make his reply with such an unequivocal intensity that it was difficult for his listener to be anything other than completely bowled over, at the time, by what he had said, even if they sometimes came to other conclusions later when they had had the opportunity to digest his words at a distance. But by then, of course, it was too late to argue with him.

When Paris was liberated in August 1944 André found himself part of the bodyguard accompanying de Gaulle in the triumphal march into the city. He was to remain a great admirer of the general (much as he was to become an admirer of Margaret Thatcher) and years later was still encouraging his clergy in England to read his writings.

The entry into Paris was a moment of mixed emotions. On the one hand, all that he had fought for had been won. On the other, more practical hand, he found himself nervously dodging sniper fire – in contrast, he admitted readily, to de Gaulle who, in typical proud pose, marched forward ignoring the bullets.

At work, André was becoming increasingly aware that surgery, despite its prestige, was primarily a matter of technical skill, which he felt he possessed in adequate measure, although he admitted it was never exceptional. What was exceptional, however, was his rapport with his patients. He developed a reputation for sitting with the dying – sometimes all night, after a full day's work – and before long he was in demand to do the same on other wards. It was this human contact with patients that he came to see as important and which was to direct him towards the decision, when the war came to an end, to go into general practice.

He set up a practice in a Russian quarter of Paris. The house had the distinction of having another tenant who seemed to spend all her time cooking Russian cabbage soup. One day André offered to give some medical advice to an acquaintance, but forgot to give him the exact address of the surgery, so he was surprised when the man turned up nevertheless.

'How did you find me?' he asked.

'I could smell the cabbage!' came the reply.

Like post-war Britain, France was struggling with austerity measures in an effort to put the country back on its feet. The government set out minimum standards of food and shelter for its citizens. André saw them not as a minimum but an ideal maximum; and not only for someone leading the monastic life. He came to an agreement with his mother – in fact there were occasions, many years later, when he said the suggestion was originally hers – that so long as there remained one hungry person in the world their household would not live above this standard. He set aside from his salary sufficient money to live accordingly and gave the rest away.

He came to see such an attitude to possessions as essential to Christianity, ideally to be followed by all believers. As a priest he would preach a powerful sermon on the subject from time to time. 'Because of your excesses, people elsewhere in the world – and here in Britain on the streets – are actually dying,' he would remind his congregation. He would urge his parishioners, including those with families, to live according to the same rule of poverty as himself.

The end of the war was not to be the end of either physical or spiritual hardship. He would describe a certain incident that he witnessed as 'a dark day at the end of the war' when he was visiting the wife of a friend who had been declared missing in action, presumed dead. They were sitting drinking tea with a third person when suddenly the door opened and the husband walked in. André never forgot the pain of what happened next. The woman jumped up and said to her husband, 'We thought you were dead!' The words came out as an accusation, leaving unsaid the terrible truth behind them: you should have stayed dead. My life has moved on. I have married another man.

This story formed the basis of a sermon Metropolitan Anthony preached years later, one of those chilling moments when he spoke with passionate conviction about the tough side of Christianity – rejection, betrayal, death – that he saw as essential to the understanding of the sacrificial nature of divine love. Grim though this particular event was, it was not the worst that André was to witness. One of the tasks he took on was to care for survivors of German concentration camps. They were broken mentally as well as physically.

Another terrible aftermath of the war was the retribution meted out to collaborators with the Germans. André was to witness a man being sentenced to death, and the terror on the victim's face as he was led off to be shot was something he never forgot. When a bishop he would sometimes recount this story during Holy Week or in Lenten retreats, to remind his listeners of the horrors of execution and the very real human suffering that was Christ's.

He was given deserved recognition for his wartime work when he was awarded the bronze medal of the Societé d'Encouragement au Bien.

Gradually, things in Paris began to return to normal and he settled into life as a general practitioner. There were occasions when he found seeing a continuous string of people in his surgery an emotional drain. He developed a strategy that not only helped him but also, he thought, made an impression on his patients.

'I had a rule when I saw large numbers of people, if I felt they had emptied me of my collectedness. When the next one entered I would say, "Will you please sit down and wait a moment; I must recollect myself. If you are a believer, pray with me. If you are an unbeliever, keep quiet!" Then I knelt down before an icon to pray for a few moments, before getting up and saying, "Now, what's the matter?" And I think several people reacted to the fact that I did that in all simplicity.'

Since he did not have a car he made his house calls by bus during the week and bicycle on Sundays. He claimed to have little road sense, and gave as an example an occasion when, cycling down a hill he saw in front of him a woman with a pram crossing the road. Concerned at the expression of terror on her face, he looked over his shoulder expecting to see a car careering madly down behind him. But the road was empty; it was he who was the cause of the woman's fright. He was to remain a non-driver for the rest of his life.

André had by this time developed an interest in homoeopathy and he tried to set up as a homoeopathic doctor, without success. The time was not ripe for alternative medicine. He retained his enthusiasm, however, and would often treat himself with homoeopathic remedies.

As well as his medical work he continued his youth activities, including leading Bible study sessions in his house. These were a source of inspiration to the young people, one of whom was Nicholas, the son of Vladimir Lossky.

Vladimir Lossky had chosen to remain a layman, despite being a renowned theologian. He was, in Metropolitan Anthony's words, one of the people in Paris who did most to promote Orthodoxy, not only among his fellow theologians but also in the world around him. He had refused to become a priest, saying that he accepted instead to be a lay theologian and, in the freedom that gave him, to convey Orthodoxy to whomever wished to hear about it. He was married, with a family of four children. How he and his wife treated them was something André was never to forget.

'I called for them one Sunday – I was living across the street from them at the time on the Isle St Louis – on the way to the Liturgy. When I went into the house I found the parents kneeling in front of their children asking their forgiveness for any wrong they had done them during the week. I have no doubt that action had more impact on their faith than any theological teaching Lossky might have given them.'

However, the young André was not above disagreeing with his friend when he thought fit. At one time, Lossky's opinion was that the Eastern religions had no proper knowledge or experience of God. André did not dare to argue openly with such a distinguished person. 'But what courage couldn't achieve, cunning could,' he later said, and he decided to make his point in a way that his friend could not fail to respond to. André slipped home and wrote out eight quotations from the Upanishads. He took them back to Lossky with an apparently innocent query.

'Could you help me? I have some sayings of the Fathers here and I can't remember who said what. Can you identify them for me, please?' Lossky went through the list and without hesitation wrote beside each quotation the relevant name: St John Chrysostom, St Basil the Great and so on. When the theologian had attributed them all, André dropped his bombshell.

'It's the Upanishads.'

From then on, he said, Lossky began to look much more sympathetically at other faiths and came to find in them truths he had never before been able to acknowledge.

Still a member of the Russian Student Christian Movement, André took a group of students to England in 1947 – despite his childhood protestations that he would never go there – to the conference of the Fellowship of St Alban and St Sergius (FSASS), travelling with his friend, the Orthodox theologian Elisabeth Behr-Sigel and her son.

The FSASS had been founded in 1928 by members of the Russian Student Christian Movement and members of the Anglican Church as an informal means of rapprochement between the two churches. It attracted notable churchmen on both sides. Vladimir Lossky was a regular attender, and senior Anglican clerics were enthusiastic members. Despite his lack of English, André was assured there would be enough people who understood French to make his participation viable. The Orthodox chaplain to the Fellowship was Father Lev Gillet, a priest André had first met on the day he had graduated from the lycée.

During this visit to England André gave his first talk to what was to become his future parish in London. It was not an auspicious beginning. Lossky had been invited to speak but at the last moment he had to withdraw, and André was sent as a replacement. When the parishioners began to assemble and discovered the substitution some of them reacted angrily.

'We were promised a great theologian, and now we're presented with a totally unknown doctor in his place. Let's all leave before he gets here so that he finds no one when he arrives!'

Those who did stay, however, were pleasantly surprised by the young unknown. He was certainly not a theologian in Lossky's mould but his vibrant and heartfelt portrayal of Christianity created an immediate response of approval.

He took the opportunity to renew his acquaintance with some old friends from his youth camp days who were living in England. One of them was Mariane Greenan, Elisabeth Behr-Sigel's daughter. Another was Natalia Scorer. Her father, the Russian philosopher Simeon Frank, was by that time very deaf, so communication was difficult. But André was impressed by his collectedness, and his open attitude towards his faith.

'He was not a prisoner of social Orthodoxy,' he summed him up, 'he was a universal Christian belonging to the Orthodox Church.'

On his return to France André began deliberating about his future. His original vocation to the priesthood had never left him but his medical training and the war had occupied him and the years had slipped by. Now, at last, all the conditions for fulfilling his intention of becoming a worker priest had been met. He was established in general practice; he had served more than his fifteen years of studying the Fathers imposed by Father

Georges Florovsky; he had passed the canonical minimum ages of ordination to the diaconate and priesthood. And he was still a layman. Just as he had begun to lose hope of ever becoming a priest, things began to move dramatically. Exactly how it happened was something Metropolitan Anthony described in different ways to different audiences.

During the Fellowship conference Father Lev, impressed by André's development, was said to have urged him to be ordained. But many years later Metropolitan Anthony recounted how the initiative had come from his bishop, who was also one of his patients.

'I'd like to ordain you,' he said one day. 'You may not be theologically trained but you are an educated man with the capacity to learn. But the real reason is that as you have a good job and a good salary, we will not have to pay you, and we can send you out to distant parishes at your own expense!'

That was not, André felt, the most uplifting of motives. He began to sound out his friends. Some, like Vladimir Lossky, urged him forward. Others, impressed by his medical career and his youth work, regretted his prospective loss of freedom to pursue these different but complementary aspects of Christian action. 'You will just become a slave to your bishop or some priest,' was their response.

He claimed to have deliberated for a year. One day, when he was sitting in his surgery with a gap between patients, he opened the Bible to find not an instant answer but certainly some guidance. His eyes fell on a passage from Isaiah chapter 58, which, he recounted later, he simply misread. The actual words were, 'Feed the souls of the hungry' but what he thought he saw was 'Give your soul as food to the hungry.' He sat back and reflected that up till then he had kept his soul to himself, walled about in its own *pairidaeza*. Now God was telling him to share with others all that he had so carefully nurtured in private. There seemed to be no further reason for delay. Without André's having to embark on any formal theological training – as could be the case with ordinations in the Orthodox Church where academic qualifications in theology were not obligatory and the shortage of priests was acute – a date was set.

On the evening before, André came to his bishop. Just as they were about to part the bishop suddenly asked him, 'How does your mother feel about your ordination?'

'She's very unhappy about it,' André felt bound to admit. Xenia was proud of her son's career as a doctor, which contrasted sharply with the lowly status of the priesthood in the average Russian consciousness. The bishop's response was immediate. 'In that case I cannot ordain you tomorrow.' It was a cruel culmination to so many years of struggle. There was nothing André could do but return home in intense pain, to learn the ultimate lesson of the uncompromising nature of God's call – which had to be learnt without any resort to un-Christian recrimination or bitterness. A natural depressive, he had to ride out this disappointment in the knowledge that divine love was not sentimental, pandering to his desires however earnest. The impact of this never left him. He would quote a saying from the Shepherd of Hermas, 'God will not finish with you until he has broken all your bones.' He also took to heart his bishop's insistence on following what he considered to be the right course of action, seeking to do the will of God rather than pleasing men. When he himself became a bishop he was likewise prepared to defer an ordination or a reception into the Church at the last moment if he felt circumstances were not right, and no amount of sympathy with the candidate's distress, which he had once shared, would make him change his mind. He would go so far as to warn people how a certain man had arrived with friends and family to be received one morning, and after making his confession was astonished to hear Metropolitan Anthony say, 'I'm sorry, I can't receive you today after all.'

'His family all thought, "Whatever has he done?"' the Metropolitan would tell the next potential victim. But despite the humour in his voice when he recounted this story, he was deadly serious; they, too had to be prepared for an eleventh-hour postponement if he judged it necessary. He never demanded from others either more or less than he had endured himself.

In his case it was agreed that his bishop should keep in close contact with Xenia, and that the ordination would not proceed until she was adequately reconciled to it.

'And I think in the end she accepted my being a priest,' Metropolitan Anthony said towards the end of his life. What influenced her favourably was the proposal André received from the Fellowship of St Alban and St Sergius that he should come to work for it in England as a lecturer on Orthodoxy. Xenia felt that clergy in Britain were treated with more respect than among the Russians.

There was, however, one thing she felt she could never accept: to see her son bearded in the Orthodox clerical manner. André therefore promised her that so long as she was alive he would not grow the traditional beard, and he remained shaven until after Xenia's death. It was a concession that satisfied his bishop, and the ordination duly took place three months later. His secret vows as a monk now came into the open, since an Orthodox ordinand must marry or take monastic vows before being made deacon. Henceforth he was known openly by his monastic name of Anthony, after St Anthony Pechersky, the reclusive founder of the Monastery of the Caves at Kiev. The choice of patron seemed not inappropriate.

Ordination to the priesthood followed very quickly. Traditionally at least a year should elapse between the two, but in the exceptional circumstances of the Russian Church in the twentieth century, both in Russia and in the emigration, this was sometimes reduced. In André's case the reduction was for the most unedifying reason. An Orthodox deacon's role is to lead the people in prayer – chiefly, in modern practice, by singing the litanies. Andre's terror of music was as strong as ever and, unschooled in singing, he made a complete mess of the services. Just how bad the situation was he discovered on overhearing what he described as an unpleasant conversation between his bishop and his parish priest.

'Father Mikhail, how long do you want him to remain here as a deacon?' asked the bishop.

'As short a time as possible. He's ruining the choir every time he opens his mouth!'

So his ordination to the priesthood took place almost at once. His early priestly duties included celebrating the Liturgy at a Russian old people's home. After the first service there, an old lady came up to him with a request for some advice on the Jesus Prayer, which she had used for fourteen years without receiving any spiritual benefit. His first thought was to direct her to someone more experienced, but she replied that all the knowledgeable priests had failed to give her an answer, so perhaps he in his ignorance might by chance blunder out the right thing. His reply, which he repeated in his book *School for Prayer*, was that she should stop all her pious activity and instead spend time each day just sitting quietly enjoying the peace of her room. 'Sit and knit before God. But I forbid you to utter one word of prayer,' he said. The result, which he claimed surprised him, was that this old woman discovered in the ensuing silence the divine presence to which she had previously been oblivious.

On another occasion he told a similar tale, this time of a young child whose mother led him through certain of the set prayers at bedtime, and who one evening announced with relief as she came to the end, 'Now we have finished all that prayering, we can pray!'

Although he had no personal experience of a child's faith, he was sensitive to the way that believing children could be influenced by adults. He would describe another incident. A mother used to pray with her young son each evening, and one prayer in particular had caught the child's imagination; he called it 'the beautiful one'.

'Then the boy "made a puddle" on the dining room carpet. His mother was very angry with him, and when bedtime came the child, still feeling guilty, said sadly, "I suppose now we won't be able to say the beautiful one."

'His mother, seeing her mistake, replied, "I was the one who was angry with you; God was not angry with you."'

Many years of priesthood were later to teach him that children often came to confession bound by the guilt foisted upon them by angry adults. He would then turn to the child and explain that this did not come from God. What was important, he would say, was how close they could feel to Jesus. It was the things they felt he would be ashamed of that they should talk about in confession.

Sometimes parents tried to prepare their children in other ways. One earnest mother made her two sons write out lists of their misdeeds, which they duly presented to Father Anthony.

'Are you sorry for what you've done?' he asked them.

'Yes,' they replied.

'I'll tell you what we'll do, then. To show that God has forgiven you, let's burn the lists.' He found a little bowl and some matches in the sanctuary, came out, placed the boys' lists in it and solemnly set them alight. Someone must have been burning incense in the bowl because as the lists caught fire a beautiful scent began wafting upwards.

'What's that?' asked the boys.

'It's the sweet smell of repentance,' he replied.

The new Father Anthony began to develop skills as a preacher of sermons, in which he initially employed an idiosyncratic technique possibly linked to his synaesthesia. He would close his eyes when he began speaking and would then 'see' in his head what he termed arabesques: a line of blue curves and squiggles on which he would focus his attention. Starting from one end of the line he would follow the marks in his mind's eye, talking as he did so almost as if spellbound, until he reached the far end, when he would stop. The technique seemed to work, in that he became a popular speaker.

There was another reason he was popular. He was able to celebrate in French as well as the traditional Church Slavonic. The younger generation of Russians, born in France, found the Slavonic difficult to follow, and a priest who celebrated in French was soon in demand elsewhere. One Sunday he was invited to another parish specifically so that the congregation could hear a French sermon.

He read the Gospel in both languages, first French and then Slavonic, and proceeded straight into the sermon, using his customary technique. It was only after he had climbed into bed that night that he was disturbed by the thought that he was not aware of anything he had said. Concerned, he telephoned the parish priest to ask him what he had preached on.

'I don't know,' came the disgruntled reply.

'What do you mean, you don't know? Why not?'

'You preached in Russian!'

It was an abrupt end to his contact with that particular parish; they never asked him back.

Nevertheless, he continued to preach according to his strange technique, at first accepting it in wonder as a gift. It was only some time later that he spoke about it to Father Sophrony, the revered founder of the Orthodox monastery at Tolleshunt Knights in Essex, who said to him, 'You know, this is very immature.'

In giving this counsel Father Sophrony was following the Fathers, who were always quick to impress upon their disciples that such mystical occurrences were for beginners, to be left behind with growing spiritual maturity. That the young Father Anthony took this to heart could be seen in the outcome. The arabesques disappeared, immediately and for good.

He still found relationships with the Roman Catholic Church difficult. One evening he attended a meeting at which a Roman bishop began to rubbish Orthodoxy. The young Father Anthony opposed him with spirit, but inwardly he was deeply wounded. On the way home, as he negotiated the dim tunnels of the Paris Metro, he prayed in the words given to him from the psalms: may his ways be dark and slippery. That, he told his congregation in England towards the end of his life, was at least an example of an honest prayer, expressing the genuine feelings of the heart and not the false piety of someone saying what he thought God wanted to hear. He recommended this bold approach rather than that of misplaced piety.

Father Anthony was invited back to the Fellowship's conference in the summer of 1948. As in the previous year he met up with some old friends, including Anna Garrett, née Duddington, whom he had known at camps in France. Now married, she had just given birth to her third child, and was delighted to have him visit. Despite the fact that he arrived at her house in civvies, the midwife recognised him as a 'man of God'.

At the conference he made an impression in more than one way. Invited to give a paper, he had written down the text and had asked someone to translate it into English. He then struggled to read it out, with predictable results. Afterwards Father Lev Gillet came up to him and said, 'Father Anthony, in my whole life I have never heard such a boring lecture.'

'Well, what can I do?' he replied. 'Since I don't know the language I can't do anything else but read out a text.'

'No, I forbid you to write down a single word, even notes.'

The young priest was horrified. 'If I try to speak unprepared, people will laugh.'

'Indeed we will, and what's more we'll be laughing at your expense. But then at least we won't be bored!'

Not everyone at the conference shared this negative reaction and he was urged to accept the job with the Fellowship. Six months later, in the last days of January 1949, he and Xenia packed up their few belongings and sailed for England.

PART THREE

LONDON –
THE EARLY YEARS

CHAPTER SEVEN

PRIESTHOOD

(1949–1957)

T he leading lights in the Fellowship of St Alban and St Sergius on the Russian side were the lay theologian Nicolas Zernov and his wife Militza, a formidable couple whose influence in bringing an awareness of Orthodoxy to the West can scarcely be underrated. When the Fellowship was founded very little was known about Orthodoxy in Britain and there were few books available. It was largely the tireless work of the Zernovs that gradually changed this situation. Nicolas was an impressive but very humble man, who, for instance, was content for everyone to sit on him in discussions on intercommunion – something he believed in passionately. He had a great interest in and love for people, and relished making new acquaintances at Fellowship conferences.

The Russians had been delighted to find in England a native church in which they could recognise much of their own faith, and the Fellowship soon became a lively and enlightened instrument of early ecumenical activity. On the official level an Anglican–Orthodox Joint Doctrinal Commission began working in 1931. In its early years there were great hopes for a formal reconciliation, which was not, however, to materialise.

In 1943 the Fellowship had purchased a house in Ladbroke Grove as its headquarters. A unique joint Anglican/Orthodox chapel on the ground floor was dedicated to St Basil the Great, and St Basil's House also housed a library, the Fellowship's chaplain Father Lev and its two secretaries, Joan Ford and Helle Georgiadis.

For the first few months after Father Anthony's arrival Olga, by this time eighty-six, remained in Paris, looked after in the household of the Losskys. The secretaries enlisted the help of the choirmaster of the

Russian parish to find accommodation for the Blooms in sympathetic surroundings. The Russian community in London, unlike its Paris counterpart, was small. Following the Revolution the British government had only accepted one or two thousand people into the country. There had been heavy British investment in the imperial Russian economy and many people were aggrieved at the loss of their money; so Britain had not been a very welcoming haven for Russian émigrés. However, those who did come tended to integrate into, and intermarry with, the host community much more than their compatriots in Paris. The Blooms would find life very different and not a little strange.

A flat fell vacant in nearby Ladbroke Square at No 13, which already housed some London Russians. The tenant on the top floor had taken up the offer of a 'Stalin amnesty' and returned to her homeland. This fourth-floor flat, small but pleasant, was to become Father Anthony's home for the next couple of years. He spent some time getting it ready, enlisting the choirmaster's daughter Mariamna Theokritoff to help him with the painting. While they worked they talked, and his words were eventually to bring Mariamna back to faith.

Olga was brought over from Paris and settled in with her daughter and grandson. The people on the ground floor were the Kirillovs, who were delighted with their new neighbours. Their daughter Irina, about to go up to Cambridge, first met Father Anthony when, as a young man in plus fours and carrying two buckets of rubbish, he appeared at the door asking, 'Where can I deposit this?' The two families became friends, regularly taking tea in each other's flats.

Father Anthony soon became well known and liked among the Russian community. He renewed his acquaintance with Natalia Scorer and was to remain a friend, spiritual guide and comforter to her family for the rest of his life. In December 1950 he stayed the night and most of the following day with Natalia's dying father, Simeon Frank, in the same way as he had comforted dying patients in Paris.

This was just one example of the time, energy and support he gave to many of the families of the Russian parish. Some of them could be very demanding. Throughout his ministry his warmth and compassion led vulnerable people to rely on him to a degree that was sometimes more than desirable or possible.

The arrival of Father Anthony was to open a new chapter in the Fellowship's history. Ironically he took on the mantle of the distinguished Orthodox theologian who before the War had been the Fellowship's 'inspirer', according to Nicolas Zernov – Father Sergei Bulgakov, the very man whose off-putting talk to the teenaged André had driven him to read the gospel. But whereas the focus of Father Sergei's vision was the restoration of sacramental Communion between the Anglicans and Orthodox, Father Anthony's was much more focused on calling the individual Christian to seek a personal relationship with Christ, regardless of which church he or she belonged to.

That was not to say he was dismissive of Church differences. He remained passionately Orthodox – he loved both its theology and the church on the ground – but he was always willing to acknowledge Orthodoxy wherever, and however incompletely, he found it. He was, in his own words, entranced by what he found in the Anglicanism of the time, although in his later years he became increasingly pessimistic about the Church of England and began to feel more empathy with the Free Churches. But in 1949 he threw himself into ecumenical activity, very quickly endearing himself to everyone who met him. He recognised Fellowship members as kindred spirits. Some were very close to Orthodoxy and went on to convert, although neither the Fellowship nor Father Anthony ever set out to proselytise. His enthusiasm for the Anglican Church was in contrast to his earlier contacts in France with Roman Catholicism and French Protestants. His distrust of the Church of Rome was still such that the first time he found himself in an English ecumenical gathering that included a Roman Catholic his reaction was to think: this man cannot be a Christian if he's a Catholic! He recounted this anecdote with mock horror in his later years. Nevertheless, it took some time before his opinion changed, and he always maintained a wariness of the Roman Church, even though he revered individual Catholics such as Dom Bede Winslow and later Cardinal Basil Hume, whose funeral he insisted on attending in preference to an important meeting at his own church.

At first Father Anthony celebrated mainly at St Basil's House, serving the full monastic services since he had neither the knowledge nor the experience to abbreviate them, but he also served as an unpaid assistant priest in the London Patriarchal Parish of the Russian Orthodox Church, joining with it on Sundays and for Easter and other feasts to concelebrate and frequently to preach.

There had been a Russian church in London, in one form or another, since the time of Peter the Great. The parish was dedicated to the Dormition of the Mother of God (the Assumption). During the nineteenth century it had been resident in a mews behind 32 Welbeck Street in the West End. However, in the 1920s the parish had split into two

worshipping communities, one recognising the authority of the beleaguered Church in Russia – known first as the Evlogy and later the
Patriarchal Parish – and the other fiercely independent of what it thought
of as the 'Soviet' church: the Karlovatsky, later known as the Synodal or
Church in Exile Parish (now the Russian Orthodox Church Abroad). In
1923, under the leadership of the Russian Student Christian Movement,
the two communities began to share an Anglican building, St Philip's in
Buckingham Palace Road, each using it on alternate Sundays. They were
able to rescue some of the furnishings from the earlier chapel, including
the Royal Doors of the icon screen.

In 1929, again on the initiative of the Russian Student Christian
Movement, the Evlogy Parish, under their priest Father Nicholas Behr,
began to hold services in a drill hall above a garage in Earls Court on the
weekends when St Philip's was given over to the Synodal Parish. With
little money at their disposal they were able to raise just enough for the
modest rent and to put together an altar table, an icon screen and a couple
of icon-desks, all of which had to be stored behind a curtain when the hall
was in secular use. This formed the basis of a chapel which they dedicated
to St Sergius, the great Russian saint.

During the Second World War, when they had had to leave the hall, the
St Sergius chapel found a temporary home in Brechin Place before being
dismantled and its contents stored. Meanwhile, worship at St Philip's continued, despite bomb damage that sometimes meant having to use other
churches. Father Nicholas died in early 1940 and was succeeded as parish
priest by Father Vladimir Theokritoff.

Father Vladimir was a remarkable man, very austere and of great personal integrity. One incident serves to show something of his qualities. As
a result of the Yalta Conference, an exchange was to take place of prisoners of war. There had been a number of people who had changed sides
when Hitler invaded the Soviet Union, hoping it would be their passport
to freedom in the West; and some had eventually ended up as prisoners in
Britain. They were due to be repatriated to the Soviet Union, and all knew
it would mean death. They asked to have confession and Communion
before they left, and Father Vladimir arranged for them to be brought to
him. He spent almost two days and nights without a break hearing their
confessions, before celebrating the Liturgy on the last morning and giving
them Communion. Then they were taken away to begin their overland
journey back to their homeland. As soon as they crossed the border into
Soviet territory they were taken off the train and shot. The politician

Richard Crosland was said to have been haunted by the tragedy for the rest of his days.

Father Vladimir continued his work caring for his small flock. In 1947 the parish was able to raise enough money to buy premises of its own, a terraced house at 34 Upper Addison Gardens, a few minutes' walk from Shepherd's Bush. There, the small St Sergius chapel was reinstated on the ground floor in what had been two inter-connecting living rooms. The French windows at the rear gave on to a small garden and thence a garden square, and could be opened on a summer's day to provide fresh air for the worshippers and the sound of Russian chant for the bemused neighbours. The upper two storeys housed Father Vladimir and his family, and the basement his brother Michael the choirmaster and his family.

This Parish House would become Father Anthony's home a year or so later. In the meantime he was settling in to his work at the Fellowship, where he soon began to make a favourable impression. A young Anglican student (later Canon), Donald Allchin, found him a powerful person, full of energy and with an extraordinary combination of different elements to his character. A few years later the two men were to share a sleeper on a train returning from Scotland, and Donald Allchin recalled that it was 'Like having Aslan in the bunk above, he was so spiritually radiant and larger than life.'

But to begin with there was one obvious drawback to his work: his lack of the English language. The decision he had made at the lycée came back to haunt him: his avowal that he had no use for English because he would never go to England. He was not daunted by his age – by this time he was thirty-five. As he put it, if fifty million people had learnt to speak English, why not one more? So he began to spend several hours each day reading English with a dictionary, in much the same way that his grandmother had learnt Russian nearly seventy years previously. And, like her, he initially spoke in the idiom of his reading matter — in her case Turgenev, in his case the Authorised Version of the Bible.

The first lecture he was called upon to give in English was at King's College, London. He crafted the talk very carefully – in French – to ensure it would take up exactly the time allotted to him so that he would not have to answer questions, something he knew would be beyond his language skills. He then asked his mother to translate it into English, intending to read it out as best he could. However, when it came to the lecture he was nervous and spoke faster than he had anticipated, with the consequence that he finished with a couple of minutes to spare. He was aghast when the unfeeling student in the chair announced, 'As we have two minutes in hand, has anybody a short question to ask Father Anthony?' A hand shot up: 'Could you explain the difference between the Roman Catholic and Orthodox theology of the Holy Spirit?' He managed to say, 'Roman Catholic Church: Spirit is love between Father and Son,' and turned to the blackboard, where he chalked up: $1 + 1 = 2$ not 3. 'And that', he would tell listeners years later, 'was my first lecture in theology!'

He began to progress with his language study, plainly in a more systematic way than he admitted, because his grasp of English grammar and idiom was to end up nearly faultless. But that was not enough. He saw the need to get out among English people in order to pick up the pronunciation.

'I walked the streets, trying to reproduce the sounds I heard people making,' he recounted. This sometimes led to embarrassing misunderstandings. 'I remember walking along Upper Addison Gardens repeating to myself "Horse, horse, cow, cow" when a woman walked past and rounded on me indignantly, thinking I was addressing her! "Why are you calling me a cow?" she asked, threatening me with her umbrella. "No, no, you – not – cow, you – not – cow," I managed to stutter, and luckily she did not beat me.'

Unfortunately, what he did not fully appreciate was the difference between the English of the Authorised Version and modern speech, and his earliest efforts at conversation were decidedly quaint. When he thought he was beginning to make a little progress he accepted an invitation from Donald Allchin to give a talk to students at Oxford. He spoke with great intensity about the gulf between the infinite God and His fallen creatures, a chasm bridged by Christ; and he could not understand why every time he mentioned in all earnestness this 'great abyss' – words he knew from the Bible – the students disappeared under the benches in tears of laughter. At the end Donald enlightened him: his Franco-Russian accent had rendered the words 'great abbess'.

Yet another difficulty he soon discovered was that words could not always be taken at face value. On a train journey he put his head out of the window and a young man shouted at him, 'Look out!' Obediently he leaned even further forward, only to find himself grabbed by the scruff of the neck and hauled back into the train. Later in the journey he made another discovery: that to a foreigner, station names were not easily distinguishable from some of the other signs. For, when the same man asked him casually where they were, he looked up, caught sight of the most prominent notice and announced solemnly, 'This station is called Bovril.'

He soon realised, however, that the laughter generated by his mistakes in English could act as a way of breaking down barriers of reserve. What was important was that he should be able to communicate on a deeper level than mere words to reach the hearts of his listeners. He found that particularly important in his increasing contact with English people. Not only were they more inhibited temperamentally than Slavs, they were, he discovered, quite ready to discuss Christianity in abstract terms and explore God as a theoretical idea so long as it all remained at one remove from life. Father Anthony, on the other hand, was adamant that there could be no divide between an intellectual grasp of theology and a living relationship with Christ. He always insisted on the reality of the experience of faith, including his own, whatever the background of his audience. His style was markedly different from what English Christians were used to hearing from clerics, and he could not fail to make an impact.

He also made an impression on the Patriarchal Parish, so that many of its congregation began wondering how they could find the financial means to offer him a permanent place in their parish when his two-year appointment with the Fellowship ended. At first he offered to support himself by setting up a medical practice or working as a male nurse. After a life of pushing himself to the limits of physical endurance he was not afraid of hard work. This, however, proved unnecessary when their prayers were unexpectedly answered. In July 1950 Father Vladimir died suddenly and Father Anthony was asked to become the vicar of the parish. He accepted without hesitation, moving into Parish House with Xenia and Olga, although he continued his involvement with the Fellowship, making an enormous contribution to its life and speaking at its conferences almost every year.

From time to time visitors came to stay overnight. Father Anthony developed a system whereby he allowed them to sleep in the basement and provided tea and sugar but no meals – they brought in bread and cheese to make their own sandwiches. One visitor from France was a Parisian-born Russian, Michael Fortounatto, to whom Father Anthony chatted informally. It was the beginning of the young man's long association with the parish: he was eventually to marry Mariamna Theokritoff, become the choirmaster and, in 1969, priest.

While Father Anthony's English began to improve, another drawback remained. It was the very one that had foreshortened his diaconate: his apparent inability to sing. Since every Orthodox service is sung unaccompanied throughout, he felt this to be a continuing source of embarrassment. The choirmaster understood his dilemma and insisted Father Anthony attend choir practices for a year. Nevertheless, the young priest continued to have an inferiority complex about his singing and to profess a profound dislike of music. He even went so far as to say that he wished there were no music at all in Orthodox services. His one consolation was his conviction that, as he put it, 'It doesn't matter how badly people sing, God in His mercy always hears it in tune.' Yet his own intonation was very good, he knew how to project his voice and he developed a pleasing vibrato that enhanced its quality. It was his lack of confidence that occasionally let him down. A priest celebrating alone without a deacon has the task of pitching the opening blessing without any aid; there is no organ to give him a note. He followed his own idiosyncratic way of setting the pitch. Utilising his synaesthesia, the strange gift of 'seeing' sounds as colours that he shared with his late uncle the composer Scriabin, he would sing green, brown or the appropriate hue. He talked about this in a matter-of-fact way without elaborating on it further and as if it were a commonplace ability.

Music apart, Father Anthony relished his new position. He set about training his small parish to become the Christian body which was his vision of the Church, with enthusiasm, energy and the persistence to see his plans realised.

Since both Russian parishes continued to share St Philip's on alternate weekends, worshippers dodging the coaches to get to the church – it was adjacent to the old Victoria Coach Station – Father Anthony decided it was only right for him to make the acquaintance of the priest of the Church in Exile, which was still vehemently opposed to the Patriarchate of Moscow. He arrived at Father Vitaly's house late one evening, rang the bell and was confronted by the silhouette of a figure whom he presumed to be the priest's wife because in the darkness he could make out a long skirt and hair down to the waist.

'Matiushka, is Father Vitaly in?' Father Anthony began. And 'Matiushka', in the deepest bass voice he had ever heard, replied, 'I'm not Matiushka, I'm a deacon.'

After this inauspicious start Vitaly himself appeared. It was the beginning of a strange relationship. Although the two priests agreed to meet once a month to discuss practical questions, Father Vitaly was never able to relinquish his dislike of the Patriarchal Church – he eventually went to the United States and became head of the Church in Exile there. He insisted, for instance, on blessing St Philip's every time after Father Anthony had celebrated the Eucharist, even though, illogically, he did not reconsecrate the Communion vessels they both shared.

At one meeting Father Anthony asked Father Vitaly what he thought of him as a priest of the Moscow Patriarchate. He claimed Vitaly made the following reply: 'I think you are an honest man, so I will be straight with you. If I wanted to be polite I would say you are no priest. But as I want to be truthful, I will tell you what I think: you are a priest of Satan.'

When Metropolitan Anthony on various occasions repeated those words to his parishioners decades later, the pain they had caused was still apparent in his voice.

'I am aware of my unworthiness as a priest', he would say, 'but I have never been a priest of Satan.'

The small Russian community remained sharply divided. As was to be expected, the aristocrats tended to belong to the Church in Exile. Apart from Russian politics, the other big issue that divided the two parishes was their position on ecumenism. The Church in Exile was vehemently opposed to ecumenism. As a member put it, very genuinely, 'Better to be divided in truth than united in error.' This split meant that it was impossible for Xenia, despite her education at Smolny, to be on social terms with people such as Princess Galitzine.

As the Cold War deepened and the Church in Russia was forced, in exchange for continuing existence, to make official pronouncements in line with Soviet policy, some people were to show their hostility towards Bishop Anthony by dubbing him the 'Red Bishop'. He tried to play this down in practical ways, such as making sure he was never driven anywhere in a red car. Since the only political view he held was implacably Russian monarchist, he was hurt by such accusations. Nevertheless, he was adamant that the persecuted Church in Russia needed support and not condemnation, and he felt he was able to be more influential from the inside. Although he knew that the Church was enslaved by the Soviet government, he also knew that in its religious life it had kept the Apostolic faith intact. He could not leave a Church that had not fallen into heresy. 'You do not abandon your family when it is in trouble,' was how he put it. He saw its sinfulness compensated for by martyrdom.

He personally kept on good terms with the Church in Exile, never speaking detrimentally about it and, towards the end of his life, established an excellent rapport with its Bishop Mark of Berlin.

The split between the two parishes was not to be resolved. Turning his attention to his own, Father Anthony looked at the make-up of his congregation. It consisted mainly of elderly people, Russians who had come to England following the Revolution (in what came to be known as the First Emigration). Some had married into English families, or had otherwise begun to be assimilated into the surrounding society, with the result that many of their children, now young adults of Father Anthony's own generation, had abandoned Russian Orthodoxy for the Church of England or for no church at all. In traditional fashion the old Russian women would bring their grandchildren to the Liturgy but the parents did not come; and the children stopped attending as soon as they reached their mid-teens. 'A whole generation was lost,' Metropolitan Anthony described the situation. But it did not remain lost. He set about bringing it back to the Church by refashioning the parish from a dwindling ethnic outpost into a living community of people dedicated to serving the Living God. Among them were the English spouses and half-English children of Russians who had 'married out'. Up to this point, the Orthodox communities in Britain, in common with most Orthodox in the diaspora, were very ethnic in character. They tended to forget that Orthodoxy was the Universal Church open to all, seeing it as a series of closed congregations of Greeks, Russians and other Slavs. That this equation of Orthodoxy with nationalism had been condemned as the heresy of ethno-philetism cut no ice at all.

It was definitely not Father Anthony's view. If Orthodoxy was the true expression of Christianity, which he firmly held it to be, then, as his years at the Rue Pétel had taught him, it was the faith of the Gospel, and the Orthodox Church was the Body of Christ given for the salvation of the whole world and not for any exclusive cultural group. He determined that his congregation should be like those of the Early Church, echoing St Paul's vision of a congregation where there was neither Jew nor Greek – nor Russian, nor English, nor French.

He began slowly to receive into Orthodoxy those English spouses of his Russian parishioners who, after instruction, felt a genuine desire to accept the Orthodox faith. The English version of the Service Book (translated by Florence Hapgood before the Revolution) contained a Service for the Reception of Converts for those already baptised in another church. After making a formal statement repudiating their former heresies and accepting the tenets of the Orthodox Faith, the candidates were then received into the Church by chrismation, the second Orthodox sacrament of initiation. Those requiring baptism would undergo the traditional Orthodox triple immersion; or in the case of Father Anthony's parish the nearest an adult could get to immersion in a tin baby bath.

The lapsed younger generation of Russians began to hear about the vigorous new priest, came to see what was going on and stayed to become members of the parish. For their benefit – for some of them Russian was no longer their mother tongue – and for the sake of their English spouses and families, Father Anthony began to give talks in English. Gradually he transformed the congregation from being a potentially dying community into a growing one, as an increasing number of people were awakened to faith by the new priest's preaching, teaching and example.

In his new role as a full-time parish priest, Father Anthony experimented with ways of organising his time. For a while he tried celebrating the Liturgy daily, with a consequent congregation of just two stalwart women on most days. This prevented him from doing any visiting and he discontinued the practice after a year. It had also been a strain for another reason. By inclination he was an infrequent communicant; as a layman his practice had been to receive Communion perhaps only four or five times a year, which was customary Russian behaviour. It was also in his case personal choice because he felt able to commune with Christ in his heart to such a degree that he did not often feel the need for physical Communion. That was one reason why, as a bishop with priests serving under him, he would leave them to celebrate weekday services.

One of his early initiatives was the setting up of a 'Sunday' school, actually held on Saturday afternoons. About twenty children began to make the weekly trek from various corners of London to the basement of the house in Upper Addison Gardens where Father Anthony gathered a dedicated group of helpers. Mother Alexia, the widowed mother of a young member of the congregation, Sergei Hackel, whom Father Anthony was later to ordain, taught Russian history and language. Tatisha Behr, neé Sakharova, daughter-in-law of the late Father Nicholas Behr and none other than the lively young woman Father Anthony had taught in Paris, ended the afternoons with singing, which was always popular. She and Anna Garrett provided sandwiches. They also provided some of the pupils, as their children made up the core attenders.

Father Anthony taught religious instruction and was extremely popular with the children. He peppered his lessons with wonderful stories and was always full of energy and fun; as well as teaching religion he also enjoyed playing games. This was, however, all within a framework of old-fashioned discipline. When a young boy, Peter Scorer, who was to grow up to become a much-respected deacon, accidentally broke the glass of a large picture, Father Anthony had no hesitation in giving him a good spanking.

One of his teaching methods was to pretend to be a little African girl and invite the children to tell her about God. In this way he drew out their own beliefs instead of imposing dogma on them. While he was always there to inspire, he was also ready to let the older children discuss, and voice their opinions.

The mothers sat in on the lessons, without taking part. One day there was an unwelcome interruption. A beggar rang the doorbell and Father Anthony, annoyed at having his class disturbed, got up from his chair with such force that he sent it flying, as he stormed upstairs to confront the man.

There was another story about beggars that his pupils later recounted. He had once offered one half a crown, a generous sum at the time. The man looked at the coin and said, 'Is that all?' Astonished at the ungrateful response, Father Anthony put out his hand and took the money back.

The Saturday school children were to become lifelong friends. In the summer of 1956 Tatisha Behr took a group of them to a Russian camp in France. Father Anthony was enthusiastic about this development, and over the next few years the trips continued.

The more Father Anthony's English improved the more he found himself in demand as a preacher and speaker at a variety of churches and institutions. One event in particular was to have a lasting effect on his ministry. He was invited to take part in a discussion at Kensington Town Hall between two believers and two unbelievers – as he put it later, 'I was one of the believers, believe it or not!' Things were proceeding on a rather high philosophical level when suddenly they were interrupted from the back of the hall. A workman in overalls shouted out: 'Stop it, all of you! I can't understand a word of what you are saying! It means nothing.' Then he pointed to Father Anthony in his cassock and went on, 'What I want to say is this. Let this man who is dressed like no one else in the hall tell us why he is a believer.' It was a terrible moment of decision. Until then he had kept his conversion experience completely to himself:

> I thought: I can keep my secret garden whole and intact, but then I will answer before God for what happens to this man. He may remain an unbeliever, he may later find God; but that is not my responsibility. My responsibility is to respond to the question. Shall I say, 'I am sorry, it's too holy a thing for me to speak in public?' Or shall I do something else? And I prayed to God: 'Well, if you want my soul to be completely laid waste in order for this man to receive a message, then let my soul be laid waste.' And so I told the man the story of my conversion.
>
> 'When I had finished he simply said, 'Thank you.' I have no idea

what happened to him. But at that moment I felt I could not keep my walled garden under lock and key. I had to say what had happened; otherwise it would have been a betrayal.

His *pairidaeza* had been breached. He was to spend the rest of his life recounting his conversion experience, not only to individuals but also to thousands through his talks, his writing and his broadcasts. Despite that, it remained for him an extremely personal and costly exercise which he likened to allowing people to touch or embrace him. 'You cannot allow a person to plunge into you spiritually, just as you cannot let a person handle you unless you are in a relationship of friendship or affection,' was his analogy. When he did speak about his encounter with Christ it was invariably with a lump in his throat, whoever his listeners were.

Still active in the Fellowship, he had within a few years become known to an increasing number of English Christians. There was a time, he said, when he would be speaking somewhere or other five times a week. In particular, individual Anglicans and the Anglican Church took him up in a big way. Over the years he reckoned he had given several thousand lectures and talks. He did not speak about Orthodoxy. His aim was to preach the Gospel, from an Orthodox point of view. He also spoke of the Russian Church and of its true situation, something that could not be done in the Soviet Union: its persecution, the courage of believers and the harsh conditions they faced. He showed people what it meant to follow Christ, to death if necessary, projecting a vision of Christianity that was courageous, inspiring and uncompromising.

This convincing and stimulating portrayal of what it meant to be a Christian encouraged a number of English people to investigate Orthodoxy further and soon some of them began to seek instruction. At first the Fellowship was not happy. Father Anthony had become such a popular figure that there were people who only attended the annual conference on the days he was going to be present. More than anyone he was becoming the public face of Orthodoxy to the non-Orthodox in Britain, and was beginning to build up a circle of admirers. When he received into Orthodoxy a prominent English member of the Fellowship, Barbara Morshead, its Council felt it necessary to hold a meeting to decide whether or not she could remain a member. Father Anthony, ever mindful of the coercive tactics of the Roman Catholics in France, was at pains not to be seen to be proselytising. He 'neither chased after anybody nor tried to entice anybody', as he put it, and always made the conversion process a deliberately long and sometimes difficult one. This continued throughout his ministry, and it was not unknown for catechumens to wait four years before they were received into the Church. The process was never very methodical. Some might be given a rule of prayer, books to read and a series of private appointments in which he or she could discuss their questions. It never resembled, say, Anglican adult confirmation classes. Furthermore, it was always on a one-to-one basis, never in a group. People were often left for long periods after the appointments dried up, simply to come to the Liturgy and absorb the prayer of the Church. Then suddenly Father Anthony might come up to them one day when they had almost given up hope of ever being received, and say, 'All right, next Sunday.' The only part of the process that did seem to have some system to it was Father Anthony's insistence on drawing it out so that anyone who was insufficiently motivated would not persist.

Barbara Morshead was to become a staunch member of the congregation and a great friend of Xenia. She took on the role of housekeeper at Parish House and for many years was also Father Anthony's driver. This duty was later taken over by Irina Kirillova and, in Metropolitan Anthony's old age, by Father John Lee.

Over the years a steady stream of converts was to become a feature of Father Anthony's parish, but at first it seemed an odd situation. He was convinced that his preaching was a message for all and that England needed Orthodoxy. His parishioners had to come to terms with this unexpected turn of events. Under Father Anthony's inspiration and guidance, the Russian Patriarchal Parish took a conscious decision to open its doors to non-Russians, with all the implications of potential loss of culture which that entailed. It was a heroic and generous decision.

The first converts – and this was to remain largely true throughout his ministry – were middle-class, young-to-middle-aged people. Apart from some who wished to convert from active Anglicanism or other churchmanship, many had no real church allegiance. Others were theologically inclined but could not accept the doctrines or arguments of the other churches.

'They came with questions,' Father Anthony said, 'and we told them that it was our conviction that the Orthodox faith was the basic faith of the gospels in its purity and fullness, which had been handed down to us. But it was a faith handed down in earthen vessels. We could speak of it but we could not incarnate it.' He remained acutely conscious that however persuasively he spoke, he found it just as difficult as anyone else to live up to his faith.

A problem he encountered with potential converts was their tendency to keep things on a cerebral level. They often read and studied a great deal. However, what Father Anthony was interested in was moving the centre of their faith 'from their brains to their hearts', and from their emotions to their lives. He was also wary of people who came to him for negative reasons: because they disbelieved this or that doctrine of their own church, or found its pronouncements or the theological opinions of the day uncongenial. He always insisted that potential converts must have the feeling not of coming to an exotic place but of coming home, and that they should come with gratitude to the church that had originally nurtured them. It was no surprise, therefore, that over the years quite a few would-be converts were put off – generally with an air of relief on both sides.

One of the other tasks Father Anthony set himself was to organise the parish on a proper administrative footing. Although he himself never claimed to be an administrator, he realised the importance of having parish statutes and appointing a parish council to organise the running of the church. He used as a basis for these reforms the 1917–18 statutes of the Russian Church, which had been drawn up after the fall of the Imperial Government, when the Church had briefly enjoyed the freedom of dis-establishment, but before the Bolsheviks began the persecution which was to prevent those statutes being implemented. The parish statutes made provision for the election of a parish council: in Russian 'prikhodski soviet', since the word 'soviet', although hijacked by the Bolsheviks, merely means a council. Some of his congregation did not entirely understand this. Two women he later described as 'stupid' – he found suffering fools difficult – came to him and said they wanted to join the Church in Exile because his parish was Soviet. His instinctive personal reaction, he later admitted, was to think 'Good!' Out loud he said that of course their allegation was not true, but why did they think as they did?

'Well,' they answered, 'you are organising elections to a 'prikhodski soviet' so there, you must be Soviet.'

Church discipline was another area of parish life that he undertook to change. He was determined to tackle the Orthodox custom of arriving after the beginning of the service. Throughout his ministry he preached that no one should receive Communion unless they had been present in church to hear the opening blessing of the service.

A second point of discipline was the tendency for the congregation to be less attentive than Father Anthony wished, as people walked about lighting candles and greeting their friends. This was something he was adamant he would stamp out in his parish, to the extent that one evening, at the point where the service of Vespers slips quietly into Matins with the intoning of six psalms by a lone reader, he heard a couple of women chatting noisily at the back of the church. He strode out of the sanctuary, clapped his hands and said, 'Mrs N and Mrs N: would you please be quiet!' To which one of the women retorted in indignation, 'Father Anthony, you don't know anything! It's allowed to talk during the Six Psalms!' He would subsequently tell this story against himself, although he was really in no doubt about being in the right. His congregation was eventually to become known throughout Europe for its air of prayerful silence.

This was not discipline for its own sake. He was always keen to point out that discipline was not at all the same as drill; it had its root in the word 'disciple' and was nothing less than the training that St Paul described as being an athlete for God, intent on attaining the Kingdom. Silence in particular was something dear to him – that deep, prayerful silence in which one could commune with God: the stillness of the Desert Fathers and the hesychasts. Gradually his parishioners came to understand exactly what lay behind his youthful enthusiasms. Here was a vibrant priest who was not merely ministering to their needs as exiles but was guiding them through their cultural vulnerability to the vulnerability of the God who had become a helpless babe in arms. He would never try to rebuild the externals of Orthodoxy that had existed in pre-Revolutionary Russia: the Christ of the great cathedrals and the beautifully 'architected' Liturgies, as he put it; but the humble Christ who had been rejected like them. Year by year, in the weeks preceding Lent, he would remark at the singing of the psalm 'By the waters of Babylon' how those words hit home to the Russian community because they too were exiles; but he would always add that the psalm was also speaking of life as exile from Paradise, to which they were given the opportunity of returning through the ascetic journey that is Orthodox Lent. Walking ahead of them, he knew, would be the Good Shepherd, of whom he, as an unworthy priest, was a struggling image.

When a Russian priest gives the absolution at the close of the sacrament of confession he says, 'And I, the unworthy priest N'. Father Anthony always spoke these words with the emphasis heavily on the word 'unworthy'. However confident he was in his vocation, he never failed to be aware that he fell far short of what his Lord required of him. From the start, despite his insistence on changing the outward ways of his congregation, which was sometimes less than fully appreciated, his parishioners could see that this young man spoke out of an inner humility. Their hope was to keep it that way. Might he not be spoiled by the unfettered authority that was his? So they – particularly the elderly ladies – were not afraid of keeping him in his place. One day he and a babushka came to a door, and she stepped forward to hold it open for him. As he sailed past her she deflated his pride by saying, 'Don't think I'm holding this door open for you because I respect you as a person. It's the office of priest I'm honouring, not you!' Thereafter he made a point of opening doors for people, and if they protested he would say, 'Children first!' It was a small thing, and an anecdote lightly told, but it summed up much of his philosophy on the place of the Christian priesthood.

In January 1953 he was appointed Igumen (and in 1956 he would be made Archimandrite). It was obvious that he had come to the Moscow Patriarchate's attention as a man with a future, who was doing great things in London. But it was not only he who was going places. The whole parish was on the move, physically, because the Church of England, unwilling to repair St Philip's, had sanctioned its demolition to make way for the construction of a new Victoria Coach Station.

For nearly three years the St Sergius chapel in Upper Addison Gardens was the only place of worship for the parish. The basement continued to be used for the school and parish meetings. Upstairs, Father Anthony saw people for private appointments in his study, and the bedrooms were on the top floor. But he, his mother and grandmother were not the only residents of the house. A serious mouse problem began to develop. Father Anthony was at a loss how to deal with it. 'If I were to lay traps it would be cruel to the mice,' he reasoned. 'And if I baited pieces of cheese with poison it would be cruel to my grandmother, because she is liable to pick up the cheese and eat it.' Olga had lost an eye and her residual sight was poor. A devout parishioner had an idea. The *Book of Needs*, a compendium of prayers for every situation, contained a prayer by St Basil for the expulsion of various pests and animals, beginning with bears and wolves, finishing with insects and including all manner of creatures in between. If Father Anthony used this prayer, surely the mice would take heed and leave the house.

'I didn't believe that for one moment,' he said, 'but the woman was insistent that if St Basil had coined the prayer, then I had no right to dismiss it.' He agreed to read it, with a proviso. He turned to St Basil, telling him frankly that he did not believe the prayer would work but that, since the saint obviously did, he would leave the praying to him. Then he put on his stole, took his stand with the prayer book and censer in front of one of the mouse holes, and waited. Eventually a mouse popped his head out.

'Stop,' Father Anthony said, 'I've got something to say to you.' The mouse sat up on his haunches and looked at him as he began to read the prayer. When he had finished he said, 'Now hurry off and tell all the others, then go away and never come back!' And the mouse scuttled back into the hole. From that day onwards there were no mice at Parish House. Father Anthony would willingly repeat this story as an example of how the saints truly intercede for the world, 'Because it was not my prayer or my faith that God heard, but St Basil's.'

Grandmother was now in her nineties and becoming increasingly senile. She was getting muddled, and sometimes wandered off or fell down the stairs. Like many old people she was tempted to feel her life was becoming a burden on her family. One of the few things she could still usefully do was the washing up – until one evening Father Anthony heard a tremendous crash, rushed into the kitchen and found Olga surrounded by broken china. She had inadvertently pushed the crockery off the draining board with her elbow and sent it crashing to the floor.

'I'm no good for anything any more,' she wailed. 'There's not one reason for me to go on living.' Father Anthony was always adamant that such a statement from an old person should be countered. No one should ever be left to think their life was worthless. He responded to Olga accordingly.

'I can give you two reasons,' he said with a smile. His grandmother perked up. Two?

'First of all, heaven is full of old ladies like you. Do you really think God wants to put up with another one just yet?'

'Oh, you're not being serious,' Olga replied.

'Well, here's the second reason. You have a function in life that is unique and irreplaceable. No one else can be my grandmother.' With these words he restored Olga's self-worth. He did indeed have a very special place in his heart for his beloved grandmother; but it was also the expression of a universal truth: that each person was precious in the sight of God and could never become a dispensable statistic, or be seen in terms of nuisance value, however old or disabled they became.

He would repeat this anecdote whenever he was asked to speak about ageing and death. When he was himself an old man struggling to find the energy to continue his work he would sometimes apologise for being more of a burden than a help, and people were quick to counter that, in line with his own advice.

Like any other family, the Blooms took holidays. Father Anthony needed a break from his parish; both he and Xenia, whose health was causing concern, needed a rest from Olga. For several years she stayed with Tatisha Behr and her husband Aliosha while Father Anthony took his mother off for a few weeks of peace. As Olga became increasingly blind and senile this created a certain amount of mayhem in the Behr household. A young Behr cousin, Mariane Greenan, often came with her young children to help look after Olga. Tatisha had embarked on taking in unmarried mothers and their babies, and one day Olga mistook Mariane for one of Tatisha's charges, causing much amusement in the household.

As Olga's memory became increasingly confused she began to imagine she was not in South London at all but back in her dacha outside Moscow. Father Anthony would come down to visit from time to time, and there would be a lot of laughter. Mariane's first contact with him had been as a girl of eight when he had visited her family's house in Nancy – she was the daughter of Elisabeth Behr-Sigel – and she had sensed even then that he was a remarkable man.

In 1956 the Anglicans came up with another building for the Russian parishes: All Saints Church, Ennismore Gardens in Knightsbridge. Designed by Vulliamy in the Italianate style it had been a daughter church of St Margaret's, Westminster. All Saints was offered to both Russian parishes on condition they continued to share premises. The Church in Exile refused a new sharing arrangement. The Cold War was at its height and they wished to sever all links with the Patriarchal Parish. Father Anthony's parish agreed to it. The church was then offered to them, rent-free, on condition that the parish maintained the building. But the Patriarchal Parish on its own was still small, and had its doubts. Father Anthony's enthusiasm overcame them and it signed a twenty-one year lease on the church on 13 September 1956.

This was the tenth building in the history of the London parish, and it was to be the spiritual, and later the physical, home of Father Anthony for the rest of his life. The exterior remained unchanged – as a listed building there was no choice – but the inside was to be gutted and rearranged to become a recognisably Orthodox church of the Russian tradition.

The consecration of the new church was scheduled for Sunday 16 December 1956. The previous evening a solemn Vigil service was concele-brated by Archbishop Nicholas from Paris (the Patriarchate of Moscow's Exarch for Western Europe), Archimandrite Anthony, and two hieromonks, Father Basil (Krivoscheine) from the small community in

Oxford and Father Kyril (Taylor), an English convert who was to serve in the London parish for a number of years. The consecration the following morning took place during the course of an episcopal Liturgy. Archbishop Nicholas, surrounded by the same clergy as had concelebrated with him the previous evening, consecrated the Holy Table (the altar) by anointing it with holy chrism, after which he went round the church anointing the rest of the building. Then came the moment when the Archbishop, bearing the relics of various saints, among them the two great Russian spiritual giants Sergius of Radonezh and Seraphim of Sarov, headed a procession of the clergy carrying the Book of the Gospels and the Cross, followed by parishioners with icons and banners, round the church to the singing of the choir. When they reached the sanctuary the Archbishop and his clergy carried the reliquary through the Royal Doors and placed it under the Holy Table. The consecration was concluded by the singing of 'Mnogaya Leta' – 'Many Years' – to the Queen, the Royal Family and all her people; the hierarchy of the Church; the rector Archimandrite Anthony, and all the parishioners.

The first Liturgy in the new church could now begin, and by its end the congregation had been standing for a full five hours. It must have been a trial for the distinguished non-Orthodox guests, who included the Archbishop of Canterbury's representative Canon Waddams, the Anglican Bishop of Kensington and Pastor Reverdin of the Swiss Reformed Church in London. Bishop James Virvos represented Archbishop Athenagoras of the Greek Orthodox community in London and the Armenian bishop in London was also present.

Before Archbishop Nicholas left for France he paid a visit to the Archbishop of Canterbury, Geoffrey Fisher. Father Anthony accompanied him to Lambeth. Ostensibly the visit was to thank the Anglican Primate for putting All Saints at the disposal of the Patriarchal Parish, although the two bishops also took the opportunity to discuss Anglican–Orthodox relations.

The new church and its rector were now very firmly on the map. The parish became known officially as The Dormition and All Saints, with its patronal feast celebrated for the first time in the summer of 1957 on the Orthodox day of All Saints (the Sunday after Pentecost). A time of optimism and hope had begun.

The Patriarchate recognised this situation and took the decision to elect Father Anthony an auxiliary bishop under Archbishop Nicholas – a decision which, Father Anthony felt, was made in a similarly unholy manner to his ordination to the priesthood had been. His immediate reaction, as he put it many years later, was to question the decision. He explained his reservations to the General Secretary of the Patriarchate's Department of Foreign Relations and asked, 'Why on earth do you want to make me of all people a bishop?' The man responded in typically Soviet manner, 'Because you have gained a reputation for being a good organiser.' That was not what worried Father Anthony. 'But have you asked yourself questions about my spiritual life?'

'Spiritual life?' the man replied in amazement. 'It never occurred to us that you had one!'

Father Anthony now had to convey the news to his mother and grand-mother. The latter was spending her usual summer break with the Behr family when her grandson arrived to tell her. She was not pleased. To her it meant only one thing: he was sure to have even less time to spend with her. In fact, Olga was not to see him bishop at all. At the great age of ninety-four she was frail and coming to the end of her life. A bout of flu developed into pneumonia. She died on 14 October 1957 after suffering a fatal stroke, on the Russian feast of the Protecting Veil of the Mother of God, and was buried in Brompton Cemetery.

So it was not without some sadness that on 29 November Father Anthony's election as a bishop was declared at the Saturday evening Vigil service. In accordance with Orthodox custom he made a discourse in which he expressed his acceptance of the call to serve his Lord and Master in a more responsible way, together with his genuine feelings of unworthiness.

The following morning at the Divine Liturgy he was consecrated Bishop of Sergievo, with Father Lev Gillet, at Father Anthony's request, leading him to the altar for the consecration. The chief consecrator was Metropolitan (formerly Archbishop) Nicholas. The second consecrator was Bishop James of the Greek Church, so it was a pan-Orthodox occasion, as grand an event as the small parish could muster.

Among the congregation that day was a young Englishman, Timothy Ware, who was beginning his own pilgrimage towards Orthodoxy. He was to be received into the Orthodox Church in the Greek jurisdiction the fol-lowing year, eventually becoming Bishop Kallistos of Diokleia and the author of the classic English work on Orthodoxy, *The Orthodox Church*. Forty years later Bishop Kallistos recalled the consecration with affection at a celebration to mark its anniversary.

The new Bishop Anthony was, in imitation of Christ, shepherd of his flock – a flock admittedly still small but growing. Now into his forties, he looked ahead with vision. If Orthodoxy was, as he was convinced, the true expression of the Gospel, it was not enough for him to minister only to his own congregation. The people of Britain needed the truth as much as his congregation did. Without losing any of his feelings for his fellow Russians or his love of the Russian language, he determined to encourage the Orthodox seed sown on English soil to take root and flourish.

CHAPTER EIGHT

⤜ ⤛

BISHOP OF SERGIEVO

(1957–1966)

Bishop Anthony was soon to face two other deaths. On 7 February 1958 Vladimir Lossky, whom he respected both as a man and a theologian, died, and he was called to Paris to take his funeral.

Back at home his mother was also near death. Three years previously Xenia had begun to suffer from serious ill health. She and her son went to see her doctor. Metropolitan Anthony later recalled how she had sat on a chair, her handbag on her lap and her hands folded neatly on top of it, listening meekly as the doctor pronounced a glib diagnosis of indigestion and sent her away with a prescription for some innocuous remedy.

'And she had a cancer!' Metropolitan Anthony would exclaim, the anguish still in his voice when recalling the doctor's incompetence after more than forty years. Eventually the right diagnosis was made and Xenia underwent surgery for stomach cancer. In later years Metropolitan Anthony described, in a series of talks on death (of which an edited version was subsequently included in the anthology *Living Orthodoxy in the Modern World*), how he told Xenia of the outcome of the operation after her return home. The doctor had rung and explained that the operation had been unsuccessful, finishing with the words, 'But of course you won't tell your mother.' He replied that, on the contrary, he would. Against the prevailing practice of the 1950s he held the view that a dying person should not be walled in by lies that cut them off from expressing their own fears and destroyed their closeness with their family. He described how he went into her room to tell her the news, to which she replied, 'And so I shall die.'

'Yes,' he replied. Then they both remained in deep silence, no words necessary to express their inner communion with one another.

'It was not a terror that had come into our lives,' he said in retrospect. 'But it was the ultimate.' He continued to nurse his mother at home, with the aid of his housekeeper, Barbara Morshead. There were occasions when he felt the approach of Xenia's death as an acute sense of loss, and he would talk to her of his feelings. At other times she was the one who spoke to him about her own fears and pain. What was important was the openness between them. At no moment was he forced into creating a barrier of euphemisms and false hopes.

By early 1958 Xenia's pain had grown to be considerable, but even at the end she still clung on to life. She wanted to see the coming spring. 'She loved life,' Metropolitan Anthony put it when he himself was old. Xenia died on Great (Good) Friday, 11 April 1958. Although her death was imminent Bishop Anthony, faced with the choice of sitting with his dying mother as he had sat with so many patients as a young doctor, or carrying out his liturgical duties, left her to take the service. When he returned she was dead.

On the morning of Xenia's funeral, which could not take place for nearly a week because of Easter, he went into the chapel in Parish House in order to pray alone for the last time before his mother's open coffin. As he came up to her he was distressed to find that in the unseasonably warm weather there were marks of decay on her hands and face. His reaction was instinctive. 'I turned away – not to turn away from my mother, but from these black marks, which were spreading.'

Metropolitan Anthony commented many years later that at the time his parishioners had accused him of being insensitive for talking about this. There was also a feeling among some of them that his insensitivity had extended to choosing to leave the dying Xenia in order to take the Good Friday service. They would have been more than willing to accept with understanding and sympathy a note of explanation on the church door, asking the congregation to pray in his absence – especially since there were many other occasions when, for far less compelling reasons, he posted notes on the door refusing to keep appointments.

There is a particular poignancy about an Orthodox funeral held during Eastertide. It resounds with the words 'Christ is risen'. For a man who claimed boldly that he knew the resurrection as a fact because he had met the risen Christ, this was a challenge. While he did not doubt the joy of his faith, he certainly admitted the paradox that bereavement brought grief to those left behind.

Xenia was buried with her mother in Brompton Cemetery. Bishop Anthony was now bereft of family and alone, a situation he claimed to have sought from his youth. He continued to live at Parish House, sometimes sharing it with clergy for long or short periods. One was a convert, Father Kyril Taylor, who served in London and Oxford for a number of years and became an important part of the parish. Another was Father Alexander Belikoff, a Serb whose wife and family were stuck in post-war Yugoslavia. This man's stay proved to be a time of trial for his host.

'I thought I could live with anyone,' Metropolitan Anthony said years later, 'but that man drove me mad.' For one thing, Father Alexander was elderly, and in his final years became confused; and without his family around him he lived a very austere life more in keeping with a monastic. He had certain annoying habits. 'During the forty days of Easter he insisted on giving me the Paschal greeting, "Christ is risen!" every time he came into the room or passed me in the hall,' Bishop Anthony would tell people. 'In the end I could stand it no more, and the next time he said, "Christ is risen!" I glared at him and replied, "I know!"

'Then he looked at me with great sadness and said, "Oh, Father Anthony, I give you the best news in the world and that's all you can answer!"'

There was one advantage to be gained by this man's stay. 'He taught me something about cooking,' Metropolitan Anthony recalled. 'He would put all the leftover food in one saucepan and cook it – fish, meat, vegetables all together. At first I thought: I'm not eating that! But I tried it and you know, it wasn't so bad.' It fitted in with his own policy of never throwing food away. After so much hunger in his youth and his awareness of the continuing hunger in other parts of the world he was always reluctant to waste anything.

His parishioners often brought him food. During the post-war era this was on a necessarily modest scale. In later years the gifts were often more varied and generous, so that it was often impossible for him to eat everything people gave him. He would sometimes leave out surplus food on Monday mornings for the church cleaners to take away, or donate a bagful to a trusted parishioner. Unfortunately he was inclined to hoard it for too long before parting with it. Inspection would reveal a strange assortment of foodstuffs – anything from the nuts and dried fruit suitable for Lent to cold meats, smoked salmon and even caviar, often weeks or months past their sell-by date.

During this time Bishop Anthony began to suffer from back trouble, which was to plague him intermittently for the rest of his life. He was hospitalised, but the doctors could do little for him and sent him home with two sticks, saying he would never walk without them again. He refused to accept the prognosis. 'I've got work to do!' was his reaction, and he found himself an osteopath who was able to treat him successfully.

His work was beginning to include broadcasting. Discovered by the BBC he was to become a regular voice on the radio, which broadened his ministry considerably, both in Britain and on the World Service in the Soviet Union. Whether he was speaking for radio, giving talks to an audience or giving sermons in church, all his work could be broadly described as preaching. This was where he excelled. His sermons in particular were invariably short: he said that a sermon should last no more than ten minutes. They were punchy, going straight to the meat of the particular gospel passage (he usually preached on the gospel reading for the day) and leaving his listeners inspired to translate what they had heard into action. They were centred on Christ, and on his loving relationship with humanity. They were exhortations to become new creatures.

In 1959 a monastery was founded at Tolleshunt Knights, a village near the Essex coast. The founder was a remarkable man, Archimandrite Sophrony, who brought over his fledgling community from Paris. Father Sophrony, born in 1896 into a Muscovite merchant family, had trained as a secular artist and had exhibited in Paris during the 1920s. He set out for Mount Athos in 1925 to become a monk at the Russian monastery of St Panteleimon under the spiritual direction of Father (now St) Silouan. After the Second World War he returned to Paris for major surgery. He had been ordained priest on Mount Athos but his vocation was hampered by ill-health until he found himself convalescing in a Russian old people's home where he assisted the chaplain. There he began to attract a group of spiritual children, both men and women, and these became the core of a community. Since they could afford few service books they used the Jesus Prayer, recited aloud, during their services, and this became a unique feature of their worship. When they outgrew the old people's home they transferred to England, to a house and land donated to them on the edge of Tolleshunt Knights, where Father Sophrony founded a double monastery of monks and nuns. It was to become a thriving centre of Orthodox spirituality and of iconography, to which Father Sophrony had turned his artistic talent. The monastery, under the Moscow Patriarchate, naturally looked to Bishop Anthony, a generation younger than its abbot, as its local authority. The two men were both individualists and the relationship was not always easy, despite their mutual respect for one another.

There was also a Russian parish in Oxford, which had had its beginnings after the war with the arrival of Father Nicholas Gibbes, the former tutor to the Tsarevich, and Nicolas Zernov, who became a lecturer at the university. They were joined in the late 1950s by Father Basil Krivoschein. In 1959 a property was bought in Canterbury Road, North Oxford, where eventually a new Orthodox church was to be built, shared by the Russian and Greek parishes.

In London the parish was increasing, with converts arriving in a steady stream. Bishop Anthony ordained Sergei Hackel deacon after instructing him to spend a year singing with the choir in the same way that he had done. Other than that the young man had no theological training, and this was to become the usual practice among Bishop Anthony's clergy. He was to be ordained priest in 1964 and spend most of his ministry in charge of a small parish in Lewes, Sussex.

The children had continued to attend various Russian camps in France, run either by the churches there belonging to the Moscow Patriarchate or by ACER, the Russian Student Christian Movement. The group was now ready for a camp of its own, and in 1959 Tatisha Behr began to organise camps in Towyn, North Wales, for about fifty children of all ages. Bishop Anthony became a regular visitor, joining in the activities and lessons, and was to go on doing so until the late 1980s. At the first Welsh camp a memorable incident occurred. During Bishop Anthony's visit, Father Sophrony sent a telegram inviting him to the monastery's patronal feast of St John the Baptist, which was imminent. Presumably the bishop made no reply, because a second and then, at the last minute, a third telegram arrived in which Father Sophrony made the dramatic threat: if you don't come tomorrow I'll take the monastery out of the Moscow Patriarchate.

'We'll go,' Bishop Anthony conceded. So a small group set out in the ancient camp van to drive for twelve hours across Wales and England to the Essex coast. Besides getting lost and running out of petrol in Birmingham in the middle of the night, the young people found being at close quarters with their bishop for so long an interesting experience. 'For the first time,' remembered Deacon Peter Scorer after Metropolitan Anthony's death, 'I understood his utter devotion to and deep love for Russia, and his passionate love and dedication to the Patriarchate.'

Archimandrite Sophrony did subsequently take his monastery out of the Moscow Patriarchate to become a stavropegic monastery under the Ecumenical Patriarchate, as the two strong-minded men decided to go their own ways.

Tatisha and Aliosha Behr purchased a cottage near Trawsfynnyd where the camps were held for the next four years. Facilities were extremely basic but this did not deter the campers, for whom the experience became a way of life. A ciné film taken at the time showed them enjoying a number of activities, including a volleyball match in which a dark-haired, newly bearded Bishop Anthony was a talented participant. However, by 1964 the first generation of youngsters were adults, there was a shortage of children of the right age to follow them and the camps came to a natural end, although the campers remained lifelong friends and church members. The cottage remained in the Behr family and Bishop Anthony spent occasional breaks there over the years.

With Bishop Anthony's continuing involvement with the Fellowship and his broader contacts he was rapidly becoming an important Christian figure far beyond the bounds of his own church. As an inspired speaker and now fluent in English – something that was unusual for an Orthodox hierarch in Britain at the time – he had attracted the attention of the BBC and was to make frequent broadcasts for many years. An early series of television appearances was on the *Epilogue* programmes, where he became a well-known face. He began to make a serious impact on the religious life of the country. In short, he became famous, and had to endure a constant clamouring for his attention on all sides.

Once a year he escaped on holiday. He would often – until precluded by illness in his mid-sixties – go to Austria. 'I would just take a rucksack and sleep rough,' he told people. A Roman Catholic priest asked whether he took his vestments in order to celebrate a daily Liturgy, which he found an amusing, if not horrifying, idea.

The year 1961 saw Bishop Anthony undertake two visits abroad which were definitely not holidays. One was to the World Council of Churches meeting in New Delhi. This was the first gathering of the WCC to which the Russian Orthodox Church, newly become a member, sent a delegation; Bishop Anthony acted as interpreter. In the Soviet Union the persecutions of the Khrushchev era were under way but the delegation was allowed to participate, no doubt for political reasons on the State's part. Bishop Anthony found the experience remarkable for more than one reason. Apart from the official business of the assembly he was impressed by India itself. This time he came not as an accepting child familiar with life in an Eastern country but as a Westerner, used to a European standard of living. His eyes were open to the poverty, and it horrified him. Despite his own experience of harsh living conditions in pre-war Paris, here in the shanty towns and the appalling unsanitary environment he found another level of human misery. It contrasted sharply with his frugal but relatively comfortable life in London. One small example, by no means the worst, passed into his store of anecdotes that, he hoped, would convey to his English listeners something of the plight of the average Indian: He and a colleague got to know one of the drivers who ferried them around. The young man lived in a makeshift shelter leaning against the side of a building. They learnt that he had a fiancée.

'Why don't you get married?' the colleague asked him. The driver replied that he had been saving up for the past year for the – for him – huge sum of £5.

'What's £5?' Bishop Anthony would tell his parishioners later. 'So my friend put his hand in his pocket and gave him the money.'

Not long after Bishop Anthony's return he was invited to speak on poverty at an ecumenical meeting in London. He put his heart into every word, knowing that this was not merely an interesting subject for discussion but a matter of life or death for millions in the Third World. At the end of the evening, when he was standing at the west door of the host church shaking hands with his audience as they left, a woman came up to him and said, 'Oh Bishop Anthony, thank you for the entertaining evening!' The idea that his words could be taken as entertainment filled him with such anger that he replied fiercely, 'Well! I hope you have given more than a shilling for your entertainment!'

When recounting this story afterwards he would mimic the woman's voice in a falsetto, and make his reply grabbing his listener by the shoulders in mock rage. Thereafter he made a point of encouraging his flock to give as generously as they could to charities targeting poverty.

He was also struck by the religion he found in India. He knew a little about Hinduism from his reading – witness his exchange with Lossky on the Upanishads – but now he had the opportunity to see it at first hand and he made a point of visiting a number of temples. One of them had a multi-faith dedication, and he went round watching all the different groups of worshippers. He was soon struck by the realisation that whatever god the people thought they were praying to, in reality it could only be the one true God who heard their prayers. This was another confirmation for him of the universality of faith, and the possibility for all people to know God, at least in an incipient way. This did not mean he reckoned Christianity to be one truth among many. The one Truth was the Lord Jesus Christ. He was aware, however, that God graciously loved and heard all his children.

The other foreign visit, in October 1961, was also to somewhere he had lived as a young child: this time Russia, now the Soviet Union, a very different place from the house near the Arbat that he had left towards the end of the imperial era. The Patriarchate had invited him to come and experience Church life, which he knew would necessarily be something of a staged occasion. As he flew in, a break in the clouds afforded him a sight that he was never to forget: the meadows, the wooden houses round the village church. It was Holy Mother Russia for him. Superficially there seemed to have been little change since pre-revolutionary times: in the cities clanking trams, cobbled streets, babushki swathed against the chill autumnal air. The same was true as he journeyed through the country-side. He drank in the landscape of vast skies. He was dazzled by the brilliant colours of the leaves drifting from the trees – precious images seen as he travelled between Moscow and the great monastery of St Sergius of Radonezh at Zagorsk. By the time he left for home two weeks later the first snows of winter had fallen, turning white the streets of Moscow, the steppes and the interminable forests. Everywhere he went he was stirred by the yearnings common to returning exiles. For the first time since infancy he was in his homeland, surrounded by his people speaking his language. Here he was no longer the foreigner, as he had always been in France or England. 'It's my language, it's my country!' was how he expressed it. And yet this vision of what he called Eternal Russia was far from being the whole picture. There were other, less congenial sights: places devastated by revolution or war; the grim Soviet buildings in the towns. 'Modern Russia is alien to me,' he described it. In this soulless, atheistic society he certainly did not feel at home.

His visit was carefully shepherded by a priest who had been designated to watch over him and, no doubt, report any irregularities. The Church's every move was overseen by the State Representatives for Church Affairs. Bishop Anthony had wished to meet with them and take stock of the situation, and was able to do so formally at the Patriarch's headquarters at Zagorsk. This was not the kind of arrangement he had in mind, and he asked his attendant priest, whom he called his 'Guardian Angel', to arrange a visit to their own premises nearby. The boss was not available but two of his underlings were. One of them was a young man with a lively mind and a good awareness of Church affairs both in Russia and abroad, to whom Bishop Anthony unexpectedly warmed. The officials might have been hoping for an opportunity to interrogate this man whom they could only have seen as a potential thorn in their flesh, with his Russian monarchist and openly anti-communist politics. Instead, he immediately turned the tables by questioning them on the Church/State divide and the anti-religious propaganda of which the West heard so much. At first the answers were chilly and slow. Both sides knew the room would be bugged as a matter of course; but despite that the conversation livened up as the two State officials discovered they had met their mark in this surprising and bold cleric. They told him to begin with, that while there was legislation to allow believers to be normal citizens, religious belief had to be balanced by atheist propaganda, although the direct sort was not as prominent as it had once been. It might work in the big cities, where it was reported in the Western media, but not in Russia's rural heartland. The State increasingly relied on the complete absence of religious teaching as the most effective way of promulgating atheism. It was only a matter of time before the last people to have had any religious instruction died off; then there would be no one left who would have even heard of the Church. Science was going to be the death of religion, the young man explained. He was an engineer himself, which naturally made him a convinced atheist. Bishop Anthony had his answer to that. 'Yet I was trained as a scientist and am a believer.' The discussion turned to the relation of the Church to the Patriarchal dioceses outside the Soviet Union. This was an important issue because the Church inside Russia was forced to spout the Party line, including on international matters, and often hoped for its own sake that its churches abroad would follow suit. Bishop Anthony made it quite clear that he did no such thing, insisting on the right to act according to his personal convictions and political views.

Only then did Bishop Anthony answer questions – with a brutal frankness despite the bugs – about the life of the Russian parishes abroad and their relations with the non-Orthodox. Bugging was to be a constant phenomenon wherever and whenever Bishop Anthony visited Russia. The Church was under constant surveillance. Some years later, when he tried staying with friends in their Moscow apartment, a team of electricians turned up on the doorstep two weeks before his visit to carry out 'rewiring'. Horrified that his friends had suffered because of him, he preferred after that to stay in the special hotels designated for foreigners, where at least he knew the rooms were bugged as a matter of routine, and he could act accordingly.

'I always recite the morning and evening prayers out loud; then I go round the room singing monarchist songs. It's an education for my listeners.'

During this first visit he celebrated services virtually every morning and evening in a number of locations, including Moscow and Leningrad (as it was then). The beauty of the churches stunned him. The Kremlin cathedrals were preserved immaculately – as museums – and the care with which they and secular monuments, like the Winter Palace in Leningrad, were kept seemed to sit oddly with the State's politics. Not too far beneath the surface was a subconscious nostalgia for all that Russia had lost.

Before his visit Bishop Anthony had been apprised of the way church life was conducted: that he would find the churches too magnificent and the ceremonial too elaborate and perfect. This was not the way of the simple church in the Rue Pétel, where he had learnt from Father Afanasy how to strip away all outward accretions in order to find Christ who had trodden the way of poverty and humility.

He described his reaction to the Russian churches in various ways, depending on his audience. Yes, he would say, he had been prepared to dislike what he found, but then after a couple of services he began to see the relevance of the beauty and perfection: it was a revelation of the glory of the eternal banquet for downtrodden Soviet citizens enduring their drab and wretched existence – as the famed emissaries of Prince Vladimir had said on their return from Constantinople, 'heaven on earth'. It was the manifestation of the eternal truth of the splendour of the love of God. The Soviets understood this, and it appears to account for the famous beauty of the Moscow Metro. Many of the stations were built on the sites of demolished churches. The State, realising perhaps of what it was depriving its citizens, tried a secular compensation in the form of chandelier-hung, painted underground halls, a parody of a Russian church interior.

However, there was another reaction that Bishop Anthony would sometimes admit to feeling. There had always been, he would explain to his flock who later visited Russia and felt uncomfortable with church life there, two poles in Russian church life: the way of simplicity and the elaborate way of the great cathedrals. Personally, he found the former to be the more congenial, and he averred he was not happy with the way services were celebrated in Russia, in particular the way the bishop could become too much the focus of a pontifical service. In London he pared down the ceremonial to the minimum, in a way that later visiting clergy from Russia sometimes found odd.

Something he did not dispute was the size of the congregations. Everywhere he went he found the churches full in the evenings and at weekends, though less so on weekday mornings when only the legendary babushki were not at work. By full he meant in the Russian manner: people standing in their thousands, shoulder to shoulder, so tightly packed that anyone who fainted remained upright, wedged between fellow worshippers.

He was impressed by the prayer. One service he attended was built around the Akathist Hymn, a series of canticles addressed to the Mother of God, in which the poetry and music are sublime. In Russia things went much deeper. He found, listening as the congregation around him joined in the singing by heart, that the words were a matter of life and death to these people who lived in constant fear of persecution.

'They prayed with a depth beyond our experience, because they prayed as people who have risked their lives for the Church of God. And when they pray to the Mother of God "the hope of those without hope", they do indeed pray because they have no other hope in life. When you hear five thousand people praying from the very depth of their souls' experience it has such a profound power and solidity, of the sort we have never experienced in England.' This was how he described his experience shortly after his return, and he was to find the same thing again and again whenever he visited Russia.

Always a visual man, he was impressed too by the icons – not so much by their artistic merit as by the power he perceived in these sacred images, before which such a tide of humanity had prayed. He was conscious that Christ, or the saint depicted, stood there receiving the kisses of the faithful; and in some cases the kisses had worn away not only the paint: the very wood had been worn into a curve.

He was not the only one to be impressed by his visit. The congregations were immensely taken with this young and fearless bishop who preached to them words they were not used to hearing. He spoke of the Church as a place of refuge – for them and also for God, who had been rejected on earth. Not only did they share his rejection and persecution: they had created and cherished these precious plots of the earth where he was at home, where he reigned, where his will was done. It was a sermon Bishop Anthony was to repeat in many places, not only in Russia, and throughout his decades of ministry.

Other topics for his sermons were no less intense. He preached on the place of the believer in a godless world; on the situation in the West where young people were leaving the churches; and on the awesome words of the Orthodox Prayer before Communion: 'I will not tell the secret to thine enemies, nor give thee a kiss like Judas' – words which in London could seem a trifle theoretical, but not in Moscow. Nearly thirty years later he described how one of the people he had got to know in Russia told him that his first childhood memories were of the desperate cries he heard during the night when the KGB came to arrest relatives or neighbours.

There was one more element to the services he attended. Everywhere he went he blessed the individual members of the congregation, wherever there was a place for it in the service. This became a long exercise, sometimes lasting a couple of hours. It was one situation where he could come face to face with ordinary worshippers, if only for a few brief seconds; but it was enough for him to be able to register something about each person, a point of contact.

'In spite of the fact that they were all dressed alike it was easy to see from the faces of the younger people whether they were factory workers, teachers, farm labourers or intellectuals. But the faces of the older ones were not so much suffering as withdrawn, as if everything they had gone through had driven all emotion deep inside them.'

All through this time of blessing the whole congregation would remain in the church. As the service ended, people would start singing spontaneously – the Lord's Prayer, the Creed, the Hymn to the Mother of God – and this would continue until the last person in the queue had been blessed. This scene was repeated every time he went to Russia.

Reports in the Western press would speak of churches crowded with old ladies. That was not the reality Bishop Anthony and others found. There were people of all ages and walks of life who were believers and who braved not just the ridicule encountered in the West but also loss of jobs, imprisonment, torture and death openly to profess Christianity. Bishop Anthony commented on one congregation that had more than the usual proportion of young members, which surprised him because its priest was in his eighties and by no means a dynamic man. Why, asked Bishop Anthony, did he attract so many young people? The answer was: because of the depth of his prayer. This was something Bishop Anthony found in the older priests who had lived through the thirties, times of intense physical persecution and horror, during which they had learnt to endure whatever was given them and through it to pray with an intensity and power unique to them. The younger priests Bishop Anthony initially described as 'magnificent'. In subsequent visits he was to become much more critical of them and also of the hierarchy, some of whom were known or suspected KGB informers or plants.

What future did Bishop Anthony see for this persecuted, decimated Church of Russia? Some people to whom he talked were pessimistic, worn down by years of hardship. Although they acknowledged that things were not so bad as in the worst days of Stalin's terror, like the State Representatives they now feared that the current more subtle form of persecution and total lack of religious teaching would have its due effect. Nothing short of a miracle would save the Church from annihilation. When he put this to Patriarch Alexis I, a man who himself was readily accused in the West of betraying the Church, the Patriarch came up with a different view. He saw the situation as a challenge, in which it took courage to be a believer. But with that courage, and God's grace, everything was possible, even a miracle.

'So will the Church die out?' the young bishop asked the old Patriarch.

'Christ has told us: this is my Church, and the gates of hell shall not prevail against it. If you don't believe that, you can't call yourself a Christian,' came the unequivocal reply.

On the final evening of his visit Bishop Anthony was given a farewell dinner, at which he spoke again to one of the State Representatives and invited him to his hotel room, where they talked into the night. Bishop Anthony put forward his own agenda for if he were to come again. 'I want to see your anti-religious work; I want to go to anti-religious meetings. I'd like to see your youth work, and talk science and religion with teachers and students.' He had been taken to the university on a staged official visit, which had been a useless exercise. The Representative offered to consider his ideas. In turn he was eager to hear what Bishop Anthony had thought of the Soviet Union and life there, and to the accusation of excessive bureaucracy he explained that the State machinery was enormous and it was politically necessary for everything to be centralised. The next point Bishop Anthony made was how strange it was to be in a purely working-class society. The Representative, surprisingly for a Marxist, agreed this was a problem. The cultural level of society had to be raised above the level of the factory floor, and through the educational system the State was trying its best. Bishop Anthony turned the discussion to the question of freedom – as defined in the West as the liberty of the individual to think, act and plan his life as he wished. The Representative agreed that did not exist in the Soviet Union, but he did not see it as a defect. 'We are building a new world,' was his answer. To someone who had lived in Occupied France during the War, that sounded chillingly familiar. Bishop Anthony trotted out the definition once given to him by a Nazi soldier: freedom is the right to fulfil one's duty unhampered. Yes, said the Representative, he would agree with that. It was by then past midnight, and the young man was wilting. Bishop Anthony, fired with enthusiasm by their frank conversation, took pity on him and offered him a drink. In true Russian fashion he refused water but accepted a glass of vodka, and the two men, of such different religious and political persuasions, drank to their strange friendship.

So ended Bishop Anthony's first visit to his homeland. He was to continue visiting Russia for the next twenty-nine years, more or less frequently depending on the waxing and waning of his popularity with the authorities there. On one trip the question would be put to him by an admirer: now that the political situation would make it possible, why are you still living over there in England when you could be here, in your own country? His reply, he claimed, was that he could not desert the flock that God had given him.

Following his own visit Bishop Anthony was able to organise a pilgrimage to Russia of Orthodox from Britain and Western Europe. Such pilgrimages were to become an intermittent feature of life in Bishop Anthony's diocese over the coming decades, and brought varying reactions. There were the somewhat romantic, gullible people who were charmed by the way they were treated: they were taken round wonderful churches, entertained by clergy who fed them the Party line on how marvellous everything was, and loaded with gifts that came ultimately from the communist authorities. Others saw through the charade and came home in spiritual despair at what they perceived was a KGB-run Church. To one of them Bishop Anthony gave an emotional appointment in which he was able to lift the young man's spirits so that he left feeling enlightened, encouraged and healed – until he reached the end of the street. Only then did he experience what others, too, sometimes felt over the years: that being in Bishop Anthony's presence had been a great spiritual experience – but what had he actually said? Once outside his room, the beneficial glow soon disappeared, leaving questions that it was too late to ask.

The new opportunities for travel to the Soviet Union that were emerging in the early 1960s drew all sorts of people, among them a young Anglican student, Michael Bourdeaux, who was sponsored by the British Council to study in Leningrad and who became deeply interested in the life of the churches there. On his return to England he set about raising the profile of persecuted Russian Christians and founded Keston College (now Keston Institute) as a vehicle for monitoring religious persecution in the USSR. He appeared not entirely sympathetic to the Orthodox, initially failing to appreciate, for instance, how the celebration of the Orthodox Liturgy can itself be a means of conversion. In 1965 he published his first book, *The Opium of the People*, which Bishop Anthony did not like at all.

Michael Bourdeaux was by no means the only non-Orthodox Westerner who found himself at odds with Russian Christianity. It was difficult for many Protestants to understand the Orthodox mind-set, even without the complications of the Church's life under the Soviet system. With a natural distrust of candles, incense and all things that smacked of

Roman Catholicism – indeed, some dubbed Orthodoxy 'Catholicism without the Pope' – and a deep suspicion of icons, seeing them as little short of idolatrous, some even went so far as to say that the Orthodox were not Christian at all. The small Russian Baptist community had vociferous supporters among their Western brethren. The desperate shortage of Bibles in the Soviet Union became a particular focus point, with visitors from the West (including those from Bishop Anthony's own flock) smuggling them in at every opportunity. Above all, Christians in the West (including some Orthodox) could not understand the Patriarchate's constant reiteration of the Soviet political line. True, they acknowledged that the Church was under the threat of persecution. But those who talked enthusiastically of basing their Christianity on the Early Church wondered aloud why true believers could not find the courage to speak out in the face of this threat.

Many years later Metropolitan Anthony would quote the case of an elderly bishop who had spent years and years in a Soviet labour camp before being released, his health broken, to take his place once more among the ranks of the hierarchy. At a session of the Holy Synod he had been expected to speak out against the latest Soviet government attack on the Church, but he remained silent. Afterwards he was asked why he, a man whose faith had been honed by active persecution, had failed to stand up and be counted in defence of all that he had suffered for.

'Forgive me,' the man replied, 'but when the moment to speak came, I felt I simply did not have the strength left to face any more torture.'

Despite all the restrictions that the authorities tried to put on Bishop Anthony, he succeeded over the years in learning, often at first hand, of the harrowing persecution that people had suffered, whether they were clergy, monastics or ordinary lay people. His reputation as a man of integrity became such in Russia that he won the trust of non-Orthodox believers as well.

He would tell of a Baptist minister incarcerated by the Soviet authorities in a psychiatric hospital. On one of Metropolitan Anthony's visits the man's wife came to tell him how her husband's brain was being systematically destroyed by drugs meted out by the doctors. Whatever ecclesial differences there were between Orthodoxy and the denominations, on a personal level Metropolitan Anthony's great Christian compassion overcame any boundaries.

With regard to his own Church, he acknowledged the sacrifice made by members of the hierarchy in having publicly to compromise their words in order to retain some measure of Church presence in the country. That was not the heroic gesture that Westerners on the sidelines imagined they themselves would have made, but it was the best practical action that the people in the front line could manage in their horrific circumstances.

Bishop Anthony's first visit had obviously made an impression on the Patriarchate. In October 1962 it awarded him the Order of St Vladimir, First Class and appointed him Archbishop of Sourozh in charge of a new diocese to cover the territory of the British Isles. Archbishop Anthony was also appointed acting Exarch (and later Exarch) of Western Europe, to oversee the parishes there. For the next twelve years he spent a good deal of his time travelling around the Continent as well as going more or less annually to the Soviet Union, which meant he could be absent from his London parish for weeks or months on end.

Precisely how Moscow arrived at this decision was to remain unclear. It has been suggested that it was Bishop Anthony's own idea to divide Western Europe into the three dioceses of France, the Netherlands and Britain, so that he could keep Britain exclusively under his control. However, the late Sir Dimitri Obolensky claimed the initiative. He maintained that he and Michael Theokritoff had gone to Paris to ask for a separate diocese to be created in Britain. In any event, Archbishop Anthony was rightly seen as its founder, inspiration and father. So, three dioceses were created under one Exarchate, which ensured Archbishop Anthony's freedom to run things in Britain without any interference.

Over the next few years a number of small parishes and Eucharistic communities were to spring up across the territory of the diocese, wherever groups of Russians, or converts, organised themselves. Archbishop Anthony began to ordain men from these congregations to serve in a non-stipendiary capacity, a policy he was to continue throughout his life. Having had no theological training himself he distrusted seminaries. Instead, he looked for people of solid faith who had leadership qualities, good experience of life and whom the congregations felt they could trust, eventually, as confessors – men might sometimes remain deacons for several years before becoming priests.

Archbishop Anthony's title was not the Patriarchate's initial choice. The first suggestion was that it should be 'of London and Great Britain'. He put this to the Archbishop of Canterbury, Michael Ramsay, whom he knew well and with whom he had a close and sympathetic relationship. Would it not be invidious for the Orthodox to claim this title when the Anglicans had their own Bishop of London? Michael Ramsay's response was that he welcomed the formation of a Russian Orthodox diocese for Britain, but that he would prefer Archbishop Anthony not to take an English title.

Relieved, Archbishop Anthony joked: 'Moscow might have appointed me Archbishop of somewhere disreputable like Soho.'

A Russian title accorded very well with his own sentiments, since he still considered himself to be Russian in spirit if not by nationality. Nor did he wish to spoil his good relations with the Church of England. The Patriarchate agreed to make him titular Archbishop of Sourozh, modern Soudak, a defunct diocese in the Crimea. The patron saint would be St Stephen the Confessor of Sourozh, and a couple of decades or so later a Soviet archaeologist excavating in Soudak discovered the relics of St Stephen and smuggled out a small piece for the London cathedral.

There were now two Orthodox dioceses in Britain, since the Greeks had their own Archdiocese of Thyateira. Numerically far larger than the Russians, because of the influx of Cypriots fleeing the troubles in Cyprus, they nevertheless maintained a low profile, so that Bishop Anthony would boast that his diocese was seen as 'the Orthodox Church in Britain'. It had English as its common language, was open to the surrounding society and was welcoming to anyone who crossed its threshold.

By this time the numbers of people who had crossed the threshold of the cathedral, the small parish in Oxford and the other communities springing up around the country had increased to the point where there was a need for services in English. Fortuitously, in early 1964 Michael Fortounatto was appointed choirmaster. The son-in-law and former assistant of Michael Theokritoff, he had been teaching at the University of East Anglia and making the journey up to London for weekend services. His appointment was to prove a great asset, as he set about imbuing the choir with his enthusiasm for and great knowledge of Church music. More than that, his excellent command of English enabled him to adapt the music to the English language.

There was some resistance to the introduction of English in the London parish. Metropolitan Anthony realised that, for both his Russian parishioners and himself, it would be a sacrifice to begin to lose the Church Slavonic. For the older Russians this was a difficult move, but for the younger generation with children the picture was different. Many years later the daughter of Anna Garrett, Xenia Bowlby, herself a former Sunday school pupil, described how she was passionate about services in Slavonic – until she had a family. Then she discovered that it was hard enough to persuade children to come to church, but it was nearly impossible if the service was unintelligible to them. In common with many London Russians she had married an Englishman and her children were being brought up in circumstances where Russian was not the dominant language. Moreover, she had to admit that Church Slavonic was not easy even for a Russian to understand.

The introduction of English in London was measured, beginning with the reading of the Epistle and Gospel in both languages, and during Archbishop Anthony's absences even that did not always happen. Nevertheless, it was a significant move, and one that was to further open his congregation to the outside world.

PART FOUR

AT THE HEIGHT OF HIS POWERS

CHAPTER NINE

9 e

METROPOLITAN OF SOUROZH

(1966–1976)

In 1966 the Holy Synod of the Patriarchate of Moscow raised Archbishop Anthony to the rank of Metropolitan. Although he was only fifty-two his rise through the hierarchy would not be as fast as some of the younger clerics in the Soviet Union, in a time when the Church was so desperately short of clergy that it had abandoned the canonical norms. What was unusual in Metropolitan Anthony's case was his integrity. Throughout his long career the KGB was never able to discredit him.

The year saw another important development in his work: the publication of his first book. *Living Prayer* was, like the books that were to follow, a compilation of talks he had given, and given in his customary manner without notes. They were transcribed, the English was polished by a suitably talented member of his congregation, Esther Williams – not enough to lose his distinctive style of speaking, which became known as 'Anthonian English' among his followers – and was accepted by Darton, Longman and Todd. It was an exciting moment. It was also a slightly edgy one as far as the Metropolitan was concerned. Before the launch he had sent out his complimentary copies to friends for their comments. To his consternation the Abbot of Nashdom replied with the one-liner: Julian of Norwich did not write *The Cloud of Unknowing*. This highlighted a characteristic failure of Metropolitan Anthony to check his sources. That was even true, as happened in later books, when the source was himself, for he showed no concern about putting into print versions of his own anecdotes that did not tally with each other in certain (sometimes significant) details.

On this particular occasion, however, he was nervous of the reaction that his thoughtlessness might provoke. Always conscious of his lack of theological education he feared it could well become another stick with which Westerners could beat the Russian Church: those of its bishops who weren't Communist plants were ignorant. A parishioner who saw him the day before the launch described him as being 'uncharacteristically like a cat on hot bricks', despite his scornful dismissal of the Abbot's criticism: 'No, Julian of Norwich didn't write it, but that's the sort of thing one just says without thinking.' He went on making similar gaffes without thinking for the rest of his life, never concerned about other people's desire for accuracy. What mattered to him was the essence of what he said, not the peripheral details. A born storyteller, he always preferred the spontaneous approach, in which checking his sources could not feature. He also admitted to thinking very much in imagery, and he painted with broad brushstrokes. This could lead to further confusion. There were some people who found him too complex and failed to understand what he said. 'I can't make head or tail of you,' someone remarked, which prompted him to ask the next person who came to see him whether she, too, found what he taught incomprehensible. She replied certainly not; but suggested the Orthodox mind-set was perhaps more readily taken up by people like herself with Celtic origins than by the more rational Anglo-Saxons.

The public found no trouble understanding what he said *in Living Prayer*. The book became a great success. The *Cloud of Unknowing* error was overlooked by his readership (and remained uncorrected in subsequent editions). Metropolitan Anthony was increasingly in demand as a speaker, broadcaster – and now writer. People began clamouring for a second book.

School for Prayer was to follow four years later and was another success, going into four impressions in the first year alone. It too was a collection of transcribed talks, this time ones given at Exeter College, Oxford during a university mission. The talks were supposed to be for unbelievers; indeed, Metropolitan Anthony claimed there had been a notice outside the hall saying, 'Believers not admitted'. 'Well, perhaps some did get in,' he confessed afterwards. One who certainly did not was a young Orthodox postgraduate student from America, Basil Osborne, who did not attend but whose wife Rachel went along to hear the Metropolitan speak on a subsequent occasion and recommended him to her husband as a man worth paying attention to.

A member of his audience recollected that in fact Metropolitan

Anthony had felt he was not giving enough of his time to the mission, and so he took to giving extra impromptu talks on the steps of the college each morning. All of them were aimed at people who were either seeking God or who were inexperienced in prayer, and since many Christians struggle to pray even after many years, the book, like the talks they were based on, fulfilled a very deep need. The most striking feature of what he said was, perhaps, his honesty. Instead of speaking in pious terms about methods of prayer, its author plunged straight in with the central problem: the absence of God that is an all too common stumbling block for unbelievers and believers alike. But, he went on to say, that absence ought to be a cause for rejoicing – because it was something real, given by God when we were not yet ready to meet him. It was only by being real that we could meet the real Living God. And, as in his sermons, he used 'we' rather than you, always insistent on including himself among his listeners.

In the book he recounted the anecdote of having been approached at the end of a sermon by a young girl who accused him of being evil. How else, she said, could he have described all their sins so well?

He spoke in a similar vein at the general confessions he held at the end of the twice-yearly retreats that began in 1971. He would stand in the centre of the church in front of the icon of Christ, surrounded by his flock, and, aloud, extemporise prayers of deep penitence that seemed to reach out to the hearts of everyone in the most personal way. Lamenting the sad fact that God had called him to glory, while he preferred to remain 'small and vile' as he put it on one occasion, he would sum up the spiritual state of his listeners as if he could see into each soul. When asked how he could do this, his response was: he was not doing it at all, but talking about himself.

The other striking feature of *School for Prayer* was the Introduction: the transcript of an interview in which the Metropolitan talked about his life, and in particular his conversion experience. This set the tone for the whole book: something challenging, alive, cutting through common conceptions of 'piety' to bring the reader face to face with what it was like truly to meet the Living God.

Perhaps *School for Prayer* had the greatest impact of any of his books. More than thirty years after its publication many people were still claiming it was the best book on prayer they had ever read. For a number of them it became the catalyst for their own conversion. Some readers spread the word about it in their own churches, wherever they were. Some found their way to the Ennismore Gardens cathedral, and stayed there, swelling the number of converts to Orthodoxy in Britain.

Interest in what Metropolitan Anthony had to say, and in his Church, was increasing all the time. He represented a challenge to believer and unbeliever alike, with his solid personal faith and his proclamation of the truth of the resurrection – which was a refreshing change from the liberalism of the day. During this period barely a week went by when he did not broadcast. His mellifluous voice was ideally suited to the radio and his impressive appearance, with his handsome face and striking beard, made him a must for television as well. In Russia some people commented that he spoke such elegant Russian and his voice was so beautiful that they found themselves just listening to the sounds without taking in a word of what he said. But many thousands took in every word, hungry to hear the Gospel message spoken with such conviction and clarity. In England he remained unusual among Orthodox clergy in having such good English, made more charming by his attractive Franco-Russian accent and occasional idiosyncrasies. This was intensified by his eyes, afire with faith and also with an expression of innocent wonder, behind which was a searing intellect. When challenged in debate his natural ability for repartee enabled him to outwit most opponents. One who did get the better of him, in a television interview, was a Roman Catholic priest who opposed the Orthodox line with Jesuitical casuistry. To this the Orthodox appeal to experiential revelation could give no intellectual answer that was intelligible to a modern secular audience. Metropolitan Anthony knew he was outwardly defeated by this man's approach, although he was also convinced that his own held the truth. He had to leave it to his listeners to judge where the voice of God could be discerned. That did not bother him. He would regularly say that his function was to speak the truth of the Gospel; and what happened as a result was God's business, not his. He was never interested in playing the numbers game, or in achieving any kind of 'success'. He was certainly not interested in being rewarded for his labours, either in monetary terms or in ecclesiastical honours.

His work on external bodies began to flourish, both in England and abroad. Besides this, his work as Exarch took him away from his London parish more and more, which he found at times both uncongenial and tiring. Despite his Italian heritage he did not like going to Italy, describing it as the country in which he would least like to live. It was too dramatic for his retiring nature and he dubbed it 'opera in life'. He also found himself at odds with the native Roman Catholic Church. At one point it was said he even received veiled threats to his safety if he did not curtail what was perceived as missionary activity.

The Patriarchate appointed him to other positions. His work with the World Council of Churches continued and in 1966 he had become a member of its Central Committee and its Christian Medical Commission. He was also a member of the Russian Church's Ecumenical Commission. Despite the fact that he did not personally find formal ecumenical dialogue congenial, this was all valuable work on two counts. Firstly it enabled the Russian Church, so restricted in its homeland, to participate in Christian affairs on the world stage; and secondly, it enabled it to do so with a voice that was authoritative and, even more important, that spoke with an integrity that would not have been possible for a Soviet citizen forced to toe the Communist Party line. Metropolitan Anthony's sincerity was beyond doubt; and he was not a man who could be intimidated. (When, some years later on a visit to Russia, he was told he might not be able to leave because the authorities had lost his passport, he enthused, 'How wonderful! I've always wanted to die in Russia!' The official disappeared into the adjoining office and 'found' his passport immediately.)

In September 1967 he accepted an invitation to visit the ecumenical community of Taizé in France. The prior, Brother Roger, invited him to participate, with other Church leaders from different denominations, in its second international youth gathering. The young people very much appreciated the clarity of his replies to their questions, especially concerning prayer, and were taken by what the brotherhood discerned as the 'spiritual radiance that emanated from his being', although one young English delegate later recalled that he tended to be too surrounded by a clique of admirers.

This was the beginning of an enduring association with Taizé. He visited the community on several other occasions. When he celebrated the Orthodox Liturgy in the Church of Reconciliation there, everyone was struck by the beauty of his singing voice and the depth of his spoken meditations. Brother Roger met him for the last time in Moscow in June 1988, during the celebrations of the Millennium of Christianity in Russia. On that occasion the Metropolitan fondly recalled his visits to Taizé.

Metropolitan Anthony's extended absences from his London parish were beginning to create difficulties. When no other priest was available either, things threatened to grind to a halt. Michael Fortounatto showed initiative and leadership in stepping in as much as a choirmaster could, and in 1969 Metropolitan Anthony, recognising these qualities among others, ordained him. His was to be a long and faithful service to the church in two capacities, because he continued as choirmaster as well as taking on a full round of pastoral duties. Noted for his peaceable and reverential manner and his sharp intellect, he was to be a much-loved priest whose temperament and personality complemented the Metropolitan's. One of his early tasks as a priest was to act as secretary to a commission on liturgical awareness. Metropolitan Anthony gave Father Michael a modern creed to look at, aware that in the other churches there was a lot of movement to which he felt the Orthodox should be reacting, although he was not prepared to take a lead himself and the project came to nothing.

Metropolitan Anthony's desire to simplify the services stemmed from his intense nostalgia for apophaticism; he felt physical things got in the way of a relationship with the Living God. For instance, he would have liked periods of silence during the services. He also said he would have preferred not to be surrounded by icons in the church. 'Give me a white wall anytime,' was how he expressed his feelings.

One liturgical move he was to make later was to invite the composer John Tavener to write a setting to the English text of the Liturgy. The music was successful in its own right but was not used liturgically.

Another new initiative, begun in 1969, was the publication of the first monthly Newsletter. In the 1950s there had been a Parish Herald, but the Newsletter was to become a more ambitious publication. Although at first it was in English only and rather meagre, it soon became bilingual and in time achieved a worldwide circulation as people from outside the Metropolitan's diocese were drawn to read his sermons, which were a prominent feature. It was to be joined eventually by a quarterly theology journal, *Sourozh*.

On the death of Patriarch Alexis, Metropolitan Anthony was called to Moscow in 1971 to take part in the election of his successor. One of the last acts of the Patriarch had been to sign the documents granting autocephaly to the Orthodox Church in America and to announce the canonisation of two Russian missionary saints, Herman of Alaska and Nicholas of Tokyo, affirming the Patriarchate's recognition of Orthodoxy outside Soviet territory.

On Metropolitan Anthony's arrival at Zagorsk for the election process a monk took him to a single room. It was a special privilege as he was a noteworthy bishop from abroad; the local bishops had to be content with dormitory accommodation. The monk explained to him eagerly, 'They've been very good to you, they've taken care of the electrics in here,' to remind him that this room had been fitted with bugs for his benefit. For the same reason he was also asked to hear a confession in the garden.

In July 1970 the BBC had televised two extraordinary debates between Metropolitan Anthony and the writer Marghanita Laski, a Jewess well known for her atheism. In fact, the two became friends afterwards, to the extent that Metropolitan Anthony accepted Laski's invitation to holiday in her house in the South of France. In turn she – like many people – claimed that she came to know him 'better than anyone else'. The interviews became celebrated programmes. They were to form the first chapter of Metropolitan Anthony's third book, *God and Man*, published the following year. Three of the other chapters were transcripts of talks he gave at Birmingham University. Again he spoke of doubt, in a different way to this different audience, but still with the assurance of a man who had met God incontrovertibly. When it came to question time, one of the students, with all the assurance of youth, said, 'Well, it's all right for you as a clergyman to speak in those terms, but I can't accept all this religious talk. You see, I'm a scientist.'

'Oh,' said Metropolitan Anthony with genuine interest. 'Tell me, what sort of scientist are you?'

'I'm a first year medical student,' replied the hapless young man, ignorant of the speaker's background.

'Well,' came the answer, 'I'm also a scientist, I was a doctor and a surgeon.'

This kind of altercation happened more than once, because it was very easy for people to listen to Metropolitan Anthony's apparently 'simple' message and fail to grasp immediately the depth of the intellectual rigour that underpinned it. He would then use his formidable intelligence and his gift for quick repartee to squash his opponents – in the nicest possible way – or at least to take the upper hand in the debate.

The longest chapter in *God and Man* was taken from talks he had given at the University of Louvain, Belgium, in 1969. Entitled 'Holiness and Prayer' it included a potted history of Russia, and the quotation of words said to have been spoken by a Russian priest who was killed in the course of Stalin's purges: 'There will come a day when the martyr will be able to stand before the throne of God in defence of his persecutors and say, "Lord, I have forgiven in thy name and by thy example. Thou hast no claim against them any more."' It was in defence of such heroes of the Faith that Metropolitan Anthony felt he had to make a stand. Despite the continuing media accusations against the unwillingness of the Russian

Church to speak out against the Soviet State's persecution of its members, and the obvious weakness of the Church itself under the communist yoke, he remained adamant that it needed his loyalty, not in any political sense but because it was the Body of Christ being broken for the salvation of the millions in the Soviet Union who were in desperate need of the Christian message.

One person on whom *God and Man* made a deep impression was Rowan Williams, a young student who was to be the Archbishop of Canterbury destined to give an address at Metropolitan Anthony's funeral. In reading this book he made the connection for the first time between the doctrine of the Trinity and prayer. Later, when he came to know Metropolitan Anthony, he described him as a man of 'integrity, warmth and acceptance, in whose gaze one felt both judged and loved inseparably'.

Another Anglican student who was impressed with Metropolitan Anthony's books was the young Richard Chartres, the future Bishop of London. He particularly appreciated what he called Metropolitan Anthony's 'fresh and original' approach to his faith, born of his scientific background. He admired the simplicity and depth of his prayer, which he described as coming out of a living stream: imagery the Metropolitan also liked to use – though not of himself. Richard Chartres first visited Russia in 1972, and found Metropolitan Anthony and his broadcasts widely talked about. He judged the people to be leading, out of necessity, an ascetic life: short of food and worldly comforts, apparently starved of spiritual support, physically enslaved by the Soviet system, they could live according to an inner freedom which he described as a great spiritual beauty. They were eager to read whatever they could get hold of about Christianity; they were eager to listen and learn.

To an extent that had also been true in the West after the Second World War. By the 1970s people in Britain were better off but they were still listening. They were also looking for new answers to the old certainties that Western theologians were busy debunking, through books such as *Honest to God*.

Amid all this Metropolitan Anthony's voice rang out clear and unwavering. His honesty to God was to talk about the God he knew 'as a fact' as he had told Marghanita Laski. And it was not the wimpish figure often portrayed in the West, but a God who had the courage to create humanity and to die for his creation. This strong, bold faith, uncomfortable and demanding, stood against the prevailing trends of the politically pinkish, theologically liberal, Gospel espoused by many other churches at the time.

Previous page: This photograph, taken in 1966, was reproduced in *School for Prayer*. *(Copyright © Sir Richard Bowlby.)*

Above: As a medical student in 1935 (middle row, third from left). *(Estate of Metropolitan Anthony.)*

Below: In scout uniform, 1927 (far right). *(Estate of Metropolitan Anthony.)*

Walking down Bond Street, 1949.
(Estate of Metropolitan Anthony.)

With Xenia, 1954. *(Estate of
Metropolitan Anthony.)*

Left: Consecration as Bishop of Sergievo, 1957. *(Estate of Metropolitan Anthony.)*

Opposite: Metropolitan of Sourozh, 1966. *(Estate of Metropolitan Anthony.)*

Below: Exarch of Western Europe, 1964. With Patriarch Alexis I. *(Estate of Metropolitan Anthony.)*

Above: With Father Michael Fortounatto, at Summer Camp, 1979. *(Copyright © Deacon Peter Scorer)*

Below: Playing volleyball at Camp, 1985. *(Copyright © Deacon Peter Scorer)*

Above: At the first service held in the Kremlin Dormition Cathedral, Moscow, since the Revolution, 13 October 1989. *(Estate of Metropolitan Anthony.)*

Below: On the 40th anniversary of his consecration as bishop, flanked by Archbishop Anatoly (left) and Bishop Basil (right), November 1997. *(Copyright © Nick Hale)*

The last photo. Metropolitan Anthony with Bishop Mark of Berlin. *(Estate of Metropolitan Anthony.)*

Metropolitan Anthony was not interested in the taking up of social causes. He had no sympathy for organisations such as the Campaign for Nuclear Disarmament. On the contrary, he spoke vehemently on a television interview in favour of the nuclear deterrent, even though, as the interviewer brought out, Western missiles were trained on his Russia and his fellow Orthodox. However, he was adamant that Christians should stand by their convictions, even if they were not his own. When a young parishioner, Irina von Schlippe, mentioned that she wished to take part in a demonstration outside the Soviet Embassy he expressed his opposition to it so forcefully that she decided against attending. He later chided her: just because he disapproved of her opinions, that was no excuse for not doing what she judged was right. He always encouraged people to think for themselves and not follow him slavishly.

In 1973 DLT published a further book, *Courage to Pray*, co-authored by Metropolitan Anthony and the French Benedictine writer Georges Lefebvre. It was typical that while Metropolitan Anthony remained vehemently anti-Catholic, his friendship with individual Catholics could result in such a book. Although he himself said nothing particularly new in it to English readers – the talks from which it was taken were originally given to a French audience – it proved another success.

Invitations to preach in non-Orthodox churches and various awards were coming thick and fast. He was the Hulsean Preacher at Cambridge University for 1972–3. In 1973 he went to Aberdeen to receive an Honorary Doctorate of Divinity at the university. While he was there he was asked to preach in the docks. This most unlikely figure – a heavily bearded Russian aristocrat turned black-robed monk – made a surprise hit with the dockers, although this strange rapport generated no obvious tangible results. 'Luckily,' he said afterwards, 'I didn't convert anyone. Suppose someone had come up and said to me, "Your words have converted me. I'd like to become an Orthodox." Where was I supposed to send him – to a Byzantine Liturgy?'

In this situation – and he preached to dockers elsewhere, too, and was always well received – he realised the need for a less academic, more pastoral kind of priest than the ones he had ordained up till then. The converts who regularly came to him were invariably educated and intellectual, so that the in-joke in his diocese was that it was necessary to have a degree in order to become Orthodox. He never succeeded in finding a less academic type of priest and he never founded any working-class parishes, such as one in the East End of London which he claimed to have envisaged from time to time. Indeed, in 1971 he had ordained to the priesthood a professor, Michael Beaumont, to serve the Orthodox community in Dublin. It was a mixed congregation of a few Russians and more Greeks. When Metropolitan Anthony first visited he decided to celebrate the Liturgy in Greek. Recalling his classical Greek from his schooldays, he used the French-accented Erasmian pronunciation with which he was familiar. This did not bear much relation to the present-day pronunciation of Church Greek. The Russians, presuming the unaccustomed language was Greek, switched off. But the Greeks were mystified. It did not seem to resemble any language they knew. Only as the Metropolitan turned to the people to give the final blessing did he see a sudden glimmer of recognition in the eyes of one old man, who added a loud 'Amen!'

For two years Father Michael Beaumont's vibrant ministry generated a lively response among the people there, before his unexpected death robbed Dublin of a highly regarded priest.

Metropolitan Anthony had been ill himself during this time. Over the years he suffered from a catalogue of ailments, some more serious than others, including recurring back trouble, which could debilitate him for weeks at a time; recurring shingles; heart trouble; and bouts of pneumonia. The London parish had to learn to cope with his illnesses and consequent hypochondria.

In 1972 had come another book, *Meditations on a Theme*, published by Mowbrays. Subtitled *A Spiritual Journey* it was in fact a series of talks on the theme of the gospel readings for the weeks preceding Lent in the Orthodox calendar: the stories of Bartimaeus, the Publican and the Pharisee, Zacchaeus, the Prodigal Son and the Last Judgement, with an introductory chapter on spiritual discipline in general and an inspirational finale on the Cross and resurrection. The latter was truly a piece of purple prose, the sort of writing that might have sent the Christians of the Early Church running into the streets seeking martyrdom – at the very least something that, once read, could never be forgotten. What had been forgotten – by Metropolitan Anthony – was an acknowledgement that this was in fact a reworking of a sermon given in 1946 by Archbishop Luke of Simpheropol, who had been a surgeon as well as a priest and had suffered a period of exile in Tashkent. It was no less powerful for that, and it was right that Metropolitan Anthony, having been inspired by it himself, should have made it available to a wider audience, regardless of his omission of an attribution.

However, a far more important omission was about to occur, this time not of Metropolitan Anthony's making. The Russian writer Alexander

Solzhenitsyn wrote a letter to Patriarch Pimen of Moscow and All Russia demanding that he condemn the lack of freedom of religious speech in the Soviet Union. The letter was broadcast on the BBC World Service. The Patriarch made no reply, either public or private, and this silence was taken up by the Western press as a stick with which to beat the Russian Church for its apparent lack of integrity. Metropolitan Anthony understood the situation better. He knew that the Patriarch lived in 'a gilded cage' to use Pimen's own words; he was simply not free to speak out. In an oblique way, his silence might have been seen as an affirmation that religious gagging did exist; but the Western media was not interested in anything but full frontal politics. Irina von Schlippe, who worked in the Russian Department of the BBC World Service, spoke to Metropolitan Anthony about it, saying she thought it was shameful to allow the enemies of the Russian Orthodox Church free rein; someone ought to speak out in its defence, even if it was impossible for the Patriarch himself to do so. Why not he? She could arrange for him to broadcast a reply. So he recorded an answer, as usual speaking without notes. However, as sometimes happened, he was carried away by his feelings and came out with such strong words that it was Irina who had to say no, he had gone too far, they would have to try again. Eventually a more suitable recording was made and approved, in which Metropolitan Anthony put forward his firmly held views: that the Church was an eternal body in a temporal world, and as such it had the monopoly on ensuring communication between God and man and man and God; and that the Church must not put that into jeopardy by engaging in politics. It was an organisation of men and women who collectively and singly had two functions: to preserve that monopoly, and to do their best to achieve God's Kingdom on earth. The Church's eternal dimension had to keep itself free of politics, while the temporal life of each believer faced him or her with the challenge of engaging with the world. It was a brilliant piece of radio journalism, depriving the Russian Church's critics of their accusation that the Church had kept silence. The Church had, in the person of Metropolitan Anthony, spoken – and with a bold and compelling voice, even if it did not say exactly what Westerners might have expected, or wished, to hear. It was the turn of its critics to keep silence. Not a peep was heard from any of them.

In 1973 Metropolitan Anthony ordained Basil Osborne as priest at the request of the Oxford parish where he had spent four years as a deacon, gaining the respect and trust of the community. This was the normal way clergy were chosen in the diocese. When the need arose for a priest the parish concerned would identify a candidate from within the congregation whom people felt would make a good pastor and confessor. Metropolitan Anthony would then make a judgement. Men who presented themselves to the Metropolitan in isolation, asking for ordination because they imagined they had a vocation, were generally given short shrift.

In London the interior of the cathedral was undergoing cleaning and redecoration. Speaking to the parish about it Metropolitan Anthony defined what churches truly were: places set aside to be God's absolute possession, his dwellings on earth, where he was Lord and Master, and where people could find consolation – places where love alone was preached, where there was no room for human hatred; where people who were disfigured by the outside world could very gradually come to their senses and to repentance and begin to change, and where joy could blossom into an earthly paradise. He was not only speaking of his own flock; he went on to pray that the decorators, too, should receive the message of God's peace. 'They are not just workmen,' he said, 'but people who will enter God's domain.' And he prayed that it should not only be the church building that was made beautiful but also the hearts of all its people, so that they might become worthy of entering God's house, not for judgement but, like the Publican, conscious of their unworthiness, and conscious too of God's all-forgiving and transfiguring love. This summed up his vision of what a church and its people should be, and he repeated it many times. It was characteristic that there was no mention of Russianness, or Orthodoxy, or pious spirituality.

After the upheaval of the redecoration people were looking forward to a period of quiet. It was not to be. In 1974 Alexander Solzhenitsyn was expelled from the Soviet Union. This time the Patriarchate went further than refusing to raise its voice in his defence. On 1 March *The Times* published a letter from Metropolitan Seraphim of Krutitsy and Kolomna in which he accused Solzhenitsyn of being a fascist sympathiser and declared that in the eyes of the believers of the Russian Orthodox Church he had 'long forfeited the right to call himself a Christian'. Metropolitan Anthony wrote a letter of reply, which *The Times* printed a week later; this time it was the full frontal approach. Writing in the name of himself as 'Head of the Russian Orthodox Church in Western and Northern Europe', and also in the name of his clergy and flock, he disowned Metropolitan Seraphim's statement and upheld Sozhenitsyn as a man who showed a 'deep and committed' love for Russia in his 'fearless struggle for human dignity, truth and freedom', which, he said, sustained the writer 'in the face of calumny, opprobrium and revenge'. He concluded by affirming that in his love and endeavour for his country, Sozhenitsyn did not stand alone, either in Russian or abroad.

In fact, he had somewhat more sympathy with Andrei Sakharov, the physicist and human rights campaigner. It was a mark of his greatness that he never limited his admiration or support to Church figures. He was also aware that, as he put it in a television interview some years later, 'to be a dissident does not mean that you are right'. Discernment was called for, and he was unhappy when on a visit to Russia he had been cornered at a meeting and asked to declare blanket support for all the dissidents.

He was invited to a prayer service for Solzhenitsyn organised by Keston College at St Martins in the Fields. He accepted but was nervous, disliking the theatrical presentation and political overtones. He was there to pray, and he did so for both the victims of oppression and those responsible for their suffering, because he was always adamant that in showing solidarity with the oppressed one must, as they should, pray for their oppressors, just as the martyrs of the Early Church prayed for their persecutors.

On Easter night he announced to his congregation that he had resigned as Exarch. *The Times*, in reporting the resignation, claimed that senior members of the Patriarchate, and perhaps the Patriarch himself, had made clear their displeasure to Metropolitan Anthony over his outspoken support of Solzhenitsyn. It was said by some that he had in fact not resigned but been sacked. At any rate, the decision seemed to have been mutually agreeable.

Later in 1974 Metropolitan Anthony went to the United States to receive the Browning Award for the spreading of the Christian Gospel. His books sold well in North America. They were also translated into a number of languages and sold all round the world.

In his own diocese several new initiatives were under way. Two communities had come into being in Devon, with clergy ordained to serve them: Father Benedict Ramsden and Father John Marks. Nicholas Behr, one of Tatisha Behr's sons, had already been ordained and was serving in Bristol. The cathedral began producing recordings of its music under its choirmaster Father Michael Fortounatto. Ikon Records, set up and run by Nicholas Tuckett, a member of the congregation working in the music industry, was over the years to raise tens of thousands of pounds for the church and to become a valuable tool in bringing Russian and other Orthodox music to a wide audience.

Another innovation was the celebration for the first time in 1974 of the annual feast of All the Saints of These Islands. This was an important affirmation of the Undivided Church of the first millennium of Christianity. The ancient saints of Britain and Ireland were brothers and sisters of their counterparts from Orthodox lands, and could be venerated with them through music, icons and the love of Orthodox people.

The children's summer camp, which had been defunct for a number of years, was restarted under a new team of people who had themselves been campers a generation earlier, headed by Father Michael Fortounatto and his wife Mariamna. The new camp was to become and remain one of the most inspiring features of life in the diocese. Metropolitan Anthony insisted on attending for part of the time and playing a full role in camp life, playing games with the children and holding discussion sessions with the older campers. Participants came from the various communities scattered over the country, the majority from situations where they were perhaps the only Orthodox at their school, to gather together as their own manifestation of the Church. From the initial blessing of the camp, via daily prayers, lessons, games, discussions, Confession and receiving Communion at the Liturgy, they were immersed in a totally Orthodox milieu.

However, the first camp appeared to the inexperienced organisers to have been a flop. Things just did not go as well as they had expected, and they had serious doubts about whether it would continue the following year. Then they gradually became aware that the children were contacting each other from one end of the country to the other, writing letters, telephoning, eager to keep in touch with their new friends and eager, too, for there to be another camp the next year. They had become a family. Some years later Father Michael summed it up: 'The Holy Spirit was there.' Camp was to become as important to the young members of the Church as the camps in France had been to people of Metropolitan Anthony's generation. The children became dedicated campers and lifelong friends, returning year after year; some ended up marrying each other.

Metropolitan Anthony was anxious to provide a similar means of making the adults in the church feel part of a family, and the following year he inaugurated a Diocesan Conference, held over the long Spring Bank Holiday weekend at St Theresa's Convent School at Effingham in Surrey. This was to prove another success, and became an annual feature of diocesan life.

All these initiatives, whether directly involving Metropolitan Anthony or not, came into being through the inspiration with which he spurred on his congregation to further the work of the Gospel. He was directing a vital and growing body, one that was increasingly fulfilling the vocation he saw for it as a community such as the Early Church had been: multinational, missionary, an expression of the Kingdom of God in an increasingly secular world.

In 1975 Metropolitan Anthony celebrated the twenty-fifth anniversary of becoming vicar of the London parish. In recognition of his achievements he was awarded the Lambeth Cross by the Church of England under its new primate, Archbishop Donald Coggan, with whom he got on particularly well. There was also a change of churchwarden on the retirement of Alexander Pickersgill. His successor, Anna Garrett, was to hold the position of starosta until her death in 1997. It involved not only the day-to-day running of parish life but also being the senior layperson, and became increasingly important as the congregation grew. There was a less joyful event: the majority of the Guildford parish, under its priest Father Yves Dubois, left the diocese after disagreements with Metropolitan Anthony.

In the same year Metropolitan Anthony moved out of Parish House into the small caretaker's flat at the rear of the cathedral. This flat, situated on the south side of the apse, was really little more than a bedsit: one room, at the back of which was a small kitchen, and a bathroom situated in the corridor which ran behind the apse. The flat had latterly been the home of Father Michael and Mariamna Fortounatto but was really too cramped for a couple, and Metropolitan Anthony decided it would be sensible for him to swap accommodation with them. The cathedral was to remain his home for the rest of his life.

His trusted driver, housekeeper and unofficial secretary for many years, Barbara Morshead, had died and from then on he looked after himself. Irina Kirillova became his driver and general aide, and was to play an influential and supportive role in his life and that of the parish and diocese.

Although Metropolitan Anthony's new accommodation was very basic he relished living in the church. For one thing, he could now enjoy far greater privacy, as the flat was too small to put up guests. People likened it to a monastic cell, or at least the Metropolitan's own *pairidaeza*, into which he could retreat in seclusion.

Parishioners coming for private appointments and other visitors now saw him in the corresponding room on the other side of the apse – known as the 'vestry' but also used as a parish meeting room, where tea was served on Sundays after the Liturgy. This enabled him to keep his flat free from what he called 'atmospheres': the remembered presence of people and their problems.

He took great delight in living in God's house. He was insistent that on entering a church everyone should stop, look around and take in the fact that they were on holy ground, in a place where God was King, where, unlike the world outside, his rule of love prevailed.

He relished the beauty and the peace of his own cathedral. Walking through the church one morning as the sunlight came streaming in through the south windows he remarked, 'Doesn't the church look beautiful at this time of day!' These words were spoken with a sense of wonder – and more than twenty years after his move there – because that sense of wonder never waned.

But the cathedral was in danger. The twenty-one-year lease on the building was due to expire in 1977, and there was talk of the Church of England selling it off to become perhaps a Chinese restaurant. Metropolitan Anthony was not the only person horrified at the thought, and he began seriously to consider whether the parish could somehow find the money to buy it. The Church of England made an offer. It would be willing to sell the cathedral to the Russian parish for the price of £80,000 with a restricted covenant preventing the building from being used for any purpose other than as a place of worship. Since this was a time of rapid price increase in the property market it was an important point; the cathedral, situated in Knightsbridge, was on prime building land. The covenant meant that the parish would not be able to sell it off for redevelopment, rebuild in a cheaper part of London and pocket the difference. When Metropolitan Anthony informed the Patriarchate of the situation he was met with a proposal: the Church was prepared to buy the cathedral and put the building at the London parish's disposal. He refused the offer, and decided his parish – numbering about one hundred and twenty people – would somehow have to raise the money itself. Towards the end of 1976 Metropolitan Anthony addressed the AGM of his parish, recommending purchase. What he had to get across to the doubters was the idea that vision was more important than good sense. If all people could see was the present parish, then to take on All Saints was foolish. But for anyone who envisaged a church for future generations of believers, alive and outward-looking, it was absolutely essential.

For property in Knightsbridge £80,000 was not a great sum; for the London parish it was enormous. He received a telephone call from the widow of Professor Frank: 'Father Anthony! I always knew you were mad, but I never knew you were quite this mad!' His reply was: on your bones and mine we will build a church that will be necessary for thousands of people. It was this prophetic vision rather than madness that impelled him to save the cathedral, and in January 1977 he persuaded the parish council to agree to its purchase and to set up a staged appeal to raise the money.

CHAPTER TEN

A MAN OF VISION

During Metropolitan Anthony's half century in Britain Western Christianity underwent dramatic changes. From the innovations spawned by the Second Vatican Council to the introduction of house churches and new theologies, a general aggiornamento took hold and flourished – accompanied, for the most part, by a relentless decline in church attendance. Matters of doctrine, even the central truths of Christianity such as the resurrection, were fudged or in some quarters dismissed, or else reduced to a fundamentalist, literalist belief in the Bible.

Against all this the Orthodox Church stood immutable in its ageless faith and worship, obstinately different – and to some outsiders hopelessly outdated – yet battling successfully in Eastern Europe against persecution.

Metropolitan Anthony was aware of all the subtle and more complex nuances beneath the surface. Too well he recognised the faults of his own Church on the ground, which he nevertheless loved and served faithfully. But he also knew Orthodoxy in all its grandeur and depth, and he spent his life bringing out of this depth a pure, unadulterated Orthodox faith, freed from the outward trappings of nationalism, superstition and political manoeuvring – things that were in danger of clipping the wings of the Holy Spirit in other places. His vision of Orthodoxy was also free from the dead traditionalism often mistaken for true Tradition. Folk customs dressed up as piety were not part of his agenda. He pared down his own episcopal celebration of the Liturgy from the modern Russian over-emphasis on the bishop, and turned it back to God. He was not concerned with outward appearances, nor with a rigorous following of the rulebook. After his death one of his young priests, Father Stephen Platt, used the phrase during an inspired retreat, 'God doesn't need the paperwork.'

Those may not have been Metropolitan Anthony's own words but they were certainly in the spirit of his teaching. Because he discovered Christianity not through the Church with all its ritual, symbolism and structures but through the gospel, in the presence of Christ, his vision of Christianity began, continued and ended with the simple truth of the Gospel message. He was more than happy to use the word 'simple' in this context, not as a rejection of intellectual discipline but of 'simply' taking up one's cross and following the risen Christ and, as best as one could, living the commandments, the Beatitudes and the Lord's example and following him to Calvary.

Metropolitan Anthony loved and revered St Paul, whom he may have taken as a model for his own life of mission. But he had no time for opposing one of the saint's passages with another, as he put it, nor for the Western academic and juridical approach to theology. He knew well the Greek Fathers and the Desert Fathers of Egypt, whose lives, simple in concept but extraordinarily hard in the living, went to the heart of the Gospel. He had a great love of the lives of the saints, especially the Russian saints and startsi, and enormous respect for the twentieth-century theologians of the Russian Emigration, many of whom he had known personally. He also appreciated and revered the great saints of Western Christianity; he was always ready to acknowledge holiness and love for God wherever he found it. He had absolutely no empathy with the nitpicking or liberalism of contemporary Western theologians. He had had his share of dissecting the dead as a doctor. Leaving the scholarly dissection of Christianity to those whose interest was the dead body of academic theology, he spoke with the fire of the Spirit from a living heart.

He was quick to emphasise that he was by training not a theologian but a scientist; and when he was awarded an honorary Doctorate of Divinity by the Moscow Patriarchate he responded by referring to it as 'a cloak of honour to cover my ignorance'. He was always happy to apply his scientist's enquiring, rigorously trained mind to matters of faith, in order to seek the reality behind the apparent truth; but for him the classic definition of a theologian was that of Evagrius of Pontus: one who prays. His theology was the knowledge of God acquired through prayerful adoration. His teaching was centred on communicating his experience, in accordance with the Gospel, of the God he knew, worshipped and followed. Very necessary. Very simple. And not at all easy. He never equated being simple with being easy, especially in the struggle to live the Christian life. He acknowledged that whatever one's beliefs or churchmanship, one could be termed a heretic by not living one's faith.

Experience was at the heart of his message. He urged his spiritual children to express their faith to others with the words: I know God because I have met him. He was adamant that unless an encounter with God had taken place, faith was something borrowed, unverified, an intellectual or emotional exercise that was likely to evaporate when challenged by people or by life. And faith had to encompass faithfulness. It was not just a matter of believing, but of following Christ with unswerving devotion.

He was very, very wary of emotion. In his eyes it was something false, easily manipulated, a dangerous substitute for feeling – that deep movement of the heart that responds to God but is not swayed by externals. Only too conscious of the attraction of Russian Orthodox worship – the haunting music, the incense, the ritual, the icons – to people who found the exotic a refuge, he deliberately made conversion a long and testing process. Answering questions on doubt at a youth conference he reiterated that people whose faith was founded on hearing of the experience of others were only at the beginning of a process which must end in an encounter of their own.

'We all recite the Creed and use the prayers of the Church. But what do I know about it except that I've heard others asserting such things? What difference does it make to my life? Then one day something we have always known becomes an experience, so deep, so explosive, that it does make all the difference to our lives.'

He would sum up the Creed: 'It says only one thing to us: we have a God who loves and who calls us to be like him.'

God's love was at the centre of his understanding of Christianity. It had overwhelmed his own life: the teenager who had experienced the world as a desolate, unloving place had been transfigured by the love Christ had shown to him in coming into his presence. That transfiguring love, unconquerable, unlike anything else, continued to resonate throughout his life. Having responded wholeheartedly to the love of God he projected the figure of a man who embodied what was said of the Apostles: someone who could turn the world upside down. This was, he insisted, the only way for a Christian to live: to become the message, someone recognisably different, someone illumined with the light of the Gospel, someone who was on fire, like the burning bush, and whose whole life radiated the Holy Spirit.

Although he was unusual among Orthodox in his quasi-Evangelical declaration of his own conversion experience, he did expect his flock to have come to know God in their own way and to proclaim the fact, if not in words then certainly in their lives. He had not the slightest doubt about the truth and purity of Orthodox doctrine, but knew that it was not enough to proclaim that truth. The saints had spoken of a God whom they had met. This was not philosophical knowledge; they were not necessarily educated people, but they were enlightened.

He was unhappy at the way adults could foist rationality on to children, stifling their response to God, and he would recount how in Paris a young boy of six had, just after Easter, driven his parents mad by continuously chanting in the sing-song way of children the words of the Easter hymn: Christ is risen from the dead, trampling down death by death; and to those in the tombs he has given life. When his parents could stand it no more and told him to stop he replied, 'Don't you understand what joy it gives him?' The boy had recognised a truth that made sense to him.

He was also impressed by an incident told him by a friend, Father Silvestre, during the German occupation of France. Among some Ukrainian families who had fled west there was a boy of eleven whose words, thoughts and attitude were those of the Gospel. Amazed, Father Silvestre asked his parents how the boy knew the Gospel so well. They replied that he had never heard of the Gospel, or of Christ, because it would have been too dangerous for them to have spoken about religion in their homeland. Instead they had made a rule never to speak anything contrary to the Gospel. In this way the child had unconsciously acquired the mind of Christ. Acquiring the mind of Christ was a recurrent theme in Metropolitan Anthony's teaching. But he was well aware of what held people back. 'We are afraid,' he would say. 'If I let myself go, what will be left?' His response to this fear was to answer:

> Be free, and let God's light shine. To be free of all things and enslaved by nothing we must act as someone living in a room cluttered by acquisitions of the past. Say: What don't I need? What things are a nuisance? Take them and give them to God. Get rid of hindrances. But this must not be a chance to pride ourselves on our generosity, because we have merely given to God what belongs to the dustbin. Then as other things surface, we must give them to God until only the essentials remain. We must gradually acquire this mastery: to give without regret, daringly, with joy. But we can let go only if we do not fear annihilation. We must let go of our self-centredness.

It was a question, he said, of acquiring spiritual muscle and tackling one after the other successive evils, giving more and more space to the vision of God within and less and less to the ugliness. This could only be achieved through prayer – not only the prayer of words but an act of placing oneself before God in silence, without making any requests or even praise, but simply listening in humility, reverence and receptiveness.

He saw Christianity as the only true humanism, in which humanity's greatness had already been seen in full measure in Christ the perfect man. He would quote the occasion when, on a visit to Moscow, he had been stopped on the steps of the Stalin-gothic Hotel Ukraina by a Party member, who, seeing his cassock, came up and said, 'I take it you're a believer. I'm an atheist.'

'Well, that's your loss,' Metropolitan Anthony replied. Taken slightly aback the man went on, 'You believe in God. I believe in man.'

'Then you and God have something wonderful in common, because he believes in man too.' The communist was not to be put down. Stretching out his arm he said, 'Show me your God in the palm of your hand.' Metropolitan Anthony noticed he was wearing a wedding ring.

'You're married? Do you love your wife?'

'Of course,' came the reply.

'I don't believe you.'

'I can prove it,' the man said. 'I bring her flowers, I buy her presents.'

'You could just be trying to get round her. That's no proof.' The man became increasingly upset as he failed to satisfy the bishop's criteria for proof of his love. Finally Metropolitan Anthony held out his own hand and said, 'Show me your love in the palm of your hand.'

He would also declare that the atheist had something else in common with God. Speaking of Christ's words on the Cross, 'My God, my God, why hast thou forsaken me?' and his descent into hell, he would say, 'Christ has plumbed the depth beyond all atheists. Even the most devastating experience of atheism is not outside the experience of Christ. So we must look at the godless world with new eyes. We can look at it with a depth it does not have itself – stranded, wounded, blinded but as full of virtual holiness as any member of the Church. The purpose of our relationship with the world is to call out of it all the meaning dormant within it. Look at the world with the eyes of Christ. Bring sparks to fruition. The Church is not an army of people proselytising. Having become Christ's incarnate presence we should become the dwelling-place of the Spirit.'

He was insistent on this non-proselytising nature of the Church;

> We do not try to win people over to Orthodoxy, but we are a missionary Church in the sense that we believe with all our hearts that

Orthodoxy is infinitely precious, is capable of bringing joy and vision to people both of things divine and of human relationships and of our total attitude to the created world, and we want to share it – whether people become Orthodox technically or not is something which is secondary to us. What matters to us is that they should become partakers of this exulting joy and wonder which Orthodoxy is. So what we should do is to be a presence that is convincing: that is, that looking at us people should see on our faces, in our eyes, in our behaviour, a dimension of wonder, joy and also of a sincere and sober desire to serve; and a disciplined mind and heart capable of serving faithfully whomever is in need of being served. And I think that if we became even a small light – if we became nothing but a handful of salt that prevents corruption – if we could bring a little hope to the hearts of people who have lost all hope, a little faith in the sense of trust and faithfulness and knowledge of God, a little love, we would be fulfilling our vocation. This is what we should bring, each of us perhaps a crumb, all of us all we possess, and express this in the readiness to give without asking any return.

He knew this was a tall order. 'It requires true saintliness to see the divine light shining in the darkness of another's personality,' he said. 'But to be seen as an icon of God could be for a person redemption. It is impious to venerate icons without venerating our neighbour, for in serving our neighbour we adore God.'

He had an exalted view of the Church as it could and should be, and a realistic understanding of how it actually was. The Church, he said, could be defined from two angles: the external view of a body united by the same hierarchical structures, doctrine and liturgy; and that of a living organism of love, a body both human and divine, the place where God and his creation were mysteriously at one. As the Body of Christ it was the temple of the Holy Spirit, but each person singly was also called to be the temple of the Holy Spirit. So both the Church at large and all its members were pervaded by the Spirit's presence to a lesser or greater extent according to their faithfulness to Christ.

The unity of the Body of Christ was the essence and the reality of the Church, and everything else, all its structures, served that purpose. But its members were at the same time citizens of the Kingdom already come, while still needing to grow towards acquiring the mind of Christ and becoming real limbs of one Body.

The vocation of the members of the Church was to become an icon of the Holy Trinity. The only real structure of the Church, the only way in which it could fulfil that vocation, was to express all the relationships – of love, freedom, holiness and so forth – found within the Trinity. The Church was called to the same dynamism of perichoresis which the Fathers had described in the Trinity.

Metropolitan Anthony defined two elements in the life of the Church: the necessity for structures because of human imperfection and the need to be guided, like a river needing banks; and the Living Water of Christ which flowed in that river.

The Church was an icon which had been painted perfect but which had, like so many other icons, been damaged over the centuries. The vocation of Christians was to restore the icon to its perfect beauty. While the action of the Holy Spirit was within each person and within the Church – both the local body and the Universal Church – there was still imperfection and frailty that necessitated outward structures to prevent the body from collapsing. But the temptation for the Church was to be structured according to the worldly principles of hierarchy and power, of enslavement and irrelevance. The laity was often seen as an irrelevance, an obedient flock to be guided by the hierarchy. That attitude was often the practice in Orthodoxy, and, he thought, the theological principle in Rome, where power was concentrated ultimately in the papacy and the Church thought of as a pyramid with the Pope at the top. That was, he said, a heresy against the Church and a blasphemy, because no one had the right to stand at the apex claimed by the Pope except Christ. It was not only foreign to the authentic collegiality of the episcopacy as understood by Orthodoxy but also foreign to the nature of the Church, which ought to be a stranger to secular power structures. It was another reason for his deep dislike of the Roman Church.

The true structure of the Church, he maintained, consisted in a hierarchy of service. It was a situation of authority, the ability to convince, in contrast to one of power, the ability to compel. Authority, he would say, was the attitude of Christ, who presented to the world all the beauty, all the holiness, all the greatness of the human vocation and potentiality and said, 'This is what you are. Look at yourself with my eyes. You are beautiful. You are great. Why do you make yourself small and ugly?' The way the notion of authority had gradually been displaced in the Church by that of power disturbed him profoundly.

The vocation of the hierarchy was to have authority but no power. To regain that would be to come nearer to fulfilling the Church's vocation of being a living body, an organism of sacrificial love. The Church had to take to heart the words of Christ, 'If anyone wants to be first, let him be a servant to all.'

The true structure of the Church was an inverted pyramid, resting on the shoulders of Christ himself. From him the structure began, pervaded by the Holy Spirit. On his shoulders stood the patriarchs and above them the metropolitans, the bishops, the clergy and people, directed upwards; each rank bearing the burdens of those above him in this inverted pyramid.

This figure of the Church as an inverted pyramid, which Metropolitan Anthony used on several occasions, was in fact a quotation from the writings of Archimandrite Sophrony of Tolleshunt Knights. It was a vision, he knew, that had largely been lost; and it could only be restored by recapturing the role and dignity of the laity. The laity – from the Greek 'laos' meaning people – denoted the whole People of God, the universal royal priesthood of all believers, including the clergy. That had largely been forgotten in practice. Until it was restored, however, it was impossible to think of Church structures being in the image of the Trinity. Metropolitan Anthony would quote an occasion when he was asked to speak at a conference to which clergy were not admitted, and was introduced as 'a layman in clerical garments'. That, he said, summed up the position of the clergy regarding their place in the *laos*.

Just as the substance of the Trinity was the total equality of the Three Persons, so there was total equality of all the members of the Church. The hierarchical structure should be one in which the person who served best as the slave of others was greatest in the sight of God. One reason it was not visible was due to the liturgical systems that had taken as their model the imperial court of Byzantium. In that context it was not difficult for the bishop to feel himself at the head of the body with lesser ministers and a flock beneath him. But that was a false picture.

His own diocese was meant to serve as a model – which Metropolitan Anthony hoped others would imitate – of how a diocese, whether Orthodox or otherwise, could be, by nature and in practice. It was a rare, if not unique attempt at realising the vision of the Church according to the Gospel and Orthodox Tradition: that is, being true both to proper ecclesiastical structures and to the simplicity of Christ's teaching, the two aspects united in a harmonious whole rather than opposed as irreconcilable differences. The diocese was also meant as a model of church life in being morally and administratively free. Metropolitan Anthony cherished its independence from the State. It was also free from interference, in practice, from the Patriarchate, another thing he cherished and hoped would continue beyond his lifetime.

In accordance with the model of the inverted pyramid he saw himself, as a diocesan bishop, carrying the episcopal load and exercising authority – but doing so from a position of service. In his eyes it was essential for him to live out, to the limits of his ability, Christ's example of authority coupled with humility. The notion of a bishop 'ruling' rather than serving, which he lamented elsewhere, was contrary to everything Metropolitan Anthony held dear. An example of the way he visibly put this into practice was an occasion, at a Vigil service which was being taken by a young priest visiting from Russia, when dressed just in his cassock he acted as a server to him, preparing the censer and carrying the candle before him at the Entrance.

He truly saw himself, as many others did, as the father of his diocese, exercising a paternal role. 'I have great affection for this congregation,' he once said, and that was true both for the parish as a whole and for individuals. He knew everyone by name and showed genuine warmth towards them, and his behaviour was absolutely devoid of airs and graces. For instance, since he lived in the cathedral he acted as its caretaker. Morning and evening he would make the rounds, checking security, making sure the gas was turned off in the hall kitchen, regulating the heating. When inconsiderate parishioners went home after a talk leaving the chairs out of place he would spend the rest of the evening putting them back. However, he might later chastise the congregation for its thoughtlessness with the words: 'I don't mind doing it – I can command chairs better than I can command people – but this is not the way for a Christian community to behave.'

When he was in his seventies he happened to let slip one year that on Easter Day, having celebrated the four-hour Paschal midnight service and then at the end having to wait for the BBC to unrig the recording equipment before locking up, he would snatch a few hours of sleep, then get up and spend seven or eight hours scraping the worst of the candle wax off the cathedral floor so that the cleaners would have less to do on the Monday morning. Immediately a group of volunteers offered to take over this chore, and in view of his age and increasing ill-health he reluctantly agreed.

He was probably unique as a bishop in being involved in the cleaning and care of his cathedral in this way. It was by no means because he was less busy than other bishops; his workload was enormous. Nor was it entirely due to the lack of paid staff. His physical care of the building stemmed partly from his devotion to it as the house of God and the deep reverence this inspired in him, and partly from his total lack of pomposity. There could be no task beneath a follower of Christ the Servant King. Just as he had cleaned out the hospital stove when he was an army surgeon, so he would tackle the sink if somebody carelessly poured tea leaves down it (and leave a hand-written notice reminding people not to do it again with the words: 'it has taken hours to unblock').

In all this he was putting into practice the words of the Russian saint, Seraphim of Sarov, who had said, 'Anything to do with the church is like an inner, kindling flame, and looking after it is the best work of all. The humblest task in the church, be it only cleaning the floor, is a nobler work than anything else', though it has to be said St Seraphim was addressing his words to nuns.

On one occasion, following a communal meal for parents and children when volunteers for washing up were slow to come forward, he announced, 'I'll do it.' Only by this very sincere offer of help were the consciences of the parents stirred, and they shooed him out of the kitchen. In his more energetic days he was also sometimes found tending the cathedral garden.

During the years of the Effingham Conferences he liked to set up the altar table himself. At the end of the conference he would pack everything away. One year, when he had been particularly exhausted, a parishioner came upon him in the vestry on the Sunday afternoon carefully wrapping up his episcopal candlesticks and vestments, whistling contentedly under his breath as he worked. When she protested that people would gladly have relieved him of the job he replied, 'No. I like to do it.' However, Metropolitan Anthony never confused personal humility with the dignity proper to the authority of a bishop. He was conscious of the charism conferred by his ordination and was never tempted, as Protestant clergy sometimes are, to let his private informality encroach on his liturgical behaviour. In services he conducted himself impeccably as a bishop, with all the reverence of which he was capable.

That did not preclude the informality which lies just under the surface of Orthodox worship. When in old age he celebrated the Vigil, where the clergy stand for some time in the centre of the nave, he would have a chair positioned to take the strain off his legs. On one occasion during Holy Week, when he was sitting flanked by several priests, each of them having to cense the church in turn, he noticed that the young boy in charge of the censer was finding it difficult to fathom to which priest he should hand it next. From then on he kept eye contact with the lad, making small gestures to him to direct him to the right priest. It was a lovely display of humanity in the midst of the elaborate and solemn ceremony going on around him.

These apparently inconsequential examples were small manifestations of something very deep: his conviction that the sacramental priesthood and episcopate had genuinely to share the characteristics of Christ's life of humility and service, not by making the occasional grand gesture – he was never one to make grand gestures – but by living the basic, simple life he had so admired among the clergy of the Paris emigration. He had witnessed how their impoverishment born of necessity had become a paragon of the Gospel and he was determined that a similar frame of mind should prevail in his own diocese. Thus the salary structure of his London clergy – virtually all the clergy in the other parishes being non-stipendiary – was also an inverted pyramid, with the priests, married family men, paid more than the bishops who, being monks, had only themselves to support and who were expected to adopt his very frugal lifestyle.

In relating the model of the inverted pyramid to the church on the ground he made it clear that the essence of the ministry was sacramental, the vocation of priests being to bring to God the elements of this created world so that they were taken out of the context of sin and brought into the context of God. The administrative aspect was something incidental. The vocation of the clergy was to create situations in which God could act. Describing the function of the clergy at the Liturgy, he said: 'The Liturgy is celebrated by no one but Christ himself. He is the only High Priest of all creation. We can say words, we can make gestures, but the one who brings forth these gifts to God is Christ, and the power that changes these gifts into the Body of Christ and the Blood of Christ, transforms the waters which we bring from the well into the waters of life eternal and so on, is the Holy Spirit.' The bread and wine of the Liturgy remained bread and wine, yet at the same time they were filled by the power of the Holy Spirit to become the Body and Blood of Christ.

He would tell the story of the young priest who one day at the beginning of the Liturgy was so overcome with awe that he felt he dare not celebrate. At that moment he suddenly became aware of an unseen presence coming forward to stand between him and the altar, so that he had to take a step back to make room. And he was able to continue the service in the realisation that it was truly Christ who was celebrating, while he only conveyed the words to the congregation.

Acknowledging this sacramental function of the ordained ministry,

Metropolitan Anthony nevertheless saw the vocation of all people, from the beginning of Genesis onwards, to sanctify creation. The dominion given to humanity by God had been misinterpreted as the right to govern and enslave. Its real meaning was not to dominate but to be a master who guided the whole creation into the fullness of unity with God.

Each human being, he insisted, was called to that vocation to bring into the realm of God everything surrounding him. It was itself a priestly function, and all members of the Church were chrismated as kings, priests and prophets. Each person was called to take the elements of the world – not only things but also relationships – that had become alienated from God, and bring them back to him, to integrate them into the mystery of communion with God.

Christ and the Holy Spirit had entered the world, and had committed to the Church the sacramental ministry in which the priest was sent like a victim into the sanctuary on behalf of the people. That, he was convinced, was the essence of the ordained ministry, which was a development within the royal priesthood of all believers and not something external to it.

A wide variety of non-sacramental work could therefore be undertaken by the laity, whether male or female – a principle he encouraged in his own diocese, where at various times the posts of Chairman of the Diocese, Diocesan Secretary and representatives to outside bodies were held by women. Metropolitan Anthony was fully aware that the Church in Russia was, for historical reasons, not currently open to ideas such as these. He realised that much time was needed for readjustment, which he thought could begin at the level of the parish priest and confessor. In particular he saw a problem of the misuse of power by newly ordained priests who had not been trained to listen to the Holy Spirit. To these 'young elders' he would say: 'A guide can lead only from a place where he has been to a place where he has been. You have never been in heaven. You can only share the little you have discovered, and not put burdens on the shoulders of people.'

He was never slow to criticise such bad practices; and in turn he received plenty of criticism. Towards the very end of his life there was a public burning of his books in one Russian town (the culprit was later duly chastised by the hierarchy) because his interpretation of the Gospel did not correspond to the ultra-conservative views of the right-wing, nationalist faction in the Russian Church.

One element of his preaching that particularly upset such hardliners was his views on the place of women in the Church. In his 1989 series of lectures on 'Man and Woman in Creation' he took as his starting point the opening chapters of Genesis. God had created man, the total anthropos containing both male and female, in a childlike state, and when this Adam had progressed sufficiently in maturity he had been divided into the two halves of male and female. Metropolitan Anthony questioned whether the notion of the rib of Adam should not be rather his side; in other words the division of the one body had been into two equal parts who could look at each other and see themselves reflected as 'alter ego – the other myself'. It was a situation, he maintained, of equality; God created Eve to be a partner to Adam, not a subordinate.

After the Fall, man and woman could no longer see each other as one in God, but as The Other. Instead of being the 'other myself', they had become 'alter' and 'ego': 'I am I and there goes another', in Metropolitan Anthony's words. 'In this tragedy of broken communion, the relationship between men and women becomes a destructive one because of fear, resentment and the desire to overpower what one is afraid of.' The obvious domination of women by men, and in a subtler way of men by women, was the result. But it was not God's first, or ultimate will.

The whole of history had consequently taken place in a twilight world where everything was equivocal. Yet God had been mysteriously present throughout history, a light shining in the darkness, culminating in his becoming tangible in the Incarnation. The Church must, Metropolitan Anthony insisted, go back to the beginnings of Genesis to find the real God-willed relationship between the sexes – a relationship that should have been restored at the Incarnation, when Christ assumed the total humanity of the anthropos, and not just maleness. But it had not been restored because, he said, humanity had not shaken off the world and its ambiguities. The duty of Christians was to work for the real integration of humanity; and not just between men and women but between all parts of society.

He was critical of the way in which this was overlooked in the Church. Undoubtedly the particular question of the ordination of women had been posed from outside, and the Church had replied negatively without any thought. But it was time, he said, for the thinking to begin.

'We must remember,' he said, 'that if the priesthood consists in being the person who makes Christ's Incarnation – his incarnate, bodily presence – possible, the first person who performed this function was the Mother of God, who was not merely a passive instrument of the Incarnation but whose faith was the condition of the Incarnation, and who in her person performed this sacramental act of the Incarnation. When we look at the Holy Gifts on the Holy Table after their consecration, if we speak of the physical presence, it is derived from the Mother of God as much, equally, as it is from the Father.'

However, he did not wish the issue of women's ordination to dominate the agenda. He considered it was time for Orthodoxy to take seriously the whole, wider issue of the place of women in creation and in the Church. He gave encouragement to women to raise their voices, although this encouragement could vary according to his mood. One day he might accuse the theologian Elisabeth Behr-Sigel of 'hiding behind me'. On another he might warn a prospective writer 'Don't be crucified for repeating what I say.' But overall he was anxious to spur women on to speak their minds and to promote them as much as he could. He even mischievously remarked, when he had refused an English convert who had come to him asking to be a priest (a situation he never liked), 'It's a pity we don't ordain women. I'd have ordained his wife any day!'

Nevertheless, while he was eager to put the subject of the place of women in the Church, and even their ordination, on the agenda for discussion, he knew that he could not go beyond that. Although he was often heard to say that the commonly held view that there was a rule forbidding women to enter the sanctuary was wrong – the rule was, he insisted, that only people with a function could enter the sanctuary – he was careful not to scandalise his congregation. He was said to have sounded out opinion in his congregation on allowing girls to serve in the altar but received a negative answer, and did not proceed further. During the last few years of the Metropolitan's life Father Michael Fortounatto organised a course for readers – that is, choir members, whether male or female, who intoned parts of the services including the Epistle at the Liturgy. At the end of the course the successful participants were presented with certificates. However, when Father Michael asked Metropolitan Anthony whether they could all be ordained to the minor order of reader his response was, 'Let's wait.'

It was not only in Russia that he was criticised. He was said to have been 'demonised' in North America by the more conservative elements of Orthodoxy there; and disapproval was voiced, too, in other places. 'I will be burnt as a heretic on a pyre of the complete works of Metropolitan Anthony,' he joked, appearing to relish the notoriety.

If his views on women were seen by some Orthodox as 'liberal', not a label he liked, his firm adherence to the central tenets of the Creed cast him as a conservative in the eyes of other churches and the media. He stood firmly against all those who wished to explain away the miracles of Christ or dispute his bodily resurrection.

The people who claimed to be too sophisticated to accept miracles were the very ones, he would affirm, who saw them in the least sophisticated way: as acts of magic, without seeing their deeper significance. Miracles occurred, he said, when circumstances arose that allowed the Kingdom of God to break through into the human situation: when, for instance, the faith of the Canaanite woman was such that, despite Christ's initial refusal to respond to her, the conditions of faith and love of the Kingdom were fulfilled.

'Every one of God's miracles was introduced, and so to speak conditioned, by the participation of man,' he said in a sermon in 1980. 'It depends on us that the Kingdom which we pray and long for is established.' That meant, in order for God to act freely, people had to open their eyes to the needs of others and be prepared to give of themselves for them to receive the Kingdom. It was not enough to wait on God, or even to pray. A human movement of faith and love was essential. The supreme example had been the Mother of God's acceptance of the angel's message at the Annunciation. Without her cooperation the Incarnation could not have happened; but it was not enough to revere her. Every Christian had to 'Hear the word of God and do it' in order for the reality of the Kingdom to be realised in the human situation. When that happened, the natural world could be fulfilled according to higher laws.

He would return again and again to the creation:

> The act of creation is not an act of power but an act of love; God loves us into existence, calls us to share not only all that he possesses but also all that he is. He offers us to become partakers of the divine nature, he offers us to become sons and daughters of his; but this relationship is possible only within the frightening category which we call freedom. The act of creation is the moment when God gives himself unreservedly, perfectly, ultimately, to us and does it with that passion, that mettlesome quality like the fire that communicates its very substance to the burning bush.

He saw that purifying fire present whenever human love could so join itself to the love of God that he was able to renew and recreate.

The creation out of nought of the material cosmos by an act of love was for Metropolitan Anthony one proof that God's care was for everything and everyone. Another was the bodily resurrection of Christ. To anyone who expressed doubts about it, he would respond that the really difficult thing to believe was Christ's death. How could someone who was, so to speak, plugged into eternal life, die?

'For Christ to die,' he said, 'was something infinitely more monstrous and contrary to nature than for us, and that is what he is confronted with in the Garden of Gethsemane. Then on the Cross "My God, my God, why hast thou forsaken me?" is not simply a cry of agony, and it is even less, I believe, the rehearsing of a psalm. One does not rehearse a psalm when one is dying a violent death. The psalm is directed towards the event and not the other way round. And the descent into hell is the ultimate point of Christ's solidarity with us.'

The ultimate glory was, he said, the bodily resurrection and ascension of Christ. He had taken his humanity into eternity. 'The fullness of God can fill matter and matter remains itself, only it is transfigured, it becomes glorious, it is freed from limitation and mortality, as we see it in the resurrection and ascension of Christ; so that Christ reveals to us both the mystery of God and all there is in this mystery which is accessible to the created world, to us and to all things.'

With this exalted understanding of the material world he developed a keen interest in environmental and ecological concerns, devoting one of his diocesan conferences to the subject. Orthodoxy, he felt, had a theology of matter that Western Christianity, plagued by the view that the physical world had been tainted by the Fall, needed to hear.

The human response to God's love for the world must be, he insisted, gratitude. 'We should be doing everything to give joy to the Lord out of thankfulness and amazement at his love,' he said in the context of the resurrection. But he was insistent, too, on gratitude for all God's gifts. The world was to be cherished, treated with respect and offered back to God by all people in their role as kings, priests and prophets.

He also saw gratitude as a useful tool with which to fight pride and vanity. He gave as an illustration the story of a young girl who came to see him with the most appalling expression on her face. He asked what was the matter and she said, 'I am a sinner. I am vain. When I see my reflection in the mirror I find that I'm lovely to look at.'

'So you are,' he replied.

'But what shall I do? I'm perishing because of this vanity.'

'Replace it with gratitude,' he said. 'Place yourself twice a day in front of the mirror and detail all the features you find lovely. Every time you find something lovely in your face, say to God, "Lord, thank you for having given me gratuitously this present." And when you will have finished detailing all your features, stop one minute and say, "Lord, forgive me that on such a lovely face I put such a horrid expression."'

He would remind his listeners that the word 'eucharist' meant 'thanksgiving' and that giving thanks to God with joy was the natural response of Christians to his love. That had been his own reaction on finding faith, and all his zeal, dedication – and in his younger days energy – stemmed from this joyful gratitude to the God who had rescued him from the hell of godlessness.

But it was definitely not a happy-clappy type of joy. It was a joy of self-giving, that had to be prepared to witness in the ultimate way, through martyrdom if necessary. Metropolitan Anthony was fond of repeating St Paul's words, 'My strength is made manifest in weakness.' The Early Church, he said, conquered the ancient world not because it was strong in human terms but because it was pliable in the hands of God. It conquered the world because it did not put the divine wisdom to the test of human sagacity but because it followed Christ to Calvary.

He called upon the modern Church – not just the Orthodox Church but the whole of Christianity – to renew itself, not by a reformation that would turn the Church away from what it had been but by recapturing the lost vision of being Christ's body, broken for the salvation of the world.

CHAPTER ELEVEN

❧ ❧

LOOKING OUTWARDS

(1977–1992)

T he appeal to buy the cathedral was a huge but rewarding effort.
Parishioners worked with passion and dedication in whatever
ways they could to raise money, from baking cakes to donating
prized possessions for sale. A professional fundraiser was
employed. The next stage was to invite donations from outside the
diocese, and the Anglicans in particular were extremely generous. Many
people were glad to be able to repay something of the debt they owed to
Metropolitan Anthony as a man who had deeply influenced their faith.

The appeal was also an act of mission, bringing the church to the attention of more and more people. A charity concert was organised at the
Royal Opera House. Ikon Records added new recordings to its list, which
encouraged visitors to come and hear the music at first hand. The sale of
icons and Orthodox books made an impact: the Cathedral Bookshop was
to become a valuable resource for English and Russian speakers wishing
to further their knowledge of Orthodoxy.

In 1977 the Patriarchate awarded Metropolitan Anthony with the Order
of St Sergius. He was honoured to receive this recognition from his own
Church, following on from the Anglican Lambeth Cross two years earlier.
The Anglicans meanwhile continued their patronage, inviting him to
preach at the Lambeth Conference the following year.

Metropolitan Anthony was keen to put his diocese on a firm administrative footing, with its own Statutes, charitable status and structures. To
this end he set up a steering committee to plan the formation of a
Diocesan Assembly, to meet twice yearly. The Assembly first met in
February 1977, with Metropolitan Anthony as President. Other members

were the presbytery of the diocese and lay members personally chosen by him. The meeting appointed a Diocesan Statutes Committee, consisting of Archpriest (later Bishop) Basil Osborne, priest of the Oxford parish, Costa Carras and Dr Andrew Walker, who presented a first text of Statutes to the Assembly at its meeting in May 1979. These were adopted, but work continued on them and several revisions were made over the next twenty years. They took into account the particular situation in Britain, and English law, especially with reference to the diocese's charitable status. During all that time the diocese received no formal acceptance of its Statutes from the Moscow Patriarchate, but it did receive permission to live by them.

The unusual aspect of the Statutes was the provision for the diocese to elect its own bishop, whose name would then be forwarded to the Holy Synod for approval. This was contrary to the prevailing Statutes of the Patriarchate, which gave the right of appointing bishops to the Patriarch and Holy Synod.

The Diocesan Assembly went on to become a largely elected body and, together with the Diocesan Council, again a mix of clergy and lay representatives, played a crucial role in the development of diocesan life.

Although these were both in theory democratic institutions Metropolitan Anthony himself was no democrat, and was liable to ignore issues that he did not find congenial. In general he was able to use his considerable charm, and the knowledge that he was much loved and revered, to do things in his own way with little opposition. Administration was never his strong point but lack of finance – the diocese remained totally self-supporting – meant he was never to have any paid staff. Metropolitan he might be, but he was also parish priest, his own secretary and administrator, and the cathedral's caretaker.

The appeal was drawing to a successful close. The purchase of the cathedral was finally concluded and the diocese became a registered charity in the summer of 1979. In the same year two joyful events took place in the name of St John the Baptist. On 18 March Deacon John Lee, a young American whose patron was the Forerunner, was ordained priest. He was to remain a loyal and much-loved supporter of his bishop and a mainstay of the London parish. The second event was the formation of the pan-Orthodox Fellowship of St John the Baptist, in which members of the Sourozh Diocese were to play a continuing part. It was to develop a full programme of meetings, a journal and an annual conference, drawing people from the various Orthodox jurisdictions.

The largest of these by far was the Greek Archdiocese of Thyateira.

Although inter-jurisdictional cooperation on a formal level remained minimal – pan-Orthodox Vespers on the first Sunday of Lent was its pub-lic face – Metropolitan Anthony enjoyed cordial relations with the Greek Archbishop. English converts and others in both jurisdictions began to hope that one day there might come into being an autocephalous Orthodox Church for Britain, which would be totally inclusive of all nationalities. The existing situation, where each national jurisdiction had built up parallel structures, was uncanonical and was the major problem of the Orthodox diaspora worldwide; and by the end of Metropolitan Anthony's lifetime it was to be no nearer a solution. There was in practice no possibility that the Russian and Greek hierarchies would unite with, say, Metropolitan Anthony agreeing to become the Greek Archbishop's second in command, or vice versa.

Another new initiative was set up: the 'Voice of Orthodoxy', a radio station broadcasting to the Soviet Union, was not directly a diocesan con-cern but it had Metropolitan Anthony's blessing, and he was to continue speaking regularly for it for years, as he was for the BBC and Radio Liberty, aware how important a part of his ministry these broadcasts were.

The farthest community of the diocese came into being, in Dunblane, where a handful of Orthodox began to come together and, from time to time, receive a visiting priest for the celebration of the Liturgy.

In early February the following year Father Lev Gillet concelebrated at the cathedral with Metropolitan Anthony and preached a sermon in which he spoke of the vocation of a bishop. In the presence of the man in whom he had seen the divine spark, had urged to seek ordination and had led to the altar to be consecrated bishop, while he himself remained a priest, he summed up his own vision of the episcopate. It was a call, he said, to a real 'spiritual suicide', the total gift of oneself not only to God but also to other people. These were to be parting words. On 29 March, the eve of Palm Sunday, Father Lev celebrated the Liturgy for the last time in St Basil's House. He died peacefully that afternoon in his eighty-seventh year. Metropolitan Anthony presided and gave the address at his funeral in the Greek Cathedral.

The two men had continued to have the greatest respect for one another during the years they were both in London – although on Metropolitan Anthony's part the respect could at times be tinged with jealousy. But he continued to value his former mentor's spirituality, par-ticularly his 'silent prayerfulness' at the Fellowship's conferences and retreats. On his part, Father Lev considered Father Anthony to be, of all the Orthodox priests in London, the one who 'carried within himself the most living spiritual flame'.

Nicolas Zernov died, aged eighty-two, in the same year, after a lifetime as an outstanding lay theologian and promoter of Orthodoxy, a founder and inspirer of the Fellowship of St Alban and St Sergius and a leading figure in the Oxford parish. According to his wife Militza he had cherished a longing to be a priest, but 'it was never given to him'.

The Metropolitan's busy schedule of talks, lectures and broadcasts showed no sign of letting up. In 1982 he had a hectic year lecturing at various British universities and institutions: he gave the Firth Lectures at Nottingham, the Eliot Lectures at Canterbury and the Constantinople Lecture in London. By the end of his life there was scarcely a university or theological college where he had not preached.

Some of these occasions were less successful than others. His habit of speaking without notes, or no more than a handful scribbled on a scrap of paper, could lead to unstructured and at times uninspired lectures in which he might bandy about a few less than accurate quotations from this or that source, giving the impression that he knew more about a subject than he actually did. He could get away with that in a pastoral context, but in an academic milieu it just would not do. This emphasised the difference between the theologian – an animal he never claimed to be – and the pastor. It was not that he did not have an analytical mind. His training as a scientist and doctor proved otherwise. Yet he knew his vocation was to speak from the heart to the hearts of his listeners rather than to their reason. His most successful sessions at universities were often the informal question and answer meetings with students, when he really came alive. One of those he liked to cite was an invitation to speak to the Christian students at Kings College, London on prayer. The meeting was relaxed, to the extent that the students were lounging in their chairs with their feet on coffee tables, eating sandwiches and drinking beer (it was lunchtime).

'Well,' he commented afterwards, 'I didn't mind the sandwiches so much, or even the beer – people do have to eat. But the casual manner they were stretched out: this is not the way to approach coming into God's presence.'

So he abandoned the talk he had meant to give and spoke, for only ten minutes, on the importance of physical discipline in a life of prayer, explaining the role of posture and the way the body and soul are meant to pray together.

'Set your alarm clock in the morning,' he told them, 'and two seconds after it rings, jump out of bed and have a cold shower to wake yourself up. Then you will be in a fit state to pray. Loafing around in an armchair will not give you the collectedness which is the prerequisite for a live relationship with God.'

The discipline he urged on his listeners did not always feature in his own life in his later years. He admitted finding it hard to get out of bed in the mornings; and sometimes he let his lethargy get the better of him in more serious ways. In particular his tendency to let people down at the last moment, whether for private appointments or for speaking engagements, gave the impression of a laissez faire attitude bordering on bad manners. For instance, he was a regular speaker at retreats held annually for Anglican clergy, which usually went well. But on one occasion he rang his driver, Father John Lee, on the evening before he was due to speak, asking him to go in his place. Father John, usually so biddable where his esteemed bishop was concerned, on this occasion refused. When Metropolitan Anthony then asked him to ring and give eleventh-hour apologies the hapless priest felt this was the last straw, and replied with a very firm no.

An even more serious non-attendance occurred when he had been invited to be the main speaker at a conference at the Episcopalian Cathedral of St John the Divine in New York. Although he plainly had no intention of making the journey, having made no travel arrangements, he did nothing about letting the conference organisers know until, the evening before he was due to speak, he sent them a telegram casually stating he would not be coming.

He was more diligent concerning his visits to the Soviet Union. The official business there was one aspect; the illegal private meetings were another, sometimes for instance under the guise of 'choir practice' in a priest's flat. Up to a hundred people would crowd into the cramped premises, and Metropolitan Anthony would speak and answer questions until he was exhausted. Thousands more, clergy as well as lay people, knew his voice from the short wave radio broadcasts he made. For years he was the voice of Russian Orthodoxy.

In between his engagements Metropolitan Anthony found some time to relax. Reading was always a favourite occupation; his room was lined with books. He also had a television (the licensing authority's computer could not, however, make any sense of his title and registered him as 'Mr M. Anthony') and he watched some surprising programmes, as was evidenced by a visit from a friend who came to collect a script from him at the cathedral.

'Have you seen the dog trainer Barbara Woodhouse on television?' Metropolitan Anthony asked the man.

'Yes.'

'Stay!' ordered the Metropolitan, running up the nave to his flat. As he went the friend, entering into the spirit of the game, shouted after him, 'Fetch!' When Metropolitan Anthony reappeared he had the script between his teeth. He ran up to his friend and released the paper on to his lap, whereupon the man patted him on the head with the words, 'Good boy!'

In the late spring of 1982 Pope Jean Paul II paid a visit to Britain. This became an ecumenical event involving the leaders of all the major churches, including the Orthodox. On 28 May Metropolitan Anthony attended a televised Mass in Westminster Cathedral, and on the following day another service, this time hosted by the Anglicans at Canterbury. He had shown reluctance to accept these invitations for more than one reason. Firstly, the weekend coincided with his own diocese's annual conference where he was always the central figure. Secondly, his antipathetic feelings towards the papacy came to the fore, and it was only with some persuasion that he agreed to take part.

At Canterbury the Pope was welcomed by the Archbishop of Canterbury, Robert Runcie, and both signed a Common Declaration setting out their plans and hopes for their pilgrimage towards future unity. Towards the end of the service they led a group of representatives from various churches in each placing a candle in remembrance of seven modern saints and martyrs. Metropolitan Anthony came forward to honour Mother (now Saint) Maria Skobtsova of Paris, and was embraced by the Pope as he returned to his seat. It was said, however, that afterwards, escaping back to his diocesan conference, he brushed his sleeve as if brushing off the Pope's touch.

Within Metropolitan Anthony's own diocese communities continued to expand and a number of new clergy were ordained. In 1983 he received an honorary doctorate from the Moscow Theological Academy, when he gave an inspired two-hour address on St Paul.

A successful initiative that had been set up by Father Michael Fortounatto was a monthly Family Liturgy at Parish House. Metropolitan Anthony had agreed to celebrate, Father Michael led the small choir of adults and children, and after the service there was a bring-and-share lunch in the basement, followed by lessons for the children, a talk for parents and games in Holland Park. This was a welcome opportunity for children to meet with camp friends and it became very popular. In 1983 the June Family Liturgy happened to fall on the nineteenth, Metropolitan Anthony's birthday. At the end of the service Metropolitan Anthony said, 'As there are several people who are celebrating birthdays or name days, let us sing "Mnogaya Leta" (Many Years) for them.' One of the choir members, a young woman, shouted out, 'It's Father Anthony's birthday, too!' When the singing was finished the Metropolitan retorted with a sarcastic edge to his voice, 'I didn't know we had a girl deacon.'

On the nearest Sunday to his seventieth birthday the following year, which happened to be the Patronal Feast of the cathedral, he was presented with a cake, made of ice cream, in the shape of a Russian church. He was very fond of ice cream; it was often served at the Patronal Feast, since one of the parishioners had access to a wholesale supply. Enough tubs were ordered so that there would be some left over to go into the church freezer housed in the cathedral, for Metropolitan Anthony's personal use later. Through the same supplier, ice cream cones would be served at the children's Christmas party each year, and, instead of a fictional bearded Santa Claus in red, the sight of a real bearded bishop in plain black cassock blessing the children as they came up to receive their presents, and later enjoying his ice cream cone, was a precious cameo.

Metropolitan Anthony was quick to acknowledge that he was 'no good at talking to children; words are my tools and they don't understand.' The Christmas party showed that to be true in the sense that when he recounted the story of the Nativity he could not adjust his language to their level. Nevertheless, they responded to his warmth and humour. One young boy, attending the party for the first time, was taken aback; the figure he had seen in church looking so forbidding in his vestments and mitre turned out to be amazingly human and showed a child-like interest in his party gift. (It was a bow and arrow. 'Are you going to shoot me?' Metropolitan Anthony asked him, with a mischievous look. 'No,' came the shy reply, and they both broke into smiles, their eyes sharing a lively innocence and sense of fun.)

The deaths of two old friends occurred in 1985. First Metropolitan Nicholas, who for nearly thirty years had been Father Anthony's bishop and who had been one of his consecrators, died in the spring. Six months later Archbishop Basil Krivoscheine of Brussels, who had spent some years serving the Oxford parish, died suddenly of a stroke in the Transfiguration Cathedral, St Petersburg, where he had been baptised nearly ninety years previously.

In the same month Metropolitan Anthony ordained to the priesthood Deacon Alexander Fostiropoulos, a Greek married to an Englishwoman and with a young family. He was to become a very welcome member of the London parish clergy and also to act as Orthodox chaplain to London University. As a former architect he was also able to give advice on building work. Parish House had needed some extensive repairs during this time, and at the Feast of the Protecting Veil of the Mother of God, 14 October, the chapel there was blessed for renewed use. It was an optimistic and peaceable time.

In the Church of England things were different. Its debate over the possible ordination of women to the priesthood seemed at first to have no bearing on the Orthodox Church. But as time went by and the issue was discussed ever more widely, Orthodox opinion was sought – and given, mainly in blanket statements of dismissal. Officially, the Russian Patriarchate expressed dismay over the possible move by the Anglicans. Metropolitan Anthony, however, began to think deeply about the subject and to come up with some surprising answers. He was not alone. The distinguished Orthodox lay theologian, Elisabeth Behr-Sigel, had already given talks on the subject of the place of women in the Church and in 1987 she published a daring and wonderful book, *Le ministère de la femme dans l'eglise*, published in English as *The Ministry of Women in the Church* in 1991. Metropolitan Anthony contributed the Preface to the French edition, in which he recommended the book 'with great joy' to 'all serious readers, to those who are ready to put aside their prejudices'. He called upon both Orthodox and Roman Catholics not to make hasty statements and suggested that, while the question of the ordination of women had for the Orthodox come from the outside, it must become one asked from the inside.

This was to be the beginning of his public support for the role of women in the Church, and he remained fearless in voicing his thoughts despite being pilloried by hardliners in both the Russian Church and the Church of England.

In the summer of 1987 the camp moved to a new site in the Brecon Beacons. Michael (Moo) Behr, a son of Tatisha and brother of Father Nicholas of the Bristol parish, had moved to a hillside farmhouse with his wife Sonia and their three children after spending many years in Africa working for Oxfam. The Behr family generously gave over their land, barns and house for half the summer holidays, and camp was to remain there, highly successfully, for more than a decade. The new location, however, proved too far for Metropolitan Anthony to travel. So ended more than sixty years of Orthodox camp life for him, although the camp was to continue undiminished in his absence as one of the most inspiring and lively parts of diocesan life.

The following year the Soviet Union celebrated the thousandth anniversary of Russian Christianity: the Baptism of Rus', when Prince Vladimir of Kiev's emissaries had famously returned from Constantinople exclaiming that in the Orthodox Liturgy they 'knew not whether they were on earth or in heaven'. The tottering Soviet system officially acknowledged this as a significant cultural event, not a religious one. But the Church was feeling its feet in the new spirit of Mikhail Gorbachev's 'glasnost' and by the end of the year few people, either in the Soviet Union or abroad, doubted the spiritual nature of the celebrations. Metropolitan Anthony described how he saw the Soviet government's stance.

> That it allowed the Millennium to become a national event is certain, and that it did so for its own reason is also certain – that reason being, as Gorbachev and Gromyko have put it, that the Church is the only body that can give a moral backbone to a nation that has broken down as far as a moral attitude to life is concerned. But on the other hand this Millennium is really a new Baptism of Russia, in the sense that millions of Russians are rediscovering God, rediscovering Christ, rediscovering a dimension of life which is the Kingdom of God, in spite of all the weakness and imperfections in the Church.

In May of the previous year Metropolitan Anthony had attended a week-long preparatory meeting in the Soviet Union. With 150 participants it was an intense programme of papers, debates and plenary sessions covering a plethora of topics ranging from Orthodox spirituality to the influence of Orthodoxy on Lutheran theology. Nevertheless the Metropolitan had found time for his usual unscheduled meetings, including one with the dissidents Father Gleb Yakunin and Alexander Ogorodnikov. Both gave him the impression that the new atmosphere of 'glasnost' provided opportunities for the revival of Christianity in Russia – something the Metropolitan witnessed himself in a meeting with twenty teenagers who were trying to set up support groups of believers of their own age. The Church was beginning to find a place in Soviet life. One of the characteristics he found was the increasing number of intellectuals and particularly scientists who were finding God and coming into the Church; and they were not coming blindly, but were asking searching and intelligent questions, and bringing a dimension of thought-out faith which the Church had lacked previously. There had been theologians at the top and very simple people at the bottom, with a dearth of mature, deep thinking in between. He saw the stirrings of this thinking, born of both tragedy and joy. He was also aware, however, that there were what he called differing opinions and undercurrents, and a resistance to change born of lack of thought.

The Western media looked on bemused at the Millennium, then saw political and other capital to be made out of the story and took it up with enthusiasm. There were articles in the press, radio and television programmes – not only discussions but services broadcast from Russia, something which would have been unthinkable just a few years earlier. Beneath the razzmatazz a deep spiritual change was going on as the Russian Church began to rattle her chains.

In Britain, Metropolitan Anthony and his diocese reacted by supporting the celebrations in whatever way they could. More than one pilgrimage to Russia was organised. Special services were arranged. The annual Pan-Orthodox Vespers took place at the cathedral and a pan-Orthodox Liturgy was held there in July. The Russian Millennium was beginning to become an ecumenical event, too. In mid-July Metropolitan Anthony was invited to celebrate the Divine Liturgy in Birmingham's Anglican Cathedral, and the following week he served Orthodox Vespers in Canterbury Cathedral in the presence of the bishops assembled for the Lambeth Conference and representatives of other denominations. In August he celebrated the Divine Liturgy at Tewkesbury Abbey. On 8 October, the feast of the great Russian saint Sergius of Radonezh, distinguished ecumenical guests were invited to the Liturgy at the cathedral, although the response was disappointing.

In June the Russian Church held a Local Council at Zagorsk, which Metropolitan Anthony and Father Michael Fortounatto attended together with Sir Dimitri Obolensky, as clergy and lay representatives of the diocese. Together with over 270 delegates there were a number of prominent ecumenical guests including the Archbishop of Canterbury.

The lay representative should have been elected by the Diocesan Assembly but Metropolitan Anthony chose Militza Zernov, the widow of Nicolas. The Patriarchate turned her down, however, saying that only men were eligible. This provoked much anger, especially since it subsequently became known that some dioceses had been allowed to send women. Metropolitan Anthony raised this question at the Council, making the point that not only had Militza, together with Nicolas, been outstanding witnesses to Orthodoxy in Britain, but that during the era of persecution the Russian Church had survived largely because of the faith and heroism of its women members and that it was monstrous for the Church to consider them unworthy to act as Council delegates.

Some interesting papers were given, including a report on the life and work of the Russian Church from 1918 to 1988, not an easy subject and one that would have been impossible before the advent of glasnost; and the draft of the new Statutes of the Russian Church, of particular interest to the Diocese of Sourozh, since the position of its own Statutes was still informal. On this occasion Metropolitan Anthony claimed to have given a copy of the Diocesan Statutes to Archbishop (later Metropolitan) Kirill of Smolensk with the request that he present them to the Holy Synod.

Mikhail Gorbachev, on behalf of the Communist Party, acknowledged publicly that terrible and wrong things had been done to believers, and he spoke of the Russian Church's need not to remain silent on that any longer. Two days were given over to open discussion, in which criticisms of both the Church and the State were voiced, in a new spirit of freedom.

Metropolitan Anthony had asked to speak, on condition he be given as long as he wanted. This was agreed, and he launched into a lengthy and bold address. He urged the Council to extend special greetings to the representatives of other Christian bodies, especially to the Russian Church Abroad. These remarks were greeted with long and heartfelt applause. He also called for the Russian Church to repent, both historically and personally, for having failed the nation in the past, and for continuing to fail to live up to its calling. 'We should be ashamed of the fact that no one meeting us would say, "This person possesses something which no one else possesses, an image of Christ and his eternal light."' It was his recurrent theme, and always aimed as much at himself as at his listeners.

He had delivered a powerful, inspirational and in places reproachful talk which brought his courageous and forward-looking outlook to a largely conservative body. Afterwards many Council members privately thanked him for his contribution.

Concluding the celebrations was a concert held at the Bolshoi Theatre and attended by the Patriarch, the delegates and members of the Soviet government. It proved a moving occasion, not only for the audience but for tens of thousands of ordinary Russians, as it was broadcast live on both radio and television. Metropolitan Anthony was less impressed. Forced to sit through what he knew would be a difficult exercise for one who professed not to like music, and exhausted by the round of engagements, he muttered to the bishop sitting next to him, 'I am going to sleep. Please prop me up if I begin to fall off my chair.'

The enthusiasm for the Russian Millennium in his own diocese was not diminished by the fact that it had reached the position of containing more English converts than Russians, although, particularly in London, there was a wide range of nationalities among its members. There was also a trickle of new immigrants from the Soviet Union, a so-called 'Third Emigration', which brought in some very welcome additions to the community. These early arrivals were quickly absorbed into parish life.

In addition, the children of the early English converts were now growing up. Having gone through the camp they were settling down into being a second generation of local people at the cathedral, together with the third generation of the original Russians who had settled in Britain. Campers of all nationalities were marrying campers. Metropolitan Anthony delighted in describing the cathedral congregation as being multi-cultural like those of the Early Church.

Underneath the harmony there lurked inevitable tensions, much the same as there had been in the Church from New Testament times onwards. A small band of converts was pressing for more English to be used in services. Metropolitan Anthony was passionate about retaining Church Slavonic but did recognise the needs of the more rational elements in the congregation. Eventually he agreed to a change of tack. Instead of having one weekend per month when the services were totally in English, and the rest totally in Slavonic, a mix of the two languages would be used every week. In this way everyone would have the chance of understanding at least part of each service without recourse to burying their heads in a book – something abhorrent to the Metropolitan.

There was also a move to introduce very limited congregational singing: just the Lord's Prayer, as is done in Russia. For a time this actually happened, but after it all but died out Metropolitan Anthony admitted that he had 'killed' the project because people were 'just making a noise' and he was not prepared to put up with it. It was another attempt to keep music at bay as much as he could – a hard exercise in Orthodox worship. He was even heard to say that he did not look forward to eternity if it was really going to contain choirs of angels.

Father Michael Fortounatto, the choirmaster, had led the congregational singing, but he and his wife were about to go on a year's sabbatical to San Francisco. Following a bout of ill-health and overwork Father Michael was in need of a less stressful environment. Their home, Parish House, was sold and another property purchased for them in Chiswick, with the bulk of the money earmarked for the building of a parish hall abutting the cathedral.

On 19 June 1989 Metropolitan Anthony celebrated his seventy-fifth birthday. A party was organised and the *Church Times* printed a tribute. According to the new Patriarchal regulations bishops had to tender their resignation on reaching the age of seventy-five. The diocese held its breath while the resignation was sent off, and then fortunately not accepted. But everyone realised that their beloved father was getting old, and what was more could now legitimately be retired by the Patriarchate at any moment.

In 1990 new ecumenical bodies were set up to replace the British Council of Churches. At first Metropolitan Anthony considered the possibility of his diocese taking only associate rather than full membership, since by this time he was largely disillusioned with ecumenism. He is said to have remarked that church unity was 'on the horizon – which never moves closer'. He was not alone in his sentiments. The Patriarchate had expressed doubts about continuing membership of the World Council of Churches, on account of its perceived liberal agenda, which appeared to fly in the face of Orthodox doctrine. This was one occasion on which Metropolitan Anthony failed to get his way, and the diocese became a full member of both CTE (Churches Together in England) and CCBI (the Council of Churches in Britain and Ireland, now CTBI, Churches Together in Britain and Ireland). Delegates were duly despatched to the inaugural meetings, where they felt not only wildly outnumbered by their Anglican and Roman counterparts but put in a poor light by not being represented by a bishop. The impression was inevitably given that the Orthodox did not set much store by the new bodies. Certainly that was true of Metropolitan Anthony himself, although not necessarily of his flock. At the local level valuable ecumenical contact continued to be made. Later on the Orthodox profile was much enhanced when Bishop Basil of Sergievo became one of the Presidents of CTE.

Metropolitan Anthony's diminishing interest in ecumenism over the years had been documented the previous year, when he gave a lengthy interview on the occasion of his seventy-fifth birthday. Asked how he viewed Anglican–Orthodox relations in the future he replied,

> I think pessimistically. Forty years ago when I came to this country I was entranced by what I saw in Anglicanism. It was the same Anglicanism basically as today, but without its present extremes. Nowadays, when I hear certain statements made by Anglican

bishops or clergy or lay people – and not contradicted by their Church at large – I ask myself whether we belong to the same Christian body. What they say is to me incompatible with being a Christian. And to the extent to which a Church can choose such men to become bishops, I ask myself questions about the faith of this Church: a sort of boneless, squeamish liberalism has now conquered such vast areas of the Church of England, so that we could not unite with it. We would have to consider every single person practically as an individual; while there was a time when one could speak of corporate rapprochement, perhaps even of corporate reunion. Now I think it is impossible, because there are people who we would not want to receive as one of us.

In the same interview he went on to discuss the relative importance of the ordination of women and the disbelief in the resurrection as issues dividing Anglicanism and Orthodoxy. He thought the latter 'an infinitely more important issue'.

'For one thing,' he said, 'I do not believe that the Orthodox are right when they simply, without giving a moment's thought and doing any research about it, affirm that the ordination of women is impossible – I'm speaking of the hierarchy and of conferences. A great deal of thought should be put into it, and I personally see no reason why women should not be ordained. And I'm not the only one in the Orthodox Church who thinks that, but I seem to be the only one who is prepared to say so and to put it in writing. But I think that if you are prepared to doubt the divinity of Christ, to be unsure about the Incarnation, to reject out of hand the Virgin Birth of Christ, and not to believe that truly the bread and wine of the Eucharist become somehow, in an inexplicable, unfathomable way the Body and Blood of Christ, then you shouldn't make an issue of the ordination of women. I know a very well-known [Anglican] bishop who would say to that: well, the heretics will die while the institution will stay. But the trouble is that history has proved that the heretics may die but heresy survives. And an institution can be undone, while the poison can run very wide and very deep into a community.'

At this point in the interview he paused, looked up with a wicked glint in his eye and went on with a chuckle, 'I'll be excommunicated by the Orthodox anyhow, so why not be excommunicated by the Anglicans as well?'

The following morning he buttonholed the interviewer to say, 'I was a little harsh on the Anglicans yesterday. I'll add a couple of remarks. First,

I am aware of course of the individual deep piety of many Anglicans. And second, the Anglican Church is not the only other Church in this country. We feel more akin to the Free Churches and the Evangelicals than to right-wing Anglicanism.'

When the article was published a number of people suggested that Metropolitan Anthony could never have said quite what was printed. He must surely have said, 'I see no theological reason why women should not be ordained.' They were wrong.

In October 1989 an Episcopal Council was held in Moscow to celebrate the four hundredth anniversary of the establishment of the Patriarchate in Russia. Deacon Peter Scorer and his wife Irina accompanied Metropolitan Anthony to the celebrations, where the initiative of so many individuals they met contrasted with the inertia in members of the old guard still to be found among the hierarchy. They attended a meeting in a private flat 'filled to bursting' at which the Metropolitan gave a talk and answered questions, and another held in the hall of the Artists' Union crammed with a thousand people, when he spoke and answered written questions for almost four hours. He also celebrated the Liturgy at a parish church where again he attracted great crowds, so that it took over an hour to administer Communion. These were scenes that were repeated again and again on every visit he undertook.

In April 1990 Metropolitan Anthony went to Oxford to ordain Deacon Maxim Nikolsky to the priesthood. Father Maxim, from an émigré family, was bilingual and was to become a significant member of the cathedral clergy when the numbers of immigrants from Russia began to increase dramatically a few years later.

The following month Patriarch Pimen died, after years of ill-health, criticism and the frustration of living in his 'gilded cage'. In a tribute to him Metropolitan Anthony described him as a 'shy, courteous and gentle, desperately lonely' man who had not been able to meet the new possibilities that perestroika had opened up for the Church because of his age and illness. But he had, he said, 'stood in prayer before God for his Church and the Land,' and been one of those people who had 'stood before the atheist world as true, if terrified, witnesses of God'.

Another Episcopal Council was called to start the nomination process for his successor, followed by a Local Council of the Russian Church. Metropolitan Anthony set out to attend both, accompanied by Father John Lee and the Churchwarden, Anna Garrett. On his return he gave detailed reports to his parish and the diocese. Only after he had finished speaking did Anna Garrett add that at both Councils his name had been put forward from the floor as a candidate. Both times it was disallowed, the reasons given being first that he was too old and second that he was not a Soviet citizen as required by law. His proposer, Father Hilarion Alfeyev, argued that his nomination was important because the Church needed to restore its tarnished image of integrity and reliability, and there was much support among the delegates. 'For about ten minutes,' said Anna, 'we feared we were in danger of losing our bishop.'

The Chair got its way; his name was not permitted to go forward and instead he was called upon to supervise the counting of the votes. In this at least he could put his integrity to good use – there had been much speculation beforehand that the voting would be rigged. The outcome was not widely anticipated. Top of the final poll was Metropolitan Alexis with 139 votes out of 317. The result was made all the more dramatic by Metropolitan Anthony's tactics in announcing it, which he recounted to his flock with his dry sense of humour.

'When we had finished the count, we sang "Dostoino Est" (the Orthodox hymn to the Mother of God) so that everyone waiting in the hall would know that we had a result. Then we sat back for ten minutes and had some sandwiches, just to keep them guessing a little longer.' The bell to announce Alexis' election was finally rung at twenty past ten in the evening, but it was another three exhausting hours before the prayers, speeches and greetings were over and the delegates were back at their hotel in Moscow.

On 10 June, his sixty-first birthday, Patriarch Alexis II was solemnly enthroned at an extremely long and tiring service. Afterwards Metropolitan Anthony felt he had had enough, so he gave his apologies to the Patriarch for not attending the final reception and took himself off to visit his cousin, something he found much more congenial.

Meanwhile, a major decision had been taken, albeit secretly, concerning his own diocese. While at the Local Council, Metropolitan Anthony had asked Father John's opinion of one of the attending bishops. When Father John raised his eyebrows, he nodded: this man might make a possible successor. Nothing was said openly, but Metropolitan Anthony made representations to the Patriarchate.

On Sunday 12 August 1990, Metropolitan Anthony came out on to the ambo at the end of the Liturgy to make the announcements as usual. But one particular announcement was far from usual. Without any prior warning he began to read out a letter, written by him on 1 August and sent out to all the communities of the diocese for simultaneous promulgation. In it he said that for some time he had been looking for a successor: a bishop who would ensure the spiritual, ecclesial, moral and political independence of the diocese, who would share its vision and guide it to its full maturity so that eventually it could grow, together with the other Orthodox jurisdictions in Britain, into the nucleus of an Orthodox Church of Great Britain and Ireland. Having searched in vain for a suitable candidate in both Western Europe and America, he had finally turned to Russia and had asked Bishop Anatoly of Ufa and Sterlitamak whether he would come to Britain, first as his assistant with the title of Bishop of Kerch and ultimately – if the diocese and he were happy about the arrangement – as his successor. Bishop Anatoly had agreed, and at last the Patriarchate and the Holy Synod had also agreed. Metropolitan Anthony added that he had made it clear to Moscow that no one else would do. The Metropolitan's plan was to settle him into his new role, and then if all went well to retire – he was, after all, seventy-six – leaving the diocese in a position where its future and independence were secure. He concluded by saying that it was joyful tidings he was announcing.

Some of his listeners were not so sure. It was not only the possibility of having their beloved bishop retire that was painful; the fact that the succession had been sewn up without any consultation and presented as a bald fait accompli made it a hurtful moment. Neither the Diocesan Council nor the Diocesan Assembly had been informed. 'It felt as if our Metropolitan had physically assaulted us; my face stung as if bruised,' one parishioner described the shock.

According to Metropolitan Anthony, Bishop Anatoly (Kuznetsov) was a monk from Zagorsk, a New Testament scholar and an able and much-loved pastor. He spoke English well, and was looking forward to life in the West. He was awaiting the necessary visas and would arrive as soon as he was able. He had, in fact, visited the cathedral at the Feast of the Exaltation of the Cross the previous year. Although nothing was said at the time, the way Metropolitan Anthony left him to celebrate the service had given the impression that something might be afoot. The Metropolitan had remained unvested and in the sanctuary until the moment when the cross was carried by the serving bishop into the centre of the church for veneration. At that point Metropolitan Anthony had slipped quietly out of the sanctuary to stand among his flock, watching the visiting bishop raise the cross in the customary way. To one observer it was an eerie foretaste of what the future might be like: as if Metropolitan Anthony were already watching his successor from beyond this world. 'Was Bishop Anatoly being sized up as the next diocesan bishop?' the woman wondered. She happened to be right.

A new venture was under way: the setting up of a pan-Orthodox charity for sending aid to Russia. The St Gregory's Foundation, with Metropolitan Anthony as its founding patron and Archbishop Gregorios of Thyateira also a patron, was in the next few years to take on a vital role in sending humanitarian aid to the Soviet Union (later the CIS countries). One of its prime movers was Irina von Schlippe, who was to devote all her time to the running of various programmes in Russia which not only sent in relief but also set up a number of highly successful self-help schemes. Metropolitan Anthony made it absolutely clear from the outset that the charity's work was to be directed towards all, not just to co-religionists, and that it should not be used to proselytise; and this was to remain central to its ethos. However, that did not preclude parishes in Russia becoming involved in the programmes, and Irina soon realised through her work just how highly Metropolitan Anthony was regarded. There were numerous communities that considered him to be their spiritual father, although their knowledge of him was only through his writings and broadcasts. But what they heard spoke to their hearts in a way that was unique. There were also further accounts from people who had met him, of unofficial meetings in private flats, with the KGB hovering helpless about the doors, and church services where his presence attracted thousands.

In December 1990 Bishop Anatoly finally arrived from Russia to be an assistant bishop in the diocese. At first he lodged with the von Schlippes until the London parish bought him a basement flat in Fulham, where he was to eke out a frugal life in not very comfortable surroundings – the flat suffered from persistent damp problems. That was entirely in keeping with Metropolitan Anthony's idea of how bishops of the Orthodox Church, necessarily monks, should live. At the June 1991 Assembly Bishop Anatoly was formally introduced to the diocesan body and gave a lengthy outline of his impressions of Britain during his first six months.

At this meeting Metropolitan Anthony also asked Father Basil Osborne to look deeply into the nature of the diocese and to come up with a vision for its future. He further announced that the post of Vicar General, held from its inception by Father Sergei Hackel, was to be abolished. Father Sergei was therefore replaced as Chairman of the Assembly by Bishop Anatoly (although because he was not confident in English he always let the Vice Chairman, Costa Carras, chair the meetings). Father Sergei also lost the chair of the proceedings at the Diocesan Conference, as this had been another aspect of the Vicar General's role. This was a hurtful episode and an example of the peremptory way Metropolitan Anthony could deal with people.

Peremptory he might be, on occasion, but he was usually very shrewd. There was, however, a particular piece of disinformation which he took up at this time, believing it to be true. Dissention had arisen in the Ukraine between the Orthodox and the Uniates (Eastern Rite Christians in communion with Rome). In a Christmas sermon broadcast live to Russia Metropolitan Anthony spoke passionately against the reported attacks on Orthodox congregations by the Uniates, discovering only later that the particular stories that had reached him had been false. He subsequently expressed his fury at having been used as a mouthpiece for this disinformation; but this failed to reach all the ears for whom it was intended. Nevertheless, he remained extremely wary of the Roman Church's position vis-à-vis the Ukraine and Russia, and went so far as to remark that a member of the (Roman) Secretariat for Christian Unity had reportedly said that Orthodoxy was only tolerated by Rome until it had been conquered completely and did not exist any more. He seemed to be convinced of this interpretation of the Roman Catholic Church's intentions and remained less than enthusiastic about the Pope's overtures to the Orthodox, particularly to the Russian Church. But while he had no sympathy for Rome he did not have total sympathy for the way in which things were done in the Ukraine.

In October 1991 Patriarch Alexis II, on a visit to Britain, celebrated a pontifical Liturgy at the cathedral. He was welcomed with great ceremony, and at the end of the service he laid two foundation stones, one bearing an inscription in Russian, the other in English, for the new hall complex. Afterwards a feast was held in the hall of Holy Trinity Church, Brompton, and concluded with an address by the Patriarch in which he spoke candidly about the Church in Russia. The following day Metropolitan Anthony, acting as interpreter, accompanied him for an audience with the Queen.

In one of his sermons that summer he told a story that he claimed he had heard in Russia, about a young boy aged about ten during the 1960s, at the time of the Khrushchev persecutions. The child told his parents that he wanted to go into the forest to pray for Russia. Their response, being devout and trusting people, was to let him go, and he went off deep into the woods to pray for the salvation of his country. During the following winter a peasant out walking came across the boy, who asked him whether he could provide some boots, as his feet were so cold in the extreme

Russian temperatures. He was never seen again, and presumably perished in the forest.

This total enthusiasm was, for Metropolitan Anthony, at the heart of the Christian calling. The boy had seen a need and responded unreservedly, at the ultimate cost to his own life. Ideally, that was how all Christians should be prepared to live. 'Respond!' Metropolitan Anthony would repeat again and again to his spiritual children. Anything less was not worthy of God.

Yet he knew how easy it was to be sidetracked by weakness and particularly by the way sin could undermine resolve. For this he had an answer. When one was a Christian, he said, committing sins became a painful accident rather than a habitual state, and so could be dealt with and left behind. He might conclude a confession by saying, 'Let it go.' Receiving divine forgiveness meant getting up after a fall and responding anew to Christ's call to follow him. In another sermon, speaking of the apostles' vocation to become fishers of men, he urged his congregation to the same vocation, adding that the people around them were 'drowning men'. In his eyes there was a compulsion for all Christians to serve the Living God with the same intensity as any ordained minister.

CHAPTER TWELVE

STARETS

'The saints,' Metropolitan Anthony liked to say, 'were not people who went from the crest of one wave to another, or even from a trough to a crest. Very often they went from trough to trough.'

He knew from his own life how the darkness of the trough was an inevitable experience; and also how a spiritual father often had to lead his children into the darkness before they could reach the light. This was vividly illustrated to a young woman one evening when, at the end of a lengthy parents' meeting, she asked the Metropolitan if she could use his phone to ring home. He took her upstairs to the church gallery where the phone was situated at the far end in the area that acted as his 'office'. Unlocking the gallery door he confronted the woman with the total darkness of the cathedral at ten o'clock at night and said, 'Follow me.' Walking ahead, his left hand behind his back clasping the woman's hand tightly, he called out encouraging words: 'Three steps down just here,' and 'not far now'. At first there was a little light behind them coming in through the half-closed door from the stairwell. But the further they walked, the more the darkness enveloped them, until there was nothing but pitch black on all sides.

'It was' she said, 'a living parable. You have to put your hand into the hand of God – perhaps realised by your spiritual father – and trust him to lead you deeper and deeper into the darkness. It was one of those moments of revelation that can shape the whole of your Christian experience.' Just as they had reached the most impenetrable depths of the benighted cathedral, Metropolitan Anthony felt for a switch

[191]

and suddenly, in the light of a battered 1940s table lamp, they found themselves at their goal.

Although the analogy was not enacted deliberately it was very much in harmony with his teaching. Belonging to that generation of Russians who had endured the darkness of exile he was always suspicious of a comfortable Christianity. The Way of the Prophet of Galilee who had nowhere to lay his head, the Way of the Cross, the Way preached and lived by the Apostles and the Christian martyrs of the early centuries and indeed in Soviet Russia, was not a way of light and happiness but something costly, difficult and at times bitter, and in which one had to be prepared to face incomprehensible situations that might seem totally devoid of the light of Christ. Again and again he talked about 'paying the price' for the costly pearl.

Yet the word he spoke most often when talking of the Christian Way was joy. The deep, inner joy of meeting God was something that, for him, operated on a completely different level from the darkness of human existence. It was nothing like the outward exuberance of, say, the Charismatic Movement, of which he was wary. It was a radiance that shone from within. And his words were not theoretical: above all, people saw this shining in Metropolitan Anthony himself, just as he had seen it in the eyes of his spiritual father at their first meeting.

Metropolitan Anthony's reputation as a starets or spiritual father grew over more than fifty years. People were drawn to him through a variety of circumstances. Once he had met them, he never forgot them – he had a photographic memory and could always recognise a face, even if he occasionally found that a name had slipped his grasp, in which case he was accomplished at bluffing his way out of the situation. An example of his ability to remember faces: on one of the many occasions when he spoke at meetings outside his church there was in the audience a young Roman Catholic woman, Bridget Hickey. When, at the end of his lecture, he called for questions she happened to be the first person to raise her hand. Some years later, searching for a spiritual director, she was invited by a friend to one of Bishop Anthony's talks at Parish House. Impressed, she approached him afterwards, introducing herself with the words: 'You don't know me.'

'Oh, but I do; we've met before,' he replied immediately. At first she told him he was mistaken. It was only when he insisted, that she recalled asking the question at Worth Abbey. She was not alone in seeking him out. During the 1960s, an average day at Parish House would find it crowded with people waiting to see him; they would overflow from the chapel into the hallway and up the stairs to his study. The same was true on his visits to France as Exarch.

In Russia, the clamour for his spiritual direction was phenomenal. He gave what time he could, knowing that good startsi were rare. For the hundreds of thousands of people whom he could never see face to face he made sure his talks and sermons were distributed via the samizdat network. In this way the vast numbers who never actually met him came to regard him as their spiritual father.

Although in his later years he saw progressively fewer people, the constant demand on his time did not let up. This reached a final peak in the last ten years of his life when his London church was flooded with new arrivals from Russia, although by then he did not have the strength to see as many of them as he might have wished.

Even in his younger days it was often an excruciating business for parishioners to arrange a private appointment. In the years when he had a housekeeper/secretary, telephone calls were deftly fielded. Sending a letter was no easier. It was said that having slit open his letters each morning he felt sufficiently virtuous to do nothing further but put them aside to be read at some other time. Correspondents were often left with the impression it was a very long time indeed.

After moving to the cathedral he installed an answering machine that for a number of years carried a message he had recorded himself. If he were expecting a call he wished to intercept he would pick up the handset and listen to the caller, butting in if he chose. Sometimes this was misinterpreted. On one occasion Robert Runcie, then Archbishop of Canterbury, duly listened to the recorded message and began his reply: 'Hello Anthony, this is Robert of Canterbury.' He was taken aback to hear the reply, 'Hello Robert, this is Anthony.'

'Fancy!' Runcie recounted to a friend – not having picked up the change between the recording and the live voice – 'he was pretending to be an answering machine!'

It was not unknown for him to cancel appointments at the last minute, when he preferred to delegate the task to a victim who was not in a position to re-book the appointment or even to give a reason for the cancellation. This was disappointing enough. Even worse was the possibility of actually arriving at the cathedral to find a hand-written note pinned to the door saying he would see nobody that day.

He did not view letting people down as anything of which he should repent; in his own eyes he had done nothing wrong. His victims, however, often found his behaviour callous, painful and bewilderingly at odds with the compassionate nature he exhibited when they did meet him. It was almost as if there were two Father Anthonys: the one, who, face to face, was full of Christian love and concern – someone truly transparent to the Holy Spirit – and the other who, out of reach in his room, was cold, indifferent and as opaque to the workings of God as was humanly possible. Most people who crossed his path had occasion, sooner or later, to go home to lick the wounds inflicted by the latter personality. But it was the former self, the warm-hearted, sensitive, caring spiritual father, who finally opened the door to his expectant visitors. When he did so he never skimped on the time he gave them; the norm was a full hour. Unlike many Orthodox he was a punctual person, with a strange ability to judge time down to the minute. If he decided to give a sermon lasting four, five or eight minutes he would do so precisely without any recourse to a clock. During the years when he made regular recordings for the BBC he could speak off the cuff for exactly as long as the producer asked.

His approach to his visitors was the same whether they were strangers or his spiritual children of long standing. Imbued with the Orthodox theology of the icon, he endeavoured to treat everyone who crossed his path as an image of Christ.

'Christ saw the beauty of the divine image in every person who came to him,' he would say. 'Perhaps it was hidden or deformed, but it was beauty nevertheless. We must do the same. Each of us resembles a damaged icon. When anyone gives us a painted icon that has been damaged by age or circumstances, or profaned by human sinfulness, we always treat it with tenderness, with reverence and with a broken heart. It is what remains of its former beauty, and not what has been lost, that is important. And that is how we should learn to treat ourselves and each other.'

His stated aim was to give people his undivided attention since that was, he insisted, the only way to a real encounter between people, just as it was in one's prayer-relationship with God. He was therefore unconcerned about externals such as social customs or his own appearance. His cassock might be fastened with a safety pin, or topped by a black jumper holed at the elbow. Warm summer days often found him without socks, and occasionally without sandals either.

Once, when he was visiting Moscow during an August heat wave, the late Patriarch Pimen took pity on his tatty cassock.

'Take that off and let me give you one of mine – we're about the same size,' the Patriarch offered. Metropolitan Anthony was wearing what he usually wore under his cassock in hot weather: nothing but a pair of shorts. Fearing the Patriarch's disapproval he tried to decline his generous offer.

'Don't be shy,' Patriarch Pimen said, mistaking his motives for refusing. 'I've seen a man in trousers before.'

'But,' Metropolitan Anthony thought to himself, 'you haven't seen a man without his trousers!' Reluctantly he took off his cassock, bracing himself for the Patriarch's shocked reaction.

'Don't you know a monk should never leave his cell without his cassock?'

'Well, I was wearing my cassock,' Metropolitan Anthony retorted. 'It was you who made me take it off!'

He recounted this incident during a similar heat wave in London some years later, much to the amusement of his listener.

Outside services he insisted on informality. If outward appearances meant little to him, visible gestures did. Especially in the last thirty years or so of his life he laid great store by bodily contact with people, preferably of a more heartfelt nature than the reserved British handshake. He hugged those he knew well; at parish gatherings he would go round kissing everyone three times in the Russian manner – men, women and children indiscriminately. Strangers he preferred to grasp with both hands or grab firmly by the shoulder than to shake hands formally. He would punctuate a one-to-one conversation with a touch of the hand, a habit English newcomers found disconcerting until they realised that his fluency in their language did not make him any less Russian, brought up in the tactile culture of the bear hug. Indeed, he would take care to remind those visiting him for the first time, 'I am a foreigner.' He was never tempted, either in manners or outlook, to play the Englishman. 'I'm not foolish enough to do that,' he remarked in a television interview with Cliff Michelmore in 1985.

Throughout his diocese people were known to him and each other by Christian names. They called him Metropolitan Anthony, or simply Father Anthony, to his face. He often referred to himself still as Father Anthony into old age. When a newcomer asked him whether she should address him as Your Grace, his reply was vehement 'No! If you call me Your Grace, I'll call you Mrs N.' He winced when people referred to him formally as Your Eminence.

When he was interviewed by the somewhat hostile French media he was asked why, given the humble message of Christianity, he was addressed as Your Eminence. He replied, 'Well, éminence also means a molehill, and that sums up my position as I see it.'

Russians might address him traditionally as Vladyka, which literally means master, but in his case the word took on the warmth of a Christian name.

He was much amused by people who did not reciprocate his informality. Visitors could be surprised that their care in preparing for appointments was not mutual. A woman arrived to see him for the first time, found the church locked and no one answering the bell. Looking through the side gate she saw a figure in old clothes and wellingtons pottering around in the garden. She called him over and said rather roughly, 'Would you fetch Metropolitan Anthony for me?'

'I am Metropolitan Anthony,' the scruffy 'gardener' replied, tickled by her surprise.

At the cathedral he used the north vestry for appointments, or sometimes the south gallery, where he saw people in an area designated as a workspace, with a small desk and telephone. The desk, old and apparently insignificant, was a treasured possession. It was the one at which he had been sitting as a teenager when Christ appeared to him.

People coming to see him for the first time often expected to be shown by staff into a suitably appointed office, to be confronted by a large desk with the Metropolitan, impressively regaled in black riassa and white klobuk, on the far side of it. It was an image that was indeed encountered in Russia, where bishops tend to be very formal; but formality was not what Metropolitan Anthony envisaged for disciples of the Master who had met people on the hills and paths of Galilee. Ringing the bell at the side door of the cathedral, visitors would generally find it opened by the man himself – he had no staff – dressed in plain cassock and bare-headed. He would show them into the vestry or the gallery, seat them opposite himself and smile. There was a common feeling that his dark brown eyes could see into their souls. Conversation would begin on terms of two people speaking to each other out of the depths. Many people experienced his apparent ability to read their thoughts, as if in some real sense they were on the same wavelength. Without any attempt on his part to indulge in the false camaraderie of the chat show, he came across as intensely human, not a prince of the Church but a man among men (or women). There was an inner stillness about him that produced a certain sense of spiritual awe, but this complemented rather than opposed his warmth and openness. Appointments were extremely intense experiences. Metropolitan Anthony always aimed to give of himself one hundred per cent, and this included his total attention and commitment to whomever he was speaking. His piercing gaze and his perceptive and invariably encouraging words contributed to the impression that speaker and hearer were inseparably held in the hand of God, and that the person's concerns where the only things that mattered to him. He never listened with one eye on the clock or half a mind on what he was going to say next. Since this is not what commonly happens in human communication – it takes training and determined effort to stop intrusive thoughts – it was a startling experience.

There was, however, a disconcerting corollary to this approach. As soon as Metropolitan Anthony had turned aside and set eyes on the next person, the first ceased to exist for him; and this abrupt loss of his attention could be upsetting. The same phenomenon is described in Dostoevsky's *Brothers Karamazov* when the Elder Zosima, a fictional starets based on real Russian startsi, meets a group of pilgrims. He too gives a word of life to one person but then turns abruptly away to focus on someone else, leaving the first pilgrim standing with a sense of being carried and then dropped.

Orthodox spirituality – and Metropolitan Anthony stressed this in his books – sees undivided concentration as the basis of a life of prayer and Christian endeavour. Certainly it is a common failing for the mind to wander in prayer, and the constant pushing away of extraneous thought is extolled by the Fathers. However, most people do not attain to such levels of concentration, and find it perturbing when they come across it in someone else. It becomes easy to receive the impression, when such concentration is turned suddenly towards another, that all the open, caring attentiveness they had received was not genuine.

There were other ways in which Metropolitan Anthony's treatment of people could be construed as inconsistent or insincere. In his advice, spiritual or practical, he always tailored his comments to specific individuals and their circumstances, and this produced startling anomalies if they later compared notes. Hearing the confessions of two women who came one after the other to speak of an incident in which they had both been involved, he concentrated on the needs and motives of each of them and came out with two entirely different sets of comments – a fact that the women discovered when, on leaving the church, they immediately and unwisely told each other what he had said. When he had finished hearing confessions he walked home to Upper Addison Gardens, and as he turned the corner of the road he found the two women waiting for him outside his house. Rushing up they burst out with indignation: 'Father Anthony! We've both come to you about the same matter and you've said different things to us. Don't you know what you meant to say?'

'Yes,' he replied over his shoulder as he made a quick getaway into the house, 'and I meant to say this to you – and that to her!'

He would quote this incident as an example of how people should not behave after confession. Nevertheless, the experience of hearing apparently inconsistent advice from him was repeated in many other situations. He might, on a Tuesday, decide someone was ready to be received into the Church, but by the following Sunday think otherwise. He might give a person the – unusual – blessing to receive Communion weekly, only to show surprise a few months later that he should ever have suggested such a thing.

He also had a policy, which had originated as advice given to him when he was ordained, of being fierce in his public speaking but gentle in dealing privately with individuals. It was another way in which he could appear to be inconsistent. However, he firmly denied that such inconsistency was ever due to insincerity on his part. He genuinely meant the words he spoke at a given moment, even if on another day he meant, and spoke, something entirely different. It was behaviour his spiritual children had to accept, because he was impervious to the annoyance and even pain it sometimes caused.

There was, however, a darker side to his nature. However much he liked to speak of the difference between power and authority, as a bishop he was in a position of absolute power with regard to his own flock. This was on two levels: the personal one, towards individuals, and the public one, when he made official pronouncements. On both levels he had the power, if he wished, to crush people, and there were rare but unfortunate occasions when he used it. From time to time he targeted people he saw as a threat and showed them the full force of his darker side. The best tactic for his victims to adopt was to remain stoical in his presence and dissolve into tears later. Why he behaved in this way was difficult to understand. It was not always in order to further a person's spiritual development, in the harsh way his own spiritual father had acted towards him. At times it was nothing more than the product of his insensitivity or inner melancholy, and he could make big mistakes in his handling of both people and situations. He could be incredibly caring to someone for a short or long period. Then he might without warning drop the person, leaving him or her hurt and wounded. Some people found the two sides of his personality impossible to reconcile, and left the church. Some suffered psychological damage from which they only slowly, or never, recovered.

His charming manners masked a social ineptitude he was never to overcome and his shyness made it difficult for him to relate to people or handle confrontational situations. Coupled with this he had a fearsome determination – to which he admitted, although he baulked at the word obstinacy. The result of this temperament was that, when because of his shortcomings he felt his authority or his personal wishes threatened, he was unable to discuss things reasonably. He would simply withdraw and refuse to shift his position, retreating into his room, staying silent for some time and, if the situation did not resolve itself, finally issuing despotic commands from a safe distance. Never a willing correspondent, he would let a situation simmer until he could no longer avoid action, at which point he would write a very firm letter. This practice intensified as he grew older, so that it was said of him by a longstanding parishioner: 'The Bishop's letters have always been stiff, but now they're positively rigid.'

Even when he was made aware of the pain he had caused, he found apologising almost impossible. Not only did he find it extremely hard to seek out people he had offended in order to put things right, he could also be unwilling even to let them make the first move and come to him.

On Forgiveness Sunday, Orthodoxy's eve of Lent, there takes place the service of Vespers and Ritual of Forgiveness, at which the clergy and people come one by one to each other to ask for forgiveness. Metropolitan Anthony was very good at preaching in a very contrite manner on this occasion, and saying a heartfelt 'Forgive me' to each parishioner who approached him to make the traditional prostration and receive a blessing. In a similar manner he would often bewail his own shortcomings in his sermons. He was ready to admit that he did not live up to the Gospel – of this he was acutely aware. But one-to-one apologies were another matter. Metropolitan Anthony could only withdraw into himself and leave his own, and sometimes his victim's wounds, to fester. He found it particularly difficult to forgive disloyalty.

A discerning member of his diocese pointed out that the photo of Metropolitan Anthony which appeared for some years on the back cover of his book *School for Prayer* illustrated the enigma of his personality: it was difficult to believe the two sides of the face belonged to the same person. There was the man of God, craving a life of prayer, loving and compassionate; and there was the other who played to the gallery, enjoyed a personality cult and showed jealousy towards perceived rivals and a cruel streak towards anyone who opposed him. There was a severe lack of integration between the two sides, a fact which made him very difficult to understand. Perhaps the nearest one could come was to acknowledge that in all things he was larger than life: he gave of himself one hundred per cent, whether what he was giving at any moment came from God or from his fallen human nature.

Many people sadly never came to any recognition of both his sides at all. Too many were prepared to see nothing but sainthood, while others found reason to demonise him. Neither group did him justice. Some saw him as 'a saint with feet of clay'. Deacon Peter Scorer summed up an enlightened attitude: that at a certain moment he stopped idolising Metropolitan Anthony and learnt to love him – in full awareness of his faults.

Despite the complex nature of his character, Metropolitan Anthony remained an outstanding spiritual father. On a practical level he was extremely generous: during the course of his ministry he gave away thousands of pounds of his own money to individuals in need. Perhaps the most striking feature of his spiritual counsel, whether during informal appointments or sacramental confession, was his lack of condemnation. While not condoning sin he was always at pains to remove any sense of guilt; for guilt, he repeatedly said, was a completely negative and destructive emotion that kept people in bondage to sin and pushed them down into hopelessness.

Orthodox theology speaks of original sin but not original guilt, and contrasts guilt with the purifying quality of repentance. The Orthodox understanding of repentance hangs on the meaning of the Greek word 'metanoia', an about turn away from the darkness of godlessness towards the divine light. It is a totally positive and joyful step, which begins with the acknowledgement of and turning away from evil, and proceeds through the – often admittedly difficult – setting out on a new path towards the Kingdom of God.

'If there are things which remain in the dark they remain dark and destructive,' Metropolitan Anthony described the process. 'If they are brought into the light they participate to the nature of light.' He was quick to add how that could be done in a variety of ways, not necessarily through a priest.

When he was a doctor one of his patients who had something very dark in his life came to him one day and said he felt that he neither knew nor trusted any of the priests but that he could talk to Dr Bloom as he trusted him. He then opened his heart in such a way that afterwards he was able to receive absolution because the priest was satisfied that the man had brought his sin into the light.

Metropolitan Anthony was fully aware that no one could leave behind the easy living of sinfulness unless presented with something more attractive. It was his purpose to reveal the attractiveness of God – not of the Christian life, which in secular terms can appear extremely unattractive, especially when it entails the persecution that was the lot of the Russian Church throughout most of the twentieth century – but of God himself. His vocation was to introduce Christ to people and lead them to experience divine love in a personal relationship, in exchange for the shallowness of sin. In this he was close to the Evangelicals, whom he also admired for their unwillingness to update Christian beliefs to fall in with the modern world.

He would therefore shower anyone who came to confession with words of love. That meant giving advice that was in tune with the spirit, rather than the letter, of the law. 'Better to break a rule than a person,' was Metropolitan Anthony's instruction to his priests.

An Orthodox confession is not conducted with any pretext of anonymity but in the open church. At the cathedral in London there is an icon-desk in the north east corner which is set aside for confessions. On it lies a rather battered and sentimental nineteenth-century icon of Christ. The priest or bishop stands to one side, generally with his head close to the penitent. He will perhaps put a reassuring hand on the shoulder of a child or anyone who is particularly upset. The role of the confessor is to act not as judge – Christ's prerogative alone – but as a witness, and to pass on Christ's forgiveness. Absolution is given with the penitent kneeling. The priest puts his stole over the person's head and makes the sign of the Cross while pronouncing the prayer of absolution. In this way the church becomes a refuge where people can admit the worst things about themselves and be accepted with love and forgiveness.

Metropolitan Anthony was sought out as a confessor for his ability to see into the hearts of people and for his deep wisdom and insight in his advice. This was not without cost to him. He would sometimes say to people he thought were being too despondent over their sins, 'Take your head out of the dustbin.' He would also describe himself as a dustbin. People poured out their hearts to him and he was left with the burden of their spiritual refuse. And it was in a real sense a burden, not only a burden of prayer for those whose confessions he heard. People often expected him to sort out their lives.

What he looked for in confessions was not the recitation of sins found in manuals of prayer. 'I don't want an inventory,' he would say. He wished rather to see the state of someone's soul and what was marring their relationship with God and neighbour. Restoring that relationship was his task, if possible. Yet he warned constantly of sweeping generalities. There was a tendency among old Russian ladies, he would aver, to make a blanket statement such as, 'I am a terrible sinner.' To one highly respectable woman who said, in tones of what he considered false piety, 'I have broken all the commandments,' he replied in a deliberate, measured voice, 'So, at the age of eighty-six you have committed adultery.'

'Father Anthony!' she retorted, eyes ablaze with indignation, 'who do you think I am?' He would tell this story as a warning to those of his spiritual children who were tempted to come out with similar platitudes.

But he pointed out other pitfalls. It was all too easy to wallow in one's sins. He recalled another woman who one day came to him and began weaving an intricate web as she recounted the tale of her misdemeanours. After a while he cut her short with the words, 'Please, if I am finding it so tedious to follow what you say, I'm sure God too has heard enough.'

He was insistent that when God revealed to someone his or her sinfulness it was a cause for rejoicing: a sign that they had reached a level of maturity where God could entrust them with a certain insight into their inner condition. That did not come all at once, but was a gradual process in which God was able to take the person deeper and deeper into the vision of their full spiritual potential and how far they fell short of it. It was not possible, he said, for a beginner in the Christian life to bear the sight of all their shortcomings. God in his mercy was content to take things slowly; and every time a new sin became apparent, people could not only be moved to repentance by what they found, but also rejoice in the fact that God's confidence in them had increased. He would remind them of the words of the theologian Vladimir Lossky: that looking into one's soul was like peeling an onion. One began by taking off the outer layers and it was only after some time – perhaps a lifetime – that the inner core could be reached.

It was no surprise that he found an unsympathetic voice for people who tried to put the blame on God for their bad behaviour, or the difficult situations he had put them in. 'Can you forgive God?' he would say, 'since you seem to think all your sins are his fault?' That was how he countered people who he felt had not really come to confession in a true spirit of repentance.

He could also be surprisingly strict when he judged it necessary, and he was never indulgent just for the sake of being nice to someone. There were certain boundaries he would not cross. For instance, to a devout Orthodox parishioner who had married a Roman Catholic he remained adamant that the Church rule forbidding intercommunion had to stand, even though he showed great personal affection towards the Catholic husband. Like Father Afanasy, he insisted on what he believed to be right.

There were times when he would give precise and practical instructions which could strike the hearer as absurd. To a young man who bemoaned the fact that nothing in Christianity seemed to be able to bring him close to God, he replied, 'Go home and for a month make a hundred prostrations daily.' This was startling enough to be followed if only out of curiosity. The man discovered that there was more to acquiring faith than an intellectual study of theology. It was something that embraced the whole person, body as well as soul; a physical placing of oneself in the divine Presence. At the end of the month he was able to return to Metropolitan Anthony with his faith rekindled.

That was particular advice for a particular person, not a blanket instruction he would issue to everyone. Thanks to his gift of discernment he understood when someone needed such advice. Yet there remained the strong theme running through his dealings with all his spiritual children: that Christianity was to be lived, and lived out by people who were unique beings of body and soul together; and so pious, cerebral counsel was not only useless, but promoted a false religiosity divorced from life.

There was a graphic image he sometimes used about sin. It was not only that the sinner had left God to go to a 'far country'; sin, he said, was like a river that bordered the Kingdom of God. In sinning we crossed that river, to find ourselves on the opposite bank, cut off from the Kingdom. Whether the stretch of water was a mere trickle or a mighty ocean, depending on the enormity of our sins, we were still on the opposite shore. We had put a barrier between ourselves and God. The sacrament of confession carried us back across the river. It was a process of reintegration, of return to communion and wholeness. Again, he insisted on including himself by saying 'we'. And he insisted on joy. What else could such a process entail?

For the tense person in the confession queue the joy was not so immediately apparent. No one could come to the icon-desk, hear the Metropolitan repeat the words of introductory prayer, then drop into a moment of silence as he leaned forward, without a sense of awe. He always gave plenty of time to each person, recognising that it was often the last thing that came tumbling out unexpectedly that was the most important. Then he would begin a wise and loving response, giving practical advice for the avoidance of the same sin in future or bolstering a person's self-confidence if he felt they were too weighed down by a sense of sinfulness – all the time speaking out of a deep personal wisdom.

'He freed me,' was a typical experience of confession with him. But it was a freedom that brought responsibility: it was up to them how they ordered or changed their lives, and having given his advice he left them to get on with things.

'He was amazing in confession,' was how Mariane Greenan, one of his longstanding Russian parishioners, put it. She had been the blameless young woman whom his grandmother had taken for an unmarried mother in the late 1950s, and after almost fifty years as his spiritual daughter she felt that he knew her better than she knew herself.

If he genuinely felt he had no helpful advice to give to a person he would say so. Occasionally, however, he got it wrong, and gave advice that was not helpful at all. He did not, for instance, seem to understand the pain of marital infidelity. He was not infallible; not always the mouthpiece of God in the way some of his devotees imagined.

His prayer was much valued. He was not only a man who could teach others to pray; many people felt his prayers could change their lives. He did not claim to be a wonder-worker but one testimony demonstrates the power of his prayer.

In the late 1980s Mariane Greenan developed a lump in her throat and her doctor organised a scan. Metropolitan Anthony was alerted to the situation and telephoned while Mariane was out, leaving a message to say he was aware of the lump and that he was praying fervently for her. The following day the tumour disappeared. The scan eventually registered only a scar where it had been.

More commonly his spiritual children recognised the spiritual healing that his prayer could effect.

One aspect of his spiritual direction that was typically Orthodox was the importance he attached to asceticism. Lay Orthodox are expected, far more than their Western counterparts, to look to asceticism to underpin their life in Christ. As a monastic living neither in a monastery nor as a hermit in the desert but very much 'in the market place', Metropolitan Anthony's own opportunities for practising asceticism were not so different from those of his flock. His teaching was therefore of particular value to them because the experience of life from which he spoke was close to theirs. This could work for or against him. For instance, he often mentioned – with disapproval at his excessive zeal – the strict regime he had imposed upon himself as a young man. He spoke of the way he had fasted so hard when he worked as a doctor during the war that he under-mined his health. While he had enough strength to walk the wards he found himself unable to walk the streets, so that on one occasion, when he had all but collapsed by the roadside, a passing ambulance stopped and the surgeon aboard hauled him in, telling him what a fool he was. 'That was not asceticism,' Metropolitan Anthony could say with the hindsight of maturity, 'that was sheer stupidity!' Moderation was a virtue he took a long time to learn.

It gave some consolation to his hearers to discover that ascetic standards were not rigid rules but guidelines to which one should aspire but which were all too often not attainable this side of sainthood. When the clergy of the diocese went for a residential meeting at a retreat house run by Roman Catholic monks they were confounded, on the first Friday in Lent, to be served a chicken supper. In the spirit of St Paul's words to 'eat what is set before you' they tucked in; and in the words of one of the priests, 'Of course we enjoyed it!'

On a visit to Durham during Lent Metropolitan Anthony took the overnight train, arrived to celebrate the Liturgy the next morning and only then found himself in the refectory, where he sniffed the air hungrily, anticipating a tasty meal.

'We know about Orthodox fasting rules, so we've cooked some lentils specially for you,' said his host.

'Lentils!' he said in disgust, unable to hide his disappointment.

Over the years his attitude to the fasting rules of the Orthodox Church varied. He went through phases: sometimes he urged fasting on people; at other times he saw it as less important. What remained constant was his insistence that fasting and asceticism in general were only tools for bringing a person closer to God. Limiting sleep or food could not of itself do this, but could change attitudes. The advice he sometimes gave to parishioners during Lent was to read and follow the words of Isaiah, Chapter 59. This, he said, was the real way to fast. Food was always meant to be eaten in moderation and with gratitude, to sustain well-being. The use of the body in kneeling, bowing, making gestures like the sign of the Cross, could awaken spiritual conditions, enabling a person to pray more easily. The whole process was akin, he said, to tuning a musical instrument. The human body was an instrument that would never allow the soul to resonate properly if it were too slack or too taut.

If the aim of the Christian life was to bring God joy it was not at all a question of 'oughts' and 'thou shallt nots', but of simply – in the best sense of the word – bringing God joy by one's thoughts, words and actions in the course of each day. To do that, he said, involved learning to live in God's presence, keeping company with him in whatever the circumstances. He recommended certain exercises for acquiring this awareness;

but he was quick to point out, in his practical way, that for a beginner to try to spend too much time in the divine presence was foolish and likely to be self-defeating. Yet the ultimate goal remained the constant awareness of God's presence.

He was wary of the amount of time the over-zealous spent in church. He might suggest to a young mother: 'Don't come to church every week. On one Sunday a month say to God, "Lord, stay at home with us today."'

There were occasions, particularly in his later years, when he took his own advice on that score. His attendance at services was not as rigorous as might have been expected. He avoided celebrating weekday Liturgies when there were other clergy available, because he was not by choice a frequent communicant. In old age he did not have the strength to celebrate a Vigil followed next morning by a Liturgy; at great feasts he would choose one or the other. He would explain to his congregation that instead he would be with them in spirit, praying in his room at the back of the church. This was not always what actually happened. In 1999, when Russian Christmas Day fell on a Thursday – when he habitually did his shopping – he went off to South Kensington as usual during the Liturgy, while most of the congregation imagined he was in his flat in prayerful exhaustion after celebrating the Vigil the night before.

So he could never be accused of being unnecessarily pious. The enforced monastic round of services would not have suited him, and his asceticism was born of a freedom, both physical and spiritual, which defied institutionalism and was seasoned with a lifetime's common sense which looked far beyond hide-bound regulations.

That was also true with regard to his attitude to the Jesus Prayer. When people sought instruction regarding the physical techniques and exercises with which the prayer is famously associated his advice was invariably: forget all you have read about techniques and just concentrate on the words. An intelligent, deep concentration was what was needed – but a concentration so hard that it would probably be impossible to sustain for more than a few invocations, at least to begin with. Not for him the recitation of hundreds or thousands of repetitions. That was something, he warned, which was only possible for the few dedicated ascetics who devoted their lives to the Jesus Prayer. The rest had to be more humble and admit their inability to keep themselves so consciously in God's presence. Such an approach was a disappointment to those people who were expecting heroic words for what they thought was their heroic piety. In fact, after a talk in which he had reiterated this advice, someone came up to him and objected to the way he had spoken. Not everyone felt like that.

Another member of the audience found his words cut through the unnecessary mystique, and told him it was the first time she had ever heard anything on the Jesus Prayer that made sense to her.

'I'm glad you told me that,' he replied in all sincerity, 'because someone else thought what I said sounded trite.' It was certainly not trite; but it was simple, direct and eminently practical advice that his hearers could take away and use rather than merely meditate on in a pious but theoretical way.

He would explain the significance of the words of the Jesus Prayer. 'Mercy' in languages such as Slavonic was far broader and deeper than the English. The phrase 'have mercy on me' could better be understood, he said, as: show me your tenderness, your loving-kindness, in whatever way it is needed. And the word 'sinner' meant one who was separated from God, who had lost touch with him, who was not so rooted in him that God's life was his life. He would point out that the original Greek was 'the sinner'. 'I am in my eyes the only sinner in the world; other people I cannot judge. But I know that I am the sinner whom Christ has come to save.'

He also emphasised the fact that if one addressed Christ as Lord, it could not be in general terms. It had to mean that he was the Lord and master of one's own life, which must become a struggle to fulfil all the Gospel, step by step, under his guidance. So the words 'Lord Jesus Christ, Son of God' were a perfect profession of faith and faithfulness.

'What matters,' he would say, 'is not the number of prayers we recite, least of all the way in which we do it; but that we sincerely turn to God and tell him something that is true – about him, about us, about what we long for. And that is really all.'

He would often begin talks on asceticism with stories from the Desert Fathers, who, by their 'simple' obedience illustrated by their 'simple' sayings – which he would recount with humour – achieved far greater Christian virtue than any complicated theology might have taught.

He was fond of the word 'martyr', again and again reminding his listeners that the Greek original meant a witness. To witness to Christ had, from the beginnings of the Church, involved giving all, often including one's life. The taking up of one's cross in order to follow Christ with total commitment was at the heart of his own struggle, as it had been, and continued to be, for Christians throughout history. Discipline was akin to the word discipleship, and asceticism was nothing more than a tool in the fight against all that prevented a person from following Christ and witnessing to him, whether in life or through death. But he would go on to say that asceticism was in a sense a universal experience. Anything that limited a person's freedom of action in order to make them live up to their calling could be described as ascetic: a musician's rigorous practice routine, an athlete's training. Christian asceticism was a sense of responsibility towards God's call: the promotion of closeness to God and the radical fight against anything that prevented it.

Christianity, he maintained, was not a world outlook but a way of relating to the Living God and of living accordingly. All Christians had repeatedly to ask themselves: is Christ the treasure of my life or not? Is the divine realm the goal of my journey? Is it my precious pearl for which I will sell everything – not only material goods or position in life but pride, laziness, indifference? There was no point in trying to be a Christian if God were seen merely as an ornament – or a troublemaker – in one's life.

He understood – and saw within himself – the sorry state of dividedness. It was easy to be wholeheartedly devoted to God when things were running smoothly, but in times of trouble God was all too often pushed into the distance.

Ascetic training had to begin in the heart rather than the emotions – not attachment to the 'sweet baby Jesus or the poor Jesus on the Cross' as he put it, but the nurturing of real, sacrificial love, and a hunger for God. A person enslaved by the world turned to God only in moments of suffering, trouble or fear. Christians should turn to him – and return after a fall – because he was their Saviour.

He saw as paramount the education of the heart into a faithfulness and purity that would allow a person to be God's own even if they fell at moments because of frailty. Only if the heart were hungry for God could the mind be brought to him. So the training of the mind followed the training of the heart. But the training of the body was also involved, because the heart, mind and body could not be separated; they pervaded one another. The total person had to take part in the life in Christ.

'A human being is not a soul imprisoned in a body which does not partake in the spiritual dimension. We are mysterious creatures: the materiality of our bodies is called into union with God, and is not just an inert carcass, a dressing gown that can be taken off, but is endowed to relate to God and to enter eternal life, in its own right, not passively.'

For Metropolitan Anthony asceticism was certainly not a matter of mystical experience. The aim of the Christian was not to go from one experience to the other but to open oneself to the action of God as completely as possible and to acquire the mind of Christ. This presupposed a profound change in the mind and heart, and a continuous effort.

Occasional efforts, interspersed with long periods of slackness, would not produce anything. Too often people's minds, he said, were like 'monkeys jumping from tree to tree'. An intense, humble and constant listening to God was necessary. Then followed a hard and ruthless struggle to allow oneself to be attuned to God's will. It was the vocation of every Christian to be the vanguard of the Kingdom of God, and to be so identified with Christ as to be an extension of his incarnate presence in the world. That could not be achieved by human effort alone. There had to be surrender to God so that he could act without any human resistance. And there was so much that resisted. The human person belonged to two worlds, the earthly and divine. The common experience of being merely of the earthly had to be outgrown. He would give practical examples of how to achieve this. Reading the Bible was essential. No new word would be given to anyone who had discarded what God had said in the past. After reading a small portion of the Gospel, one should ask honestly: what did God wish to convey to me? – and not the other way round.

'It might take hours and days to find the meaning,' he would say, 'but do not move on to the next passage in a hurry. Listen when Christ speaks; venerate him in his silence; or listen reverently when he speaks to others but not to us.'

The same was true for prayer. He readily acknowledged that there were times when one felt only coldness in prayer, but perseverance was imperative. 'In the cold it is only by rubbing our hands that we get warm,' he would say. Only by forcing oneself into the presence of the living God could one come to feel his warmth – even if, at times, that presence seemed to be an absence. But silence and word – and listening and doing – had to go together. The words of prayer, like those of the Gospel, also needed to be read and repeated until they were so deeply ingrained that a person began to live by them. 'Unless we allow the word of God to become identical with us we will never go anywhere. This is where asceticism begins,' he would say.

He recommended reading the Orthodox daily morning and evening prayers. But, he pointed out, these were not coined in a study; they had 'gushed like blood or a howl of agony or a cry of joy from the hearts of living men and women'.

'First of all, turn to the saint who wrote the prayer and ask him to pray with you, so that you may touch the hem of his experience and he may carry your anaemic prayer to God.'

He would recount how Father Afanasy had taught him: first be silent, then pray to the saint, read the phrase, and prostrate to involve the body.

Then repeat it. Doing that would make reading the morning and evening prayers into a two-hour exercise. If time did not permit, then it was far better to take a few prayers that evoked a response and pray in depth in this way, rather than to recite all of them with inattention.

'Make a rule for yourself that you can keep,' was his advice. 'Choose the prayers that give you life. But when a rule becomes a routine, change it.'

Then, he would conclude, there had to be the determination to meet every situation and person as a God-given occasion in order to learn how to live the words one had prayed. Prayer had to be rooted in the will.

Like all Orthodox teachers, Metropolitan Anthony was acutely aware of the need to establish in his listeners a spirit of discernment, which the Fathers talked of endlessly, and for good reason. The undiscerning could be carried away by seemingly spiritual things that came not from God but from the world, their own imagination or Satan.

Metropolitan Anthony made no apology for believing in the existence of the devil. He knew him as a force to be reckoned with and struggled against, and he saw the Christian life as a battle with the Adversary that never ended this side of the grave.

He told a chilling anecdote to illustrate the need for spiritual discernment. He had once spent three weeks living with Charismatics, who accepted him and told him that they did not need to lay hands on him because, they said, 'We know you are born of the Spirit.' ('Whether they were right or not is another matter!' he would add.) But he remained largely unconvinced by what he saw. Glossolalia is something the Orthodox Church recognises as having taken place in the Early Church – a tool for the Church in its infancy which was less and less needed as a certain level of maturity was reached, according to Metropolitan Anthony. He thought that one could only partake of gifts such as speaking in tongues without danger if one were possessed of a degree of discernment that, he felt, was not often present. Nevertheless, he went along to one particular Charismatic meeting with an open mind. He described the scene:

> A man began speaking in tongues in a riveting manner, in a way that was so moving that everyone listened in a spirit of worship, of adoration. Suddenly another man came into the room, paused at the door and said, 'But stop him! He is blaspheming!' The man who was speaking in tongues was, unknown to himself, speaking in the Basque language, but the man who came in was a Basque, and he told us that this man had been pouring out blasphemy and curses – but with a tone of voice that gave the impression that it

was an act of prayer and adoration. And in the given case the criterion was not even that someone had the gift of discernment – he was simply a Basque speaker. So when it happens you can not rely on the voice, the manner, the impression it makes on you. It may be from God, it may be from Satan, or it may be simply an outpouring of the best or the worst in the given person.

He readily understood how difficult it was to stand up to the assaults of the devil. He was always quick to point out that Satan was from the beginning The Liar. Like the serpent of Genesis, he moved not in a straight line, when he might easily be recognised, but from side to side, craftily weaving his way towards his unsuspecting goal, often couching his lies in the deceit of the half-truth.

If one of his spiritual children felt attacked by the devil he would offer, 'Send him to me and I will deal with him.' He once recounted how Satan had come and rattled his fireguard. 'If that's all you can do!' was his derisory response, in his habitual the-best-defence-is-attack manner.

This was a real experience of which he spoke, and not imagery. The translation of the Lord's Prayer sung at his cathedral uses the words that Orthodoxy has always understood as implied by the original Greek: deliver us from the evil one.

As a doctor he was also aware that some of his spiritual children's problems could have a physical origin, and he was quick to tell them to seek medical help when it was appropriate. On the other hand, he recognised that sometimes nothing more than a practical solution was necessary. For instance, since he himself suffered from depression he was always ready to give advice on dealing with it to other sufferers and explain his own tactics for warding it off. On a good day, he said, he would see people. If he were not feeling up to this, he would read; and when he felt he could not even do that, he would clean his room.

'That way,' he said, 'I can always look back at the end of the day and see I have done something positive.'

To people finding themselves in the grip of a really debilitating bout of depression his advice was: 'Don't fight it; you won't have the strength. Just flop.' The sudden and otherwise inexplicable notes he often left on the church door suggested he took his own advice regularly.

He was also aware both that depression was not just a matter of chemicals or being 'all in the mind' but could be caused by circumstances of life that needed to be resolved. For instance, a young woman who was in the middle of a particularly painful situation asked whether she should seek medical help to help overcome her anxiety.

'No, don't go to your doctor. He will give you tranquillisers. If someone comes to a doctor with a nail in his foot you don't give him codeine; you take the nail out.' He then proceeded to take out the 'nail' of the situation that was tormenting the woman and sent her away, as he invariably did, encouraged and uplifted.

There were however, circumstances in which his own 'nails' remained very firmly wedged.

He often referred to his parishioners as his children, and the newly received as babies. After a pensioner was received he came up to her at the end of the service and welcomed her as 'My youngest Orthodox baby'. She replied that she did indeed feel her knowledge of Orthodoxy was very much in its infancy; she felt, as she put it, 'Still below the bottom rung of the ladder.' He replied, 'So am I: and what a wonderful place it is to be!'

PART FIVE

'WEEDS NEVER DIE' – FINAL YEARS

CHAPTER THIRTEEN

◑ ◐

LOOKING TO THE FUTURE

(1992–1999)

At the 1992 Diocesan Conference Metropolitan Anthony arrived looking tired and gaunt. 'I've lost two stone,' he admitted, a fact easily substantiated from observation. His face was haggard, his once podgy hands were bony, his cassock hung limp in unaccustomed folds about him.

The Sunday morning found him serving the Liturgy almost buried beneath his white Easter vestments. Weariness was apparent in every word and gesture. It was reminiscent of the story he told of once having been so tired at a service that he afterwards apologised for having celebrated 'like a dying swan'.

'No, Father,' a parishioner had replied, 'like a dead duck.'

By the end of the Liturgy he was struggling to find the breath to sing, and instead of his customary bold and upright bearing he shuffled about, his shoulders drooping. Although he was scheduled to address the conference after breakfast that day, people wondered how he would possibly gather sufficient strength. They were in for a surprise. He began speaking with such fire that it was difficult to recognise this as the same man. Filled, it could only be said, with the power and inspiration of the Holy Spirit he held the conference's attention for a whole hour, and then asked to continue for a further fifteen minutes, as he unfolded his vision of the Church with a passion that touched everyone in the hall. It was an unbelievable tour de force. This time it was his listeners who were breathless.

Later that afternoon, even after a sleep, he had returned to his state of exhaustion. This was not just in a general way. 'My heart is tired,' he confessed. 'But', he added over a cup of tea and a doughnut, 'weeds never die.'

When he had finished his tea he struggled to his feet and before anyone could relieve him of his cup he picked it up in one hand, took a neighbour's in the other and carried them both over to the tea trolley with the words, 'I try to help whenever I can.'

Metropolitan Anthony's flock thought he was the one who needed help. His last years were to be tempered by declining health and his ability to do less and less on the practical level. The clergy had expressed their wish for him to consecrate the widowed Archpriest Basil Osborne as a second assistant bishop, and he announced this with joy at the Diocesan Assembly meeting a few weeks later.

At the beginning of August Father Alexander Fostiropoulos outlined arrangements for the start of the building work on the hall complex and the Metropolitan's new quarters. It would entail demolishing his small flat on the south side of the sanctuary and turning the existing vestry on the north side into improved accommodation for him, adding an upper floor. He would go away for a two-month extended break while the work was done. This was to be his first proper holiday since 1988, and as usual the destination was secret. He was never able to divulge where he was going for fear of being disturbed by doting parishioners who might just 'happen' to take their holidays in the same place.

He went, in fact, to a cottage in Cornwall, which he was only ready to admit after his return. When he had first arrived there he had had little strength to take advantage of his rural surroundings. He found he was only able to walk a hundred yards before he became utterly exhausted, but as time went on he grew fitter, so that he was eventually able to go for walks lasting two hours at a time. He began to get to know his new locality and to take an interest in things around him. There was a spell of rough, blustery weather, the sort he liked. Apart from walking he claimed to have done 'Nothing. I sat and thought about myself and my life. And the more I thought, the darker it seemed.' In fact, his introspection easily tended towards self-loathing, which he would only have conquered if he had ever been able to defeat his personal demons.

By the end of September it was plain that the building work was seriously behind schedule. Metropolitan Anthony's delayed return was put tentatively at mid-November. The proposed consecration of Father Basil to the episcopate began to recede.

Metropolitan Anthony did not arrive home until the second week in December. The congregation gathered expectantly on the Sunday morning, but there was still no sign of him. Anticipation began to turn to the fear of disappointment. There was a sudden rattling of the partition in front of his new home, and he appeared from behind it. Although still extremely thin he walked briskly across the nave, arms swinging with an encouraging vigour. He celebrated, administered Communion to the congregation and preached a lively sermon. He also announced that he would spend another week doing nothing but settling in, after which he promised to resume his normal parish duties. That was all that was mentioned of his long absence; no 'good to see you' from him, no official 'welcome back' from the other clergy. Just, more or less, business as usual.

There was a daunting backlog of parish and diocesan matters awaiting his attention. It had been impossible to come to any major decisions without his approval. On previous occasions he had returned from a break and set about reversing uncongenial decisions necessarily taken in his absence. In that respect he never progressed beyond the autocratic in ecclesial matters, which could be immensely frustrating.

The consecration of Father Basil Osborne as Bishop of Sergievo finally took place in early March 1993. The consecrating bishops were Metropolitan Anthony, Bishop Kallistos of Diokleia, vicar of the Greek parish at the Oxford church shared with Bishop Basil's Russian parish, and Bishop Anatoly, whom the Patriarch simultaneously raised to Archbishop. Other churches sent their representatives, making it an ecumenical event, and Bishop Basil was later that year to become one of the four Presidents of Churches Together in England. He soon began to take on an increasing workload in the diocese, as Metropolitan Anthony tried to conserve his dwindling strength.

In July the London parish held its belated Annual General Meeting after the Liturgy. By the time the meeting ended Metropolitan Anthony was very tired indeed. Nevertheless, he spoke to one of his parishioners who lived at a distance from the church and who had a pressing family crisis. Taking her up to his 'office' on the balcony he spent an hour with her, from time to time stopping to take some tablets. 'My heart is tired,' he explained, and claimed the tablets were camphor to liven him up. She offered to leave, but he insisted on giving her a whole hour's attention rather than have her make a long journey to return on a day when he was feeling stronger.

He might well have put his tiredness down to overwork, since he began telling several people that he regularly got up at 4 a.m. in order to get all his work done. He would be at his desk till 10 o'clock in the morning when he would stop for an early lunch, and then continue, not getting to bed until at least eleven o'clock at night.

At the end of the Liturgy one Sunday in August he made an

impassioned outburst against gossip, something he did from time to time. On this occasion he complained that rumours were circulating about his health. 'I am being accused,' he said, 'of suffering from a variety of diseases including diabetes, Alzheimer's disease, Parkinson's disease and even mad cow disease!' He denied them all. Ironically his health really was about to take a turn for the worse. He disappeared for several weeks and it was reported that he was unwell, with 'flu', suggesting nothing serious. Finally, on 24 October he celebrated the Liturgy for the first time since August. At the end of the service he announced he was still in a state of recuperation following pneumonia. Few people had got wind of his being quite so seriously ill.

As 1994 began the diocese pondered how to celebrate Metropolitan Anthony's eightieth birthday in the coming June. A collection was put in train for a present. But what to buy him? There was one thing he was known to want, not for himself but for the cathedral: a hand-written liturgical Book of the Gospels in English, to be used beside the Slavonic one. Father John Lee was able to locate a source and the book was purchased.

Metropolitan Anthony's birthday happened to fall at Orthodox Pentecost, and he was duly greeted at the end of the Liturgy. The Gospel Book was not presented to him then but, since it was a gift from the whole diocese, was kept until the following Sunday, the occasion of the annual Diocesan Liturgy widely attended by clergy and people from all over the country. Father Sergei Hackel stepped forward with the new Gospel Book and, with a few words to express the love and appreciation of the diocese, presented it. At the end of the service, when further congratulations were given to him, he was seen to put up a hand to wipe away a tear or two, genuinely overwhelmed by the affection of so many people.

During this time a movement was taking shape among a number of Anglicans, led by the clergy on the whole, who were opposed to the ordi-nation of women. There was a problem for many of those Anglican priests who might have considered joining the Roman Church: they were mar-ried. A number who wished to remain priests and in some cases to bring their flock with them contemplated becoming Orthodox, and formed themselves into a group calling itself 'Pilgrimage to Orthodoxy'. Metropolitan Anthony made his position clear. 'We do not receive anyone on the rebound,' he announced bluntly, reiterating his view that people should only become Orthodox for wholly positive reasons and with due reverence and gratitude to the church that had nurtured them. Besides, he continued to speak in favour of women's ordination. There were some who, not sharing his views, convinced themselves that his words were not genuine, or that he had not actually said this or that. He was branded a heretic by others, both within and without Orthodoxy. In the event the numbers of Anglicans who became Orthodox were far fewer than had been estimated, and they mostly found a home in the Antiochian Patriarchate after being influenced by converts from North America.

At the end of May 1995 the first Diocesan Conference for two years was held. Revitalised and in a new venue – Rye St Anthony School, Oxford – it attracted the largest number of participants ever seen at a Diocesan Conference. A visitor from abroad commented on the way Metropolitan Anthony had greeted individually the participants from outlying parishes. Despite his age and poor health his mind was as sharp as ever and he was still very much the man in charge.

During the early months of 1996 Metropolitan Anthony suffered a recurrence of the severe back pain that had plagued him intermittently for forty years. He spent Lent doubled over, joking that he seemed destined to spend his last years like St Seraphim, who had also been bent double in old age. This time the Metropolitan's usual recourse to osteopathy, which had helped him many times in the past and which he recommended to other back sufferers, failed to do the trick. Bravely he struggled on, celebrating the Liturgy and attending meetings, although he admitted to being in constant pain.

His congregation wondered how he would stand up to the rigours of Holy Week, and the first few days were obviously difficult. The long service of Matins and Holy Unction on the Wednesday evening was a particular marathon. Although he always countenanced against people expecting physical healing from the anointing, nothing would have pleased the congregation more than to see him relieved of his pain. Their prayers were answered. The following day he had returned to his customary upright stance, and was walking briskly and without a trace of a limp. For the remaining services of Holy Week he seemed truly renewed.

On Easter night he made an impassioned plea in his sermon for the revocation of the break in Communion between the Patriarchs of Moscow and Constantinople. This had occurred when the Orthodox Church in Estonia had elected a new diocesan bishop against the wishes of the Patriarchate, which insisted on appointing another man. The supporters (mainly ethnic Estonians) of the rejected candidate placed themselves under the jurisdiction of the Ecumenical Patriarch, while the mainly ethnic Russian parishes remained under the Moscow appointee. Squabbling over property ensued, resulting in the break in Communion between the two Patriarchates. This was a matter of concern to Metropolitan Anthony's diocese for two reasons. Firstly, it caused pain and practical difficulties for the Oxford church, shared by the two jurisdictions of Moscow and Constantinople. Secondly, it did not bode well for any future situation in Britain should Moscow not be willing to accept the diocese's nominee when it elected its own bishop.

During the final verses of Easter Matins Metropolitan Anthony was seen to take up the service book and study it intently. When he came to give his sermon he reminded his listeners of the words they had just heard: 'Brethren, let us forgive all in the Resurrection.' How could the two Patriarchs continue their feud in the light of those words?

He did not receive any direct reaction on the sermon from Russia although the service had been broadcast on the BBC World Service. But it made its impact, and was credited with the restoration of Communion between the Patriarchates which followed soon afterwards. Metropolitan Anthony was still the unfettered voice of conscience of the Russian Church and when he spoke, people listened.

After Easter he held a meeting at the cathedral with representatives of the non-Chalcedonian churches in London, with whom relations were very good. They spent an hour and a half asking him details of how the parish was run, and various questions of a pastoral nature. He described it afterwards, with a smile, to his own people: 'I thought it was an interesting meeting. And one of the interesting things was that after three quarters of an hour, one of the non-Chalcedonians said to me, "Now, Father, could you tell us: is this the church where Metropolitan Anthony celebrates?" So I had to avow, yes, well, he does.'

A new phenomenon had been impinging on the London parish over the previous few years. Following the fall of communism the numbers of new arrivals from Russia had increased from a trickle to an ever-growing wave of people. The parish set up various initiatives to accommodate the newcomers. Metropolitan Anthony contributed by giving fortnightly midweek talks in Russian to complement the English ones he had been giving for decades. The whole nature of the parish was changing, and the changes really needed a leader with energy and dynamism – just the sort of man Metropolitan Anthony had been in his youth. He still had the brains and the capacity for vision, but not the strength to see it carried out.

The following year for the first time the Easter Liturgy was served in a mixture of English and Slavonic. This was possible because the BBC had decided to discontinue their broadcast of the service. For years the cathedral had provided the only access to a church service at Easter and Christmas for millions of Russians. With the fall of communism things were reversed: the BBC broadcast Easter services from Moscow on Radio 3.

On 29 August 1997 Anna Garrett died. She had been the churchwarden of the London parish for many years and her passing was seen as the end of an era. Two days later came the death of Princess Diana. At the end of that morning's Liturgy Metropolitan Anthony preached a tribute to both. Of Anna he said that he had known her for sixty-one years, since he was twenty-two and she twenty-three, when they were both leaders at the French camps, where she was known for her truth and honesty – he said she was known as 'Anna with the honest eyes' because it was impossible to say anything that was untrue to her, or to hear anything untrue from her. When he saw her a few days before she died she had said to him that he should not be sad because their friendship and affection for one another would continue for eternity.

Of Princess Diana he said that her life had been 'tragic': 'I have tasted honey, and now I am facing death' he quoted from the Old Testament. At the following *panikhida* (memorial service) which he served for both Anna and Princess Diana he was seen wiping tears from his eyes. Anna's death brought home the fact that there were hardly any people of Metropolitan Anthony's generation left: that is, people who had been children at the time of the Revolution and who had suffered enforced emigration. By this time there were no adult survivors of the Revolution at all.

30 November 1997, which fell fortuitously on a Sunday, was the fortieth anniversary of Metropolitan Anthony's ordination to the episcopate. A very large congregation assembled for the Liturgy, together with many of the clergy from around the diocese. At the end of the service Archimandrite Theophan, visiting from Russia and representing the Patriarchate, presented Metropolitan Anthony with the Russian Orthodox Church's Order of St Sergius First Class. The following evening Festal Vespers was celebrated, at the beginning of which the Anglican Bishop of London, Richard Chartres, gave a message of tribute from his diocese. Metropolitan Anthony and the other clergy stood quietly among the congregation, leaving Father John Lee to celebrate Vespers. It happened to be the eve of the feast of St Philaret, the newly canonised nineteenth-century Metropolitan of Moscow, and the choir sang verses to music composed especially in his honour by the choirmaster Father Michael Fortounatto.

There were visiting clergy from other Orthodox jurisdictions, including

Bishop Kallistos of Diokleia, Bishop Timothy of Tropaiou (both from the Greek Archdiocese of Thyateira), and representatives from the Serbian, Antiochian and Bulgarian churches. The Russian Ambassador to London, Mr Fokine, was in Moscow, but his wife came in his stead. After the service there was a reception in the hall. The smell of borscht had been permeating the cathedral during the service and the food, generous and imaginative, although vegetarian since the Nativity Fast had begun, was welcome on a cold evening.

Eventually people were called to take a seat for some congratulatory speeches, and they gathered round. First to speak was Archimandrite Theophan, representing Metropolitan Kirill and the Moscow Patriarchate. After suitable words of praise for Metropolitan Anthony's years of work not only in Britain but also in Russia itself through his lectures, sermons and broadcasts from abroad all through the years of Soviet persecution, he presented him with a *panaghia*. Bishop Kallistos spoke on behalf of the Greek Archdiocese, and reminisced on how he had been present at the young Bishop Anthony's consecration. Bishop Basil of Sergievo spoke on behalf of Metropolitan Anthony's own diocese, and recounted how he remembered seeing an early photograph of the new Bishop Anthony 'in his cassock, with both feet off the ground, playing volleyball'.

It was also announced that the Queen had sent Metropolitan Anthony a letter of congratulation – which was loudly applauded. Father Michael Fortounatto spoke on behalf of the people of Russia, where he regularly visited.

Metropolitan Anthony had sat through these tributes looking serious and tired. From time to time he caught his breath, or coughed, or slipped a pill under his tongue. Dressed in his cassock and white *klobuk* he looked thin and weary after an exhausting two days. Finally his turn came to reply. He began by saying that he felt that despite the generous things people had said about him, he had not lived up to his potential. So he wished to put the other side of the story, not in any false humility but simply to explain his own shortcomings. Thereupon he embarked on a highly amusing speech, recounting various anecdotes to illustrate his trials when learning English as a young man. The more his audience responded with laughter, the more he came alive. It was one more example of the tour de force he could produce out of nowhere when inspired by an enthusiastic audience. He undoubtedly enjoyed playing to the gallery.

During the first week of February 1998 he fell, breaking a couple of ribs on the stone stairs, while trying to carry some heavy books down from the cathedral gallery. He did not appear in church again until after Easter. In his absence Bishop Basil was running the day-to-day life of the diocese. Known and trusted by the clergy for many years, this quiet but extremely capable man, in a very different mould from the Metropolitan, was nevertheless seen as the only person who could guide the diocese towards a full and integral part in English church life, and keep its independence intact, as well as being sympathetic to the very real needs of the new Russian community. It was assumed, with approval, that Metropolitan Anthony was grooming him as his successor.

Metropolitan Anthony did not finally reappear from his prolonged absence until 5 May, for a meeting of the Parish Council, at which he expressed displeasure with some of the decisions taken in his absence. He said he would give the Thursday talk two days later.

At half past six people began to arrive at the cathedral for the talk, but no one came to open up the church. It began to look as if Metropolitan Anthony would not be giving the talk after all. Just as the crowd of people was coming to the conclusion that it was time to give up and go home the door opened and a rather contrite Metropolitan Anthony appeared. He stood quietly holding the door while everyone filed in past him into the church. Finally he came in and began to recite the evening prayers.

It was noticeable that instead of beginning with 'Christ is risen' as is done during the forty days of Easter, he used the Prayer to the Holy Spirit which is normally not said until Pentecost, as if Easter simply had not happened for him. Before starting the talk proper he said a few words regarding his absence: that he had been 'very ill' and that he thanked all those who had sent him get well cards or messages, and 'nibbles'. He was obviously still weak and frail but he spoke well, even if he did, on his own admission, repeat a lot of anecdotes and points from previous talks.

In particular – and he spoke almost as if it were his swansong – he talked about salvation. His message on this point seemed to sum up his lifetime's teaching, based on his interpretation of St Paul: that the pagans would be saved by keeping the 'law within their hearts'; the Jews by keeping the Law of Moses; and the Christians by their faithfulness to Christ's teaching. Thus, while not preaching universal salvation, he reiterated the view found in Orthodoxy that all may be saved. Salvation was not dependent on the glib argument of the fundamentalists that only faith in Jesus Christ as one's personal Saviour mattered; it had been effected by Christ on the cross on behalf of all creation, and it was not for human beings to put limits on God's will.

However, there were hardliners in Russia who insisted on the much narrower interpretation of salvation: that only Orthodox Christians could be saved. His reply to this was an explanation which satisfied many of his critics: when a non-Orthodox, for instance a Muslim, came face to face with Christ in eternity and recognised him as what he truly was, the Son of God, at that moment he became Orthodox and so could receive salvation.

Firmly back at the helm he seemed to be greatly in favour of promoting the new Russians, and talked about bringing over a priest from Moscow to minister to them when the money was available.

The parish was still without a churchwarden, and two names, neither of them new Russians, had been put forward during his prolonged absence. At the AGM Metropolitan Anthony rejected them both out of hand, preferring to leave the decision until later in the year and ignoring criticism of what was seen as his autocratic decision, which provoked some ill-feeling.

He said he wished the parish to 'become a body of people who seek honestly, ruthlessly, the mind of Christ'. The impression he gave was certainly one of ruthlessness on his part. He had walked out of his room before the start of the meeting as 'a man of iron' according to an onlooker, steeling himself against the furore he knew would be awaiting him. In an angry and obstinate mood he had – not for the first time – taken refuge in acting despotically in order to hide his own inadequacy in dealing with difficult situations.

On the Sunday of All the Saints of Russia, two days after Metropolitan Anthony's eighty-fourth birthday, the congregation greeted him at the end of the Liturgy by singing 'Save him, O Lord'. In reply he said, in the cynical tone he often used on such occasions, that it was the congregation who needed saving more than he did. 'You need to be saved from the mistakes I make,' he said. Although people smiled at his joke, many of them were aware of the truth behind his words.

He was about to be pulled up short. Still not strong enough to see many people, he had had time for some introspection. Finally he expressed some of his thoughts in the sermon he gave on 9 August, when he spoke of how he had been looking with new eyes at an icon of the Mother of God of Vladimir.

'I was struck in the depth of my heart, I hope, by what I saw in them,' he said. 'She looked at me as though she was saying, with deep compassion and at the same time with horror, with horror: "How can you be who you are? How can your life have been, and still be, what it is now, while you proclaim that the Child whom I hold, who is leaning his cheek against mine, is your God and your Saviour?"'

He saw, he said, no bitterness or resentment in her eyes, only a deep amazement and a deeper pain. He asked his listeners to look at the Mother of God and see in her eyes the same horror and compassion. His final words were: 'I leave you the cry that emanates from this gaze: "How can you? Look at my Child. All the frailty of divine love is incarnate in Him. He is left to die because you have lost your way."'

He had given this sermon leaning on his staff, head bowed as though making a public confession. Many people were aware that his life had not always been that of the saintly figure he habitually projected, and hoped he would take his own words to heart and use the time remaining to him to change.

In March the following year, when the crisis in the Balkans was at its height, Metropolitan Anthony preached a sermon on the subject in which he called on his congregation to pray for the situation. However, he made it very plain that in doing so he was not asking them to take sides. Instead, he announced that at the end of the Liturgy there would be a prayer service for justice, peace and love to come to the Balkans, without distinction of nationality and without distinction of the congregation's own preferences. Christ died, he reminded his listeners, for all; and his body would continue to bear the marks of the crucifixion until that day when everyone would come to a knowledge of the truth – the truth being God himself – and learn to love one another as Christ had loved them.

He also added sorrowfully that most of the wars and injustices that had occurred over the past century had been perpetrated by people who claimed to be the disciples of Christ.

There were some who had looked to him to take their own pro-Serb stance in support of fellow Orthodox. His resolution not to do so displeased them. But he stood firm on the principle that their prayers must be for all.

In June 1999 the acting Chairman of the Diocesan Assembly, Costa Carras, announced his resignation, after several years as Chairman and several decades of service in a wider capacity. An extremely able, intelligent and Christian-spirited man, he was retiring to Athens and would be greatly missed. Metropolitan Anthony chose as his successor Irina Kirillova, who had acted as his long-term unofficial right-hand person and who, being a lecturer in Russian at Cambridge University, had used her bilingual skills to liaise with the Patriarchate on behalf of the Metropolitan after he had ceased travelling to Russia himself. Hers would be a strong, decisive tenure that ensured the diocese retained a high profile in Moscow.

On 2 November Metropolitan Anthony was invited to a Millennium Lunch hosted by the Lord Mayor of London. Around three hundred guests who had contributed to British life attended. The Bishop of London, Richard Chartres, who had had close contact with the Russian Church for some years, had put Metropolitan Anthony's name forward. It was a grand occasion, not the sort generally associated with Metropolitan Anthony but a fitting accolade to his fifty years' service in Britain.

How much longer he could continue to serve his church was in doubt. More than once he had tendered his resignation to Moscow, for it to be refused. The Patriarch, he said, had asked him to stay in place for as long as possible, even if most of his work had to be delegated. In terms of consecration he was the longest-serving bishop in the Russian Church, a revered figure not only by seniority but even more on account of the integrity of his ministry. His voice was the great voice of truth, the uncompromising and uncompromised message of the Gospel, which some may have wished to silence but which remained for the majority an unfailing source of hope, joy and faith.

Although he had often talked of wishing to retire he had also expressed the sentiment: we die in harness. The Diocese of Sourozh was his baby, and it is doubtful whether he could ever have stepped aside to watch another man take his place. It was just not in his nature.

CHAPTER FOURTEEN

LOOKING TO ETERNITY

(2000–2003)

Throughout February and March 2000 Metropolitan Anthony was laid low with a chest infection and he appeared only intermittently in church. He also complained of 'not feeling right in the head' and dizzy, and was under investigation at the neurological department of the Brompton Hospital. The hospital wanted to give him a brain scan following a fall in South Kensington – he had been walking along, he said, when a large woman in front of him fell backwards, knocking him over, and he hit his head on the kerb. It is possible he suffered a slight stroke.

Arriving for an appointment in good time, he was kept waiting for three hours, at which point his patience ran out; he handed in a note explaining his departure and left. When he arrived back at the cathedral he was surprised to receive a telephone call from the hospital apologising for the delay and giving him another appointment.

'They treat me well,' he explained, 'not just because they know I'm a doctor but also because of my great age.'

During this time one of his parishioners had given him a computer and he had spent a month trying to master it, without much success. It was too much to expect of a man in his mid-eighties, but despite his continuing bouts of dizziness it was not a sign that his brainpower was in any way diminishing. His mind remained razor-sharp.

Towards the end of Lent he ordained a new priest, Father Michael Gogoleff. The intention was that he would serve the fledgling community in Bristol that had remained with the Russian diocese after the majority of the parish had become unequivocally part of the Greek Archdiocese a few years previously. Father Michael would also serve in London as well, as he spoke both Russian and English and could therefore be useful to all sections of the community. In addition, Father Michael was travelling once a month to Dublin to minister to the rising numbers of newly arrived Russians there.

Metropolitan Anthony had not consulted the London parish in advance about the ordination. It was an example of the high-handedness which could mar his usual reputation for generosity of spirit, and it caused some ill-feeling. Of course, he would say, people could always put their opinions, good and bad, in writing to him. That in effect meant they would be ignored.

The size of the cathedral congregation was turning it from one that had been very much a family into something anonymous. This was nobody's fault: four or five hundred people in a crowded church cannot possibly get to know one another, especially when many of them are visitors or short-stay migrants. However, the newcomers were beginning to air their own views, particularly on the ways the parish differed from those in Russia.

Metropolitan Anthony said privately that he cared not so much for Russian culture (which may or may not have been true) but that he was passionate about the language, 'which people tell me I speak rather well', he added. By well he meant elegantly: like other émigrés of his generation he still spoke in the pre-Revolutionary style unadulterated by modern Soviet slang. He was therefore keen to retain Slavonic in the services, and sermons in both Russian and English. He was adamant that the children of the newcomers should not lose their mother tongue. Encroaching Anglicisation was something he feared, even though he was aware that the Greek Orthodox congregations in Britain had lost vast numbers of young people because of their insistence on retaining the Greek language

The Statutes were revised again to change the method of electing the Diocesan Bishop, making the Diocesan Assembly an electoral college, which was thought more likely to be acceptable to the Patriarchate. With Metropolitan Anthony's advancing age and infirmity the question of the succession was becoming ever more pressing.

At the end of July 2001 Metropolitan Anthony suffered a minor 'event', coming close to collapse during the Liturgy. He soldiered on for a few more weeks but with increasing tiredness, and it was soon announced that he was to go into hospital to have a pacemaker fitted. He said it would make him a new man, and able to be a better pastor, by the very next Sunday.

Indeed, he was home after twenty-four hours and things seemed to be going well, until he tried to get on his feet too soon and as a consequence ran a temperature. Each following week the other clergy gave a brief bulletin, saying he was 'continuing to rest' or 'improving by the day'. The truth was, instead of being revitalised by the surgery his constitution appeared to be still in decline.

Meanwhile, Metropolitan Kirill, Chairman of the Patriarchate's Department for External Church Relations, had paid a visit to London in November, with no small consequence. Immediately afterwards the Patriarchate put out a press release stating that Metropolitan Kirill, accompanied by Hegumen Hilarion (Alfeyev), had met with the Sourozh bishops and some of the clergy and had discussed the questions of organising pastoral work for the English-speaking and Russian-speaking parishioners of the Sourozh Diocese. Certainly the problems of integrating the growing Russian contingent were apparent to everyone. But real efforts were being made. Bishop Basil, who had virtually taken over the running of the diocese, was already inspecting a possible second church building for London in Clapham with Father Alexander Fostiropoulos.

On 16 December Metropolitan Anthony appeared and celebrated the Liturgy for the first time since his operation. It was plainly something of an ordeal for him, and he neither preached nor read the notices at the end of the service. A fortnight later at the end of the Liturgy he announced that he had two important items of news to share. Speaking first in Russian (and more fully than he subsequently did in English) he informed the congregation of Archbishop Anatoly's resignation as an assistant bishop but added that he would remain indefinitely in England, to celebrate and to continue his pastoral work, especially in Manchester and among the Russians in London.

The general view was that Archbishop Anatoly, nice man that he was, was nevertheless too retiring and too old – in his early seventies – to lead a diocese which had carried a bishop of advancing years for long enough. The role required a younger and more vigorous man. People had assumed, however, that he would have stayed on as an assistant bishop and not be forced into official retirement.

The second item was the news that, at Metropolitan Anthony's request, Hegumen Hilarion Alfeyev would be appointed a 'young suffragan bishop' for the diocese. He was to be consecrated Bishop of Kerch, Archbishop Anatoly's title up till then. Bishop Hilarion would also teach in Cambridge University's Faculty of Theology and in the Orthodox Institute there; but he would spend Sundays mainly in London at the cathedral.

Father Hilarion had been known to key people in the diocese for some years. He had studied for his doctorate at Oxford, so had good English, and looked set to become a useful addition to the diocesan clergy.

Metropolitan Anthony claimed he had for a long time been fishing for Father Hilarion to come to England, as a priest who would help with the new Russian immigrants. The Patriarchate's response, he said, was to insist on the young man coming as a bishop (although this was later contradicted by Bishop Hilarion, who maintained it had been Metropolitan Anthony who had demanded he come as a bishop). Bishop Hilarion was duly consecrated on 14 January 2002 in Moscow, with Bishop Basil representing Metropolitan Anthony, and arrived in England at the beginning of March. Everyone was struck by the extreme youth of the new bishop. He was not yet thirty-six and no one knew how he would mature.

At Vespers of Forgiveness Sunday a couple of weeks later Metropolitan Anthony gave a heartfelt address on forgiveness. He admitted that the congregation had much to forgive him for: he had spoken words of truth but had failed to live up to them. He asked above all that people would pray that he would have the courage, and the time, to repent. It was one of those impressive moments when one felt the utter simplicity and genuineness of the man; until one realised he had been repeating much the same words over a number of years, without apparently having come to repentance at all. This was, in fact, to be the last time that he appeared at this service, as he was too ill to do so in the following – his final – year.

When the Queen Mother died soon afterwards, Metropolitan Anthony described her in a sermon much as he had done his own mother, as being a person of simplicity and directness, for whom the whole nation was grieving. A dedicated monarchist, he had a reverence for the British royal family and, despite his tiredness, celebrated a *panikhida* for her at the end of the Liturgy.

Within a few weeks of Bishop Hilarion's arrival tensions began to surface. With Metropolitan Anthony's blessing he began a tour of all the communities of the Diocese of Sourozh, celebrating the Liturgy and talking to clergy and people. Metropolitan Anthony later claimed that on his arrival Bishop Hilarion had spoken of having power. The Metropolitan's own view of the episcopate was not a position of power but of service. 'Now I can rule', Bishop Hilarion was reported to have said to him. It was plain that he had much to learn about how an assistant bishop was expected to behave in the Diocese of Sourozh; and Metropolitan Anthony judged he was capable of learning. He had been Hilarion's spiritual father for many years, and thought he knew him. Father Hilarion had been the priest who had proposed Metropolitan Anthony for election as Patriarch.

On his travels around the country the young bishop had begun to uncover elements of dissatisfaction that had been left to fester over time. It was certainly true that Metropolitan Anthony's failing strength had led to a general neglect of all sorts of things over the preceding years; and people had suffered because of his bad handling of situations where they disagreed with him – his shy nature left him unable to cope successfully with dissent. He also tended towards a bad-mannered forgetfulness to thank people for hard work. But there were also instances where he had stood his ground on principle, and the disgruntled had only themselves to blame.

A bold young bishop who arrived to listen to grievances with promises to resolve them caught the ear of the dissatisfied. He gathered round himself a small but vociferous band of supporters, creating a faction. The diocese had never had to face such unpleasantness and Metropolitan Anthony, struggling to continue a punishing work schedule despite his age and illness, found the situation impossible, and said so.

The Holy Synod sat in mid-July and recalled Bishop Hilarion from London, appointing him to take charge of the newly formed representation of the Russian Orthodox Church to the European Union in Brussels. Archbishop Anatoly's title of Kerch was restored.

Although a period of relative calm ensued, the strain on Metropolitan Anthony's health was enormous. On 1 February 2003 an Extraordinary meeting of the Diocesan Assembly was called to discuss his wish to retire and his desire that Bishop Basil should succeed him. His reason was a serious deterioration in his health. 'I cannot carry on,' were his words at the meeting, and with one abstention the Assembly voted to accept his resignation. It also voted to petition the Synod right away to appoint Bishop Basil as permanent diocesan bishop.

The following day Metropolitan Anthony celebrated the Liturgy, at the end of which he announced the decisions of the meeting and elaborated on his health problem: he was to undergo an operation and treatment – for what condition he did not say.

Eleven days later he was admitted to the Princess Grace Hospital, for cancer surgery the following day. As a former surgeon he took an active and vociferous interest when the consultant's team made its rounds before the operation, prompting Father John Lee to say, 'Be quiet! You haven't even put a plaster on anyone since the war!'

'John,' he replied, 'I don't know how it is that you and I have managed to stay friends for so long!'

Metropolitan Anthony and the surgeon contemplated the possible causes of the cancer. One dated back to his years in occupied Paris, when in the prevailing makeshift conditions he had spent long hours operating in the radiology unit without any protective clothing. That the resulting cancer might have lain dormant for so long, only to show itself following the unpleasant events of the previous year, said much about his constitutional stamina.

People waited for news with bated breath. The immediate fear was that such a frail old man might not survive surgery; but survive he did, and on the evening of his operation he was described as sitting up in bed, positively chirpy. He was to remain in hospital for a week before returning to his flat in the cathedral.

Word began to get out as to the nature of his operation: his bladder, containing a large cancer, had been removed. The operation appeared to have been successful; all the cancer there had been excised.

Although he was still officially out of circulation he soon made one or two appearances during the Monday morning cleaning sessions, walking first with the aid of two sticks and then with one. He seemed to make good progress. However, the question of his retirement still loomed. The Holy Synod's next session was postponed *sine die* on account of the Patriarch's own poor health, leaving the question of Metropolitan Anthony's retirement and the appointment of his successor unsettled. Instead, the Patriarch circulated a letter dated 1 April in which he outlined to various hierarchs a proposal for the creation of a semi-autonomous Metropolia in Western Europe which it was hoped would include not only the existing Patriarchal dioceses but also eventually the Church in Exile parishes and the Russian churches in France under the jurisdiction of the Ecumenical Patriarchate. The letter expressed the idea that the dioceses would eventually elect a bishop to head the Metropolia, but that as an interim measure the Patriarch had appointed Metropolitan Anthony as its head.

He was said to be greatly pleased at the appointment, which vindicated everything he had stood for as a champion of Orthodoxy in the West. It had given him a new lease of life. Too ill to travel, he contacted the other hierarchs named in the letter and asked them to come to him. Bishop Mark of Berlin, of the Russian Church Abroad, was an early visitor. It all looked very promising.

Meanwhile, efforts continued at the London cathedral to bring the two communities, 'English' and 'new Russian' together. Groups began discussing ways of improving information, communication and generally getting to know one another; ideas were put forward for social events. The new Clapham community was up and running, with Father Alexander Fostiropoulos building up a good-sized, multi-ethnic congregation.

Orthodox Easter fell on 27 April. Metropolitan Anthony appeared at the Holy Wednesday service of the Anointing. This sacrament, normally reserved for the seriously ill, is given to everyone on the eve of Holy Thursday as a healing climax to the endeavours of Orthodox Lent. In this context its function is primarily spiritual, but in Metropolitan Anthony's case people were also praying for physical healing. He sat in the centre of the church surrounded by his flock, leaving Archbishop Anatoly to celebrate until the rite of anointing took place at the end. Metropolitan Anthony then approached the Archbishop and the final prayer was read with the Book of the Gospels placed on the Metropolitan's head, before Archbishop Anatoly anointed him. He then in turn anointed Archbishop Anatoly before retiring into the sanctuary while the clergy began anointing the congregation.

The following day Metropolitan Anthony again appeared at the service of the Twelve Gospels, sitting quietly in a chair beside the door into his flat and taking no part in the service itself.

He was present at Good Friday Vespers. Speculation began to mount as to whether he would appear on Easter night.

Indeed he did. Archbishop Anatoly conducted the initial service of Compline around the Shroud of Christ in the darkened church. But when the Royal Doors were opened for the start of the Paschal procession Metropolitan Anthony, fully vested in the triumphal white of Easter, led the clergy out of the church to announce the Resurrection of Christ at the West Doors of the Cathedral. Very frail, but with immense determination and courage, he was using a stick and was helped along by one of the priests. Still using a stick he joined fully in the celebration of Easter Matins, censing the church and giving the greeting 'Christ is risen!' to his congregation. At the end of Matins he struggled to read the traditional Homily of St John Chrysostom in Russian, leaving Bishop Basil to read it in English. His short sermon was given in Russian only. By then he was exhausted and said as much, apologising for not having the strength to greet the congregation at the ambo. He retired to his flat while his two assistant bishops served the Liturgy.

Easter Matins was to be the last service he celebrated, although he continued to appear informally in the cathedral out of service time. Before the Diocesan Council meeting on 12 May he came out of his flat to greet council members and give them individual blessings, though admitting that he felt shaky. Four days later he was taken by Father John to a hospital appointment, at which he was told the news that he had another tumour. Father John informed his audience at his talk that evening, adding that the new tumour would be 'dealt with' the following Wednesday and urging everyone to pray for the Metropolitan. A mood of sadness hung over the cathedral.

Six weeks of radiotherapy followed, for five days a week. Metropolitan Anthony told a parishioner that, if it worked, he might have two years; if not, two months.

He had still received no reply to his letter of resignation and his request – and that of the diocese – that Bishop Basil should succeed him. But by June it was obvious that he could no longer function in any official role. So he wrote again, saying that he now had to retire on health grounds.

One of his last public engagements was as guest of honour at a dinner given by the Nikaean Club on 5 June at Lambeth Palace, at which he was awarded the Lambeth Cross a second time, a fitting tribute to the enormous influence he had had on the spiritual life of the country during his long ministry. At the end of the evening the Archbishop of Canterbury knelt to receive his blessing.

Towards the end of June, during President Putin's state visit to Britain, Metropolitan Anthony was invited to his reception in London (a 'return match' in response to the Queen's banquet at Buckingham Palace held on 24 June, which Bishop Basil attended). His extreme weakness was only outdone by his determination to be present, although his driver for the occasion, Irina Kirillova, wondered how they would cope. Cope they did.

But by the end of June he was back in hospital, spending two weeks undergoing radiology for his spreading cancer despite a pessimistic prognosis. He was in a room of four beds, and had apparently endeared himself to the other patients, so that when Father John rang his bedside phone, a strange voice said, 'This is Anthony's bed.'

'But you're not Anthony,' Father John replied.

'Oh, Anthony's gone for his treatment. Is that Father John?'

'No. This is John.'

Having – some might say at last – escaped from the clutches of his congregation, he could briefly be just Anthony, a man among men. When Father John repeated this to a meeting of parishioners, he added, 'He's charmed them all in the hospital.'

During this time Metropolitan Anthony sometimes asked Father John to stay with him until he fell asleep at night. He had said many times that no one should be allowed to die alone; perhaps he feared that very thing himself. All through his illness Father John had accompanied him back and forth to the hospital for treatment, with a heroic devotion that was typical of the man.

Metropolitan Anthony finally left the hospital for good, to come back home to his flat in his beloved cathedral, where could be looked after privately. On arrival he was seen looking extremely thin, dressed shabbily as usual and wearing sandals but no socks, and hobbling with the aid of a stick.

Father John had arranged for him to be cared for by MacMillan nurses, but when they arrived at the cathedral Metropolitan Anthony refused to let them in. The next day they did gain entry but were unhappy about his condition and found him a place in Trinity Hospice in Clapham, South London.

The last couple of weeks were a swift and painful decline, relieved by heavy doses of morphine-derivative drugs and draining him of any interest in the diocese. By the end of July he was asleep for most of the time, and a statement was issued on 2 August saying he had received Holy Unction from Father John and was unconscious. His flock could only pray for a merciful release, and prayer services were instituted at the cathedral twice daily. At the same time, events were moving in Moscow. The Holy Synod had met on 30 July, when it belatedly accepted Metropolitan Anthony's retirement and appointed Bishop Basil as ruling administrator of the Diocese of Sourozh (that is, charged temporarily with its administration). By the time this news became official it was overshadowed by Metropolitan Anthony's imminent death. On Monday 4 August 2003, at 3.40 p.m. on a blisteringly hot afternoon, he died of cancer in Trinity Hospice.

The prayer services immediately became *panikhidas*, the Orthodox memorial services for the departed. The news was hard for many people to take in. For so many years their much-loved Metropolitan Anthony had suffered from heart problems, lung problems, one illness after another, and survived them all. Despite his advanced age, it had seemed impossible that death would ever claim him. Others were glad that his physical suffering was at last over.

By chance – or divine Providence – the BBC was about to broadcast Orthodox Vespers from St Petersburg to commemorate the three hundredth anniversary of the founding of the city. Michael Bourdeaux, the founder of Keston Institute, had been asked to give an introduction to the service. Having heard of Metropolitan Anthony's death – which the BBC had not – he arranged to turn his piece into a tribute. The broadcast went out two days after his death, and Michael Bourdeaux was deeply moved by what was surely not a coincidence.

At one of the cathedral *panikhidas* Father John Lee told the congregation, without any air of sensationalism, that in early February the consultant had been of the opinion that there was a real chance the battle with the cancer would be won and that a lengthy period of remission was possible. But after they left the hospital, Metropolitan Anthony told Father John that he knew it would not be so. The previous night he had had a dream in which his grandmother had appeared to him. She was holding a calendar and the pages, beginning with January 2003, began to turn in her hands in rapid succession. As they reached July they began to slow; and they finally stopped at 4 August. This Metropolitan Anthony took as a sign that he would die on that day.

The *panikhidas* continued. The Orthodox Church knows how to deal with death. With its life focused on the bodily resurrection of Christ and the certainty of the general resurrection, it takes seriously the meaning of baptism as dying with Christ in the waters of the font and rising again to new life. Thus physical death is only a small and less significant moment on the journey to eternity, a threshold to be crossed along the way but not a final point. This was Metropolitan Anthony's firm belief. But he, like the Church, also recognised death as a tragic separation for those left behind. The Orthodox life of prayer surrounding a death does not hide behind sentimental platitudes but it does give enormous strength to the bereaved. So the daily *panikhidas* were an opportunity for the Metropolitan's spiritual children to come, pray together as a family group and be reminded of the awesome but joyful character of the departing of a Christian into eternity.

He was brought 'home' at five o'clock on Monday 11 August. As the cathedral bell began to toll a crowd of faithful parishioners lined up to welcome him. The coffin was carried in solemnly, the lid removed, and for the first time the congregation was able to see him lying resplendent, fully vested and mitred, looking peaceful and with the same humble dignity that had so marked him out in life. A *panikhida* was taken round the open coffin, at the end of which the people came up one by one to give their beloved bishop the customary kiss, on his hand and on his mitre.

The following evening a Great Panikhida was taken by Bishop Basil and an old friend of the Metropolitan's, Metropolitan Filaret of Minsk, who had arrived with other Russian clergy to represent Patriarch Alexis and Metropolitan Kirill of Smolensk.

The day of the funeral, Wednesday 13 August, was extremely hot, necessitating the use of fans in order to keep the cathedral a little cooler. Despite rumours that plane-loads of his followers were arriving from Russia, the cathedral was full but not overflowing as the Liturgy and then the funeral service began. It was a solemn and reverent occasion, as the Metropolitan would have wished, yet in the Orthodox fashion at the same time with an underlying informality as the congregation stood around the coffin in the centre of the church, looking down for one last time at the man who for more than half a century had been their priest, their spiritual father and their inspiration.

Archbishop Gregorios of the Greek Archdiocese in Britain led representatives from other Orthodox and Oriental Orthodox jurisdictions, and gave an address at the end of the service. The ecumenical guests included the Archbishop of Canterbury, Rowan Williams, who also delivered an address; Bishop Alan Hope representing the Archbishop of Westminster, Cormac Murphy O'Connor; and representatives from the ecumenical bodies in Britain. Metropolitan Filaret read out a message of condolence from the Patriarch and another from Metropolitan Kirill. Finally Bishop Basil of Sergievo covered Metropolitan Anthony's face with a veil and delivered a final tribute, before leading the clergy, guests and congregation in giving the Last Kiss to the singing of 'Eternal Remembrance' in a procession that lasted for well over an hour.

When the cortege arrived at Brompton Cemetery's north entrance the hearse made its way at walking pace down the long avenue, followed by a procession of the clergy of the diocese, choir and mourners to the simple grave where Olga and Xenia had been buried more than forty years previously. For the last fifty yards the coffin was borne on the shoulders of six of his priests, men whom he had ordained and nurtured in their spiritual life, who were now carrying him to his earthly resting place.

After the final prayers people came one by one to throw a handful of earth on to his coffin to the spontaneous singing of the Easter hymn: 'Christ is risen from the dead, trampling down death by death, and to those in the tombs he has given life.'

Although there had been tears at the funeral as hundreds of people said goodbye to the man who had been a real father to them, there was also a sense of peace and of completion: Metropolitan Anthony had finished the work given him by Christ, and was entering his rest as a good and faithful servant. He might himself have put it otherwise, aware of his sins and his inner dividedness. But he was also, always, aware of the unbounded love and forgiveness of the God he served.

He once described how he imagined he would face his Creator in eternity. 'Standing before God I will be overcome by sorrow at my sinfulness and my failure to live up to his calling. But when he sees how sorry I am, that will pass away.'

Over the years the thrust of Metropolitan Anthony's missionary zeal varied according to the circumstances in which he found himself. The constant background was the vision formed in Paris under Father Afanasy: of an open Church welcoming to all people regardless of ethnicity. This was tempered by another constant: his love of Russia, her people, her language. He had a special affection for the 'old Russian' core of his London parish, some of whom he had known since his teenage years and with whom he felt particularly at ease. As the congregation had begun to draw in converts, his focus widened so that for most of his ministry he might well have been called the Orthodox apostle to the English. At the same time his work in Russia presented a different picture to the people there, for whom he was an apostle to them, using England as a springboard.

In the twilight of his life his focus changed again as, overwhelmed in London by the new arrivals from Russia, his Russian fervour came to the fore and he concentrated his attention on ministering to them.

As astute as ever, he was well aware that within a generation the children of the immigrants would have integrated into British society and the cycle would begin again for the parish. But that was beyond his concern. With his physical decline he could only concentrate his mind where his heart immediately was.

He undoubtedly felt great gratitude to England and a certain affection for the English. But for Russia he felt a passion.

He was content to remain a foreigner, never taking out British citizenship (he retained French nationality). In turn, his enormous contribution to the religious life of this country remained unrecognised by successive governments.

In old age he sometimes said he would like to go to sleep and not wake up. Indeed, he had gone through a stage, in the early 1990s, of telling people, 'I would like to die,' whenever conversation gave him the opportunity. He admitted, however, in May 1998 that he had grown beyond actively wishing for death. 'I am now prepared to carry on for as long as God wants me to,' he said. As other elderly people came to face death with resignation, he had become resigned to life. Or at least, that is what he had said. Father Michael Fortounatto summed it up differently after his funeral: 'He loved life', echoing the words Metropolitan Anthony had said about his own mother when she too lay dying of cancer. She had, he said, been prepared to put up with all the pain, just so long as she could go on living. 'She loved life,' were his own words on that occasion, unaware that both the words and the situation would one day apply to himself.

Over twenty years earlier Metropolitan Anthony had described in a couple of radio broadcasts his vision of eternal life and his attitude to his own death. On entering eternal life he had said: 'In moments of prayer, moments of elation, the spirit wells up, up, up – and breaks down against the frailty of the body. A day will come when life will burst triumphant. And that is what I believe about eternal life.' And, regarding his own death: 'Although I want to go on preaching, teaching, reaching people, I rejoice at the thought that one day they will be free of me; and nothing will be left except the Word of truth.'

Certainly his greatest achievement was as a preacher of the Gospel: the pure, heroic and loving Gospel message that is Orthodoxy's joy; and it is no exaggeration to say that his preaching converted thousands, in Britain, Russia and all over the world, wherever he spoke in person or his books were sold.

EPILOGUE

'You could have called me a pig, which is also true.'

When Metropolitan Anthony spoke those words to me in 1989 I replied, 'It may be true, Father Anthony, but it's the sort of thing we keep in the family.' Our eyes met and we exchanged the briefest of smiles.

Like many people who knew Metropolitan Anthony I had occasion to see his less than holy side, and at times to be bruised by it. His congregation was very much a family, and, as families do, we saw the roughness of each other's characters, but were bound together by an instinctive feel for what should remain personal to us.

In his book *God and Man* Metropolitan Anthony wrote that holiness was our absolute vocation. His life was a movement towards that end, but it was punctuated by the same reversals that plague the life of all Christians. He knew, however, that the path to holiness lay through prayer: the placing of oneself – one's true self, totally vulnerable – in the presence of God. Despite his personal failings his desire to be with Christ, the love of his life, remained his ultimate goal.

Towards his brothers and sisters in Christ he was also vulnerable, accepting criticism as a man and not as a hierarch beyond reproach. Although he was capable of pride in his own abilities he never, ever, put on airs. A great many people meeting him for the first time counted the event as a turning point in their lives.

My own first meeting with Metropolitan Anthony took place when he was already in his mid-sixties. I had been deeply moved by *School for Prayer*, especially the account of his conversion experience. The realisation that just a few miles from me there lived someone who had encountered Christ much as St Paul had done filled me with longing. If only I could meet him, judge whether or not he was a man I could believe and, if so, catch something of his faith at second hand! So I wrote to him. Eventually – it was over three months later – he telephoned and asked me to come to the cathedral three days later. I had no idea what to expect.

When I rang the bell a woman wearing an apron and with a duster in her hand opened the door: it was Monday, cleaning day. She took me into the church. After a while a door opened and a short, bareheaded man appeared.

'At last!' Metropolitan Anthony strode up and grabbed me by the shoulder. 'I'm going to take you somewhere you shouldn't see,' he went on, hauling me upstairs to the gallery. It was a curious sight. We made our way between cupboards, books, and piles of rubbish including an old cooker, to a clearing just big enough for two chairs. In fact he used the chaos as an analogy. Life seemed different according to one's perspective, he said; it was like climbing a mountain, where the view altered the higher one progressed. The church downstairs looked beautiful, but upstairs it was another matter. And yet the beauty was still there. Later on I was to make my own analogy when I made my first confession. This was a church where one could bring the rubbish of one's life into the presence of God, and find acceptance.

He said nothing shattering. He spouted no theology (and never would). We talked instead of where I was in my tentative life of faith, and he listened, and answered, with a compassion such as I had never met before. It was not so much his faith which impressed me; that was taken for granted. What eclipsed everything else was the awareness I felt, for the first time in my life, of the love of God. I also came to realise that it was the indwelling of the Holy Spirit that enabled a person such as Metropolitan Anthony to become a channel for God's love.

There would be other occasions when I experienced the sad fact that his openness to the Spirit was by no means constant. Sometimes he could be as opaque as anyone else. But the one situation did not negate the other. Both existed, like the two sides of his face in the photo.

This book has afforded a glimpse of Metropolitan Anthony's life in Christ. It cannot be taken as the definitive account. That, I believe, will never be written, because he was much too enigmatic a personality to be confined to paper. He had his secrets. Either by accident or design he was not always strictly truthful. As well as narrating some of the incidents in his life in the third person, as if they had happened to someone else, he was also capable of appropriating other people's experiences and recounting them as his own. The anecdotes he told about himself were tinged with nostalgia for the budding saint of his youth, who perhaps had never quite existed, and idealised by the worn and over-painted icon he had later become: a man, in a sense 'holy', as Archbishop Methodios recognised, but with many flaws unconquered. Did he really have time as a young man, as he averred, to pray for eight hours a day when he was spending several more giving lessons, as well as coping with full-time study? Where did fact end and hyperbole begin? He was a master at seeing the potential in people; and he saw the potential in himself, and expressed it in words and outward behaviour, even though he knew he fell short in reality.

Over the next few years more of Metropolitan Anthony's talks will be published, his work will be re-evaluated, and more details about his life will come to light. Uncritical devotees will embrace the hyperbole and wish to see him canonised. The demonisers will have their say. He once avowed in a broadcast that he decried 'seeming to be what I am not' although he guarded his – sometimes unjustified – reputation jealously. To my comment to one of his priests that he seemed to be two people came the answer, 'Oh, at least five!'

But what was one and true and constant was his message. When he received his honorary doctorate from the Moscow Theological Academy in 1983 he repeated words that he had used when he was ordained reader as a teenager: how could he speak about a holiness he had never experienced, or preach what he did not practise? His answer was to quote St John Climacos: that at the Last Judgement men who were unworthy of their preaching would be upheld by those who could say, 'Lord, had he not preached I would never have known thy life-giving Truth.'

He was such a man; and his preaching was his glorious vision of the Gospel, which he proclaimed with authority, with conviction and in the power of the Holy Spirit, not as a prince of the Church on an ecclesiastical pedestal but as a servant of the Living God; and as a king, priest and prophet of the Kingdom of Heaven, which is the vocation of every Christian.

GLOSSARY

Apophaticism	Theology which speaks of God by negative description, saying what he is not rather than what he is
Archimandrite	A rank of the monastic clergy, senior to an igumen
Autocephaly	The principle of self-government of a local Orthodox church
Exarch	The bishop with oversight of parishes outside the geographical territory of a local Orthodox church
Hesychast	One who practises the Jesus Prayer and a life of inner stillness, after the teachings of St Gregory Palamas
Hieromonk	A monk who is also a priest
Igumen	A rank of monastic clergy – an abbot; a title often given to senior hieromonks in charge of parishes
Klobuk	The black headdress (white for a Russian Metropolitan) worn with a veil by monastics
Orthodox hierarch	A senior member of the Orthodox clergy (bishop, archbishop, metropolitan, patriarch)
Panaghia	A small circular icon of the Mother of God worn around the neck of a bishop
Perichoresis	The 'circle of love' of the Three Persons of the Trinity, their coherence or mutual indwelling
Starets (pl. startsi)	A wise elder, consulted by the faithful for spiritual guidance
Starosta	A churchwarden (and senior layperson) of a parish
Stavropegic	Of a monastery, directly under the head of an autocephalous church and not the local bishop

RECOMMENDED READING

Metropolitan Anthony's books:

Living Prayer
School for Prayer
Courage to Pray
God and Man
Meditations on a Theme
Compendium: The Essence of Prayer

Recommended Listening: CDs of services at which Metropolitan Anthony celebrates:
IKOCD 9006: The Liturgy of St. John Chrysostom
(Choir of the Russian Orthodox Cathedral in London directed by Father Michael Fortounatto, celebrant Metropolitan Anthony of Sourozh. Sung in English with a very good introduction to the Liturgy)
IKOCD 9009: Matins for Holy (Good) Friday
IKOCD 9010: Vespers for Good Friday
IKOCD 9012: Christmas Vigil
(These three CDs are sung in Church Slavonic by the Cathedral Choir directed by Father Michael Fortounatto, celebrant Metropolitan Anthony of Sourozh)
All books and CDs are obtainable from the Russian Cathedral Shop, 67 Ennismore Gardens London SW7 1NH

The website www.sourozh.org includes the Cathedral Newsletter, which regularly carried Metropolitan Anthony's sermons until his death.

The website www.metropolit-anthony.orc.ru/eng contains a list of his published works and the texts of a number of his talks and sermons.

The journals *Sourozh* and *Sobornost* contain numerous articles.

INDEX

⁘

Afanasy, Father *see* Nechaev, Father
    Afanasy
Alexis I, Patriarch of Moscow and All
    Russia 60, 128–9, 142
Alexis II, Patriarch of Moscow and
    All Russia 186, 189, 237
Alfeyev, Bishop Hilarion 186, 229–31
Allchin, Canon Donald 99–100
Anatoly, Archbishop of Kerch 187–8,
    217, 229, 231, 233

Beaumont, Father Michael 146
Behr, Aliosha 113, 115, 121–2
Behr, Father Nicholas (elder) 98, 105
Behr, Father Nicholas (younger) 149,
    178
Behr, Michael 178
Behr, Sonia 178
Behr, Tatiana (Tatisha) 57–8, 105–6,
    113, 121, 149, 178
Behr-Sigel, Elisabeth 86, 113, 167, 178
Bloom, Boris Edwardovich 7–8, 10–11,
    15–17, 21, 23–4, 31, 35, 54, 65, 77
Bloom (née Scriabin), Xenia 6–8, 13,
    17–20, 23–4, 26–7, 29–30, 34–5, 72,
    87–8, 92, 101, 108, 113, 117–19, 237,
    239
Bourdeaux, Canon Michael 130,
    235–6
Bulgakov, Father Sergei 40, 42, 96–7

Carras, Costa 172, 188, 225

Chartres, Bishop Richard 80, 144, 221,
    226
Coggan, Archbishop Donald of
    Canterbury 151
Crosland, Richard 99
Curie, Marie 55
Curie, Maurice 55

De Gaulle, Charles 72, 82
Dostoevsky, Fyodor 55, 197
Duddington, Anna *see* Garrett, Anna

Elizabeth II, Queen 114, 189, 222, 234
Elizabeth, Queen Mother 230
Evology, Metropolitan 46–8

Fernandez, Olga Ilyinichna *see*
    Scriabin, Olga
Filaret, Archbishop of Minsk 236–7
Fisher, Archbishop Geoffrey of
    Canterbury 114
Florovsky, Father Georges 53, 55, 86–7
Fokine, Ambassador, 222
Fortounatto, Father Michael 101, 133,
    141–2, 149–51, 167, 176, 180, 182,
    221–2, 239
Fortounatto, Mariamna 96, 101, 150–1
Fostiropoulos, Father Alexander
    177–8, 216, 229, 233
Frank, Simeon 86, 96, 152

Garrett, Anna 58, 91, 105, 133, 151, 185, 221

Gibbes, Father Nicholas 121

Gillet, Father Lev 32, 47–8, 86–7, 92, 95, 115, 173

Gogoleff, Father Michael 227–8

Gorbachev, Mikhail 179, 181

Greenan, Mariane 86, 113, 204

Gregorios, Archbishop of Thyateira and Great Britain 188, 237

Gromyko, Andrei 179

Hackel, Father Sergei 7, 105, 121, 188, 218

Hansen, Cecilia 57

Hope, Bishop Alan 237

Hume, Cardinal Basil 97

John Paul II, Pope 176

Kallistos, Bishop of Diokleia 115, 217, 222

Khrushchev, Nikita 122, 189

Kirill, Metropolitan of Smolensk 181, 222, 229, 237

Kirillova, Irina 96, 108, 151, 225, 234

Krug, Father Gregory 48–9, 73

Laski, Marghanita 143–4

Lee, Father John 108, 172, 175, 185–6, 218, 221, 231–2, 234–6

Lefebvre, Georges 145

Lossky, Nicholas 63, 79, 85, 95

Lossky, Veronique 75

Lossky, Vladimir 47–8, 85–7, 95, 117, 123, 202

Mark, Bishop of Berlin 103, 232

Methodios, Archbishop xi, 242

Michelmore, Cliff 195

Molotov see Scriabin, Vyacheslav Mikhailovich

Morshead, Barbara 107–8, 118, 151

Moscow Patriarchate 102–3, 113–15, 120–1, 124–5, 131–2, 137, 141–2, 148–9, 152, 155, 171–2, 185, 187, 219–22, 225, 228–30, 232

Nechaev, Father Afanasy 45–6, 48–50, 61–2, 64, 66, 68–70, 76–8, 80–1, 126, 203, 209, 238

Nicholas, Archbishop (later Metropolitan), Patriarchal Exarch to Western Europe 113–15, 177

Nikolsky, Father Maxim 185

Obolensky, Sir Dimitri 132, 180

O'Connor, Archbishop Cormac Murphy 237

Ogorodnikov, Alexander 179

Osborne, Bishop Basil of Sergievo 138, 147, 172, 183, 188, 216–17, 222–3, 229–31, 233–7

Osborne, Rachel 138

Ouspensky, Leonid 48–9

Peter the Great, Tsar 7, 97

Pimen, Patriarch of Moscow and All Russia 147, 185, 194–5

Putin, Vladimir 234

Ramsey, Archbishop Michael of Canterbury 132

Roger of Taizé, Brother 141

Runcie, Archbishop Robert of Canterbury 176, 193

St Maria Skobtsova 76, 176

St Paul 104, 110, 155, 170, 176, 205, 223, 241

St Silouan 120

Sakharov, Andrei 149
Scorer, Deacon Peter 105, 121, 185, 200
Scriabin, Alexander Nikolaevich (the composer) 3–6, 9, 102
Scriabin, Lyubov 4
Scriabin (née Fernandez), Olga Ilyinichna 3, 5–6, 8–9, 14–15, 17–19, 34, 59, 72, 79, 95–6, 101, 103, 111–13, 115, 237
Scriabin, Nikolai 3, 5–9
Scriabin, Vyacheslav Mikhailovich 10
Sergius, Metropolitan 46
Solzhenitsyn, Alexander 146–9
Sophrony, Archimandrite of Tolleshunt Knights 91, 120–1, 161
Stalin, Joseph 96, 128, 143, 158

Tavener, John 142
Thatcher, Margaret 82
Theokritoff, Father Vladimir 98–9, 101

Theokritoff, Mariamna see Fortounatto, Mariamna
Theokritoff, Michael 99, 132–3
Timothy, Bishop 222
Tuckett, Nicholas 149
Turgenev, Ivan Sergeivich 6, 32, 99

Von Schlippe, Irina 145, 147, 188

Walker, Andrew 172
Ware, Timothy see Kallistos, Bishop of Diokleia
Williams, Archbishop Rowan of Canterbury 144, 237
Winslow, Dom Bede 97

Yakunin, Father Gleb 179

Zakharovna, Tatiana see Behr, Tatiana
Zernov, Militza 95, 174, 180
Zernov, Nicolas 95–6, 121, 174, 180